His Darling Kitty

In Loving Memory

Jean Flannery

Copyright © 2022 Jean Flannery

All rights reserved.

ISBN: 9798843205560

DEDICATION

Dedicated to the memory of my mother Kitty and father Jack, to my sister Carole, to all Kitty's family - past, present and future, and to all who loved her.

CONTENTS

Acknowledgements	i
Foreword	1
Little Kitty Wallis	3
Momentous Times	13
A Home of Her Own	47
The Family Completes	66
Back to Bletchley	76
Early Years in Stewartby	86
Moving On	102
A Different Tack	114
Bess	124
Back to Kitty's Life	128
All Her Family Reunited	133
Bungalow Living	150
Wedding Anniversaries	158
Final Years in the Bungalow	162
Endings	169
Family Tributes and Memories	181
In Memoriam	192
Picture Gallery	193
Epilogue	292
Appendix	293

ACKNOWLEDGMENTS

My grateful thanks to all whose memories contributed to this book. I'd like to especially thank my sister Carole for prompting my memory in many instances, as well as contributing her own.

My cousin Brenda provided more memories of Kitty's family and early years. My cousin Pauline and friend Lana, who was once a next door neighbour, also made their contributions.

Other friends, along with members of several community Facebook groups, have been of real help to me in a variety of ways.

Heartfelt thanks again to Carole, with thanks also to Brenda and to my friends Bev and Lana, for proofreading. Any remaining errors are mine alone.

Last but far from least, my grateful thanks as ever to John for his unfailing patience, love and support.

Jack's Darling Kitty, 1945

FOREWORD

Whose darling was my mother Kitty?

Until the end of his life, she remained my father Jack's darling. No circumstance could alter his love for her. They had an unbreakable bond.

Having recently completed a tribute to my father: "Jack Blane," published to Amazon, I knew that I couldn't leave it there. I think Dad would haunt me if I didn't also write a tribute to my lovely mother.

This is Kitty's story, told as best I can. I am only too painfully aware that there is no way I can do anything like full justice to her memory. I don't know if the words even exist to truly describe her character. Jack's darling, our lovely, loving mother, Kitty enriched the life of everyone who knew her.

Where I speak of my own memories, I know that others may vary. Memory is subjective and all are equally valid.

I have included some family history and memories from other family members and friends. Having written each of my books to stand alone, there is inevitably some repetition. Please forgive that and just skip over anything that looks too familiar.

The appendix contains notes on some of Kitty's forebears, along with family trees and records. I have also added maps and information on the towns and villages where Kitty lived.

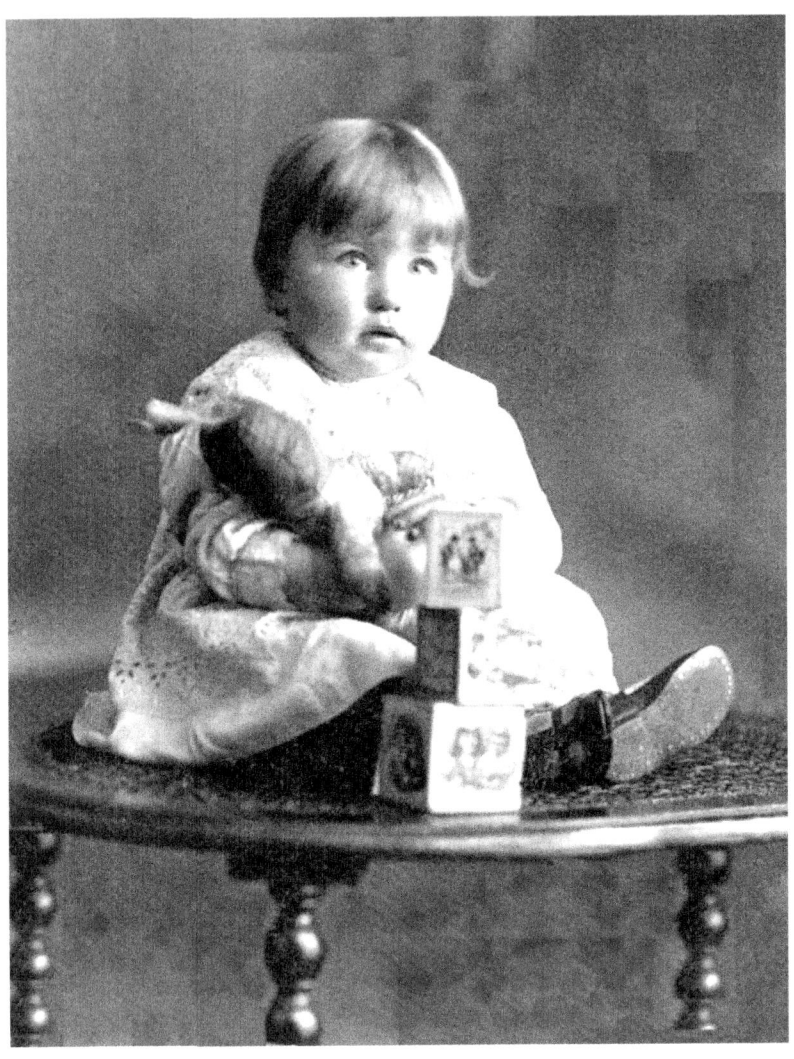

Little Kitty Wallis 1920

LITTLE KITTY WALLIS

My mother Kitty was the youngest of the five children born to Thomas Charles and Bertha Annie Wallis.

The eldest, Florence Ellen (Nellie) was born 15 June 1903, followed by Annie Edith 18 August 1908, Frederick (Fred) 12 December 1912, and Thomas (Tom) 13 September 1915.

Kitty was born 19 February 1920 in Hackenthorpe, then a village in Derbyshire in the Parish of Beighton, now considered a historic township of Sheffield, Yorkshire. Kitty looked so small, scrawny and weak at birth that her father is said to have commented, "Let the poor little bugger dee (die)."

Happily for all, the "poor little bugger" didn't die, although she didn't enjoy the best of health as a child.

She certainly looks a bonny enough baby in the picture you see of her, some time before her first birthday.

But Kitty always did remain small, never more than five feet tall. She shrank to become even shorter as she aged. And the crooked little finger, with which she was born, never changed.

When Kitty was two years old the family moved to the small mining town of Beighton itself, now also swallowed up by the city.

Kitty lived in Beighton until she left school at fourteen years old. The first family home there was 26 Cairns Road. They moved into the second, 172 Robin Lane, on some promotion of her father.

School - Kitty hated it! What nobody realised was how poor her eyesight was. She couldn't see the blackboard properly and didn't do well academically. But in later life it became obvious that she was very bright, just badly taught.

In order to avoid going to school, when living in Cairns Road Kitty would sometimes run round and "hide" next door, at number 24. She was always seen by Mrs Clarke, who lived there. "Mrs Wallis, your Kitty's here!" And that was Kitty found.

A brief digression: Many years later Kitty's niece my cousin Brenda, and her husband Keith, moved into 24 Cairns Road where they lived for some years. It was there that, thanks to their generosity towards me, I spent the few months with them as described in my book, "In No Particular Order."

Now back to Kitty's story. She has memories of a kind and loving mother. But when Kitty was retrieved from next door on these occasions, I think Bertha felt both annoyed and frustrated.

She took her young daughter to school, walking behind and slapping Kitty's legs from time to time as they went. I imagine that only added to Kitty's dislike of school.

Kitty was in some ways rather a timid child. She was very afraid, even terrified, of the graves in the churchyard, despite her mother telling her in her Yorkshire accent, "Eee m'lass, it's not the dee'd 'uns as'll hurt thee."

In later life, Kitty had a fear of being buried alive and asked me to make sure she was dead before she was placed in a coffin.

I don't know if Kitty's fear was connected to Bertha's work as the local "hatcher and dispatcher." That is to say, firstly that Bertha was an unqualified midwife. Money was tight for many families and so it wasn't "Call the midwife," but "Call Mrs Wallis."

Bertha also laid out the dead, washing and dressing them, making them look presentable, for families in the village. As soon as she arrived home from a laying out Kitty would ask, "Have you washed your hands, Mother?" She hated the thought of Bertha touching dead bodies.

Bertha made pork pies for the local butcher, and brawn for both the butcher and for her own family, as well as taking in washing when money was even tighter than usual. She certainly kept busy.

Another pet hate of Kitty's was when she had to accompany her mother to the butcher to collect a pig's head, or half a pig's head, for making the brawn. She always walked on the far side of Bertha to the one on which her mother held the bag with the head.

Then there was something that as a recollection still made Kitty cringe many years later. I don't know if Bertha was occasionally given a steak by the butcher or if it was cheaper then. How did she like her steak cooked? She said that "T'blood should follow t'knife." All her life Kitty had to have her meat well cooked!

What else? For some reason Kitty really disliked the taste of milk and butter. She took milk in her hot drinks: tea, coffee and cocoa, but never alone.

She liked cheese - but butter (and margarine)? She shuddered at the thought. Pork dripping, meat and fish paste, sometimes marmalade and jam, were always Kitty's spreads.

Kitty's father Thomas had a deformed spine and hated having his picture taken. Kitty and indeed it seems the family, had just one photograph of him, which has sadly become lost.

Thomas wasn't born with the deformity and there are two family stories about how his spine was damaged. One is that a nursemaid was taking him out in his pram and let go of the handle on one of the hilly Beighton streets. The pram ran down the street, tipped over and threw the baby out, causing the damage.

The other story is that a young male relative was tossing the baby up in the air and catching him, a good game enjoyed by both. However, on the final attempt the young man didn't catch Thomas and he fell to the ground, this causing the deformity.

Thomas was able to obtain employment as a Checkweighman, described in the 1911 census as "Coal Mine Weighman Above Ground," at Birley colliery, Woodhouse - not far from Beighton.

He couldn't do any heavy work but his job was a responsible one. He distributed the tally (identity) discs to every man going down the mine at the start of a shift, collecting them when the men returned to the surface. All had to be accounted for. It was something very necessary in the event of accidents.

Sadly, Thomas also became an alcoholic - or at least a very heavy drinker. This was why Nellie always hated to see anyone drunk. The General Strike of 1926, the immediate cause of which was a miners' strike, ended 12 May.

The miners continued to strike in an attempt to achieve better pay and working conditions. But by the end of the year they were completely defeated. They had to return to work to lower wages and longer hours. This disappointed and embittered all the men.

Thomas had a small private income, the source of which is unknown now. Apparently his workmates ostracised him because of this and he was very hurt, became even more bitter. That's when he started to drink so heavily.

One story goes that Tom could not stand to see how his father acted when drunk, confronted him, whether physically or not I'm unsure, and the heavy drinking stopped. Another is that Bertha confronted him and laid down the law.

I do wonder if Kitty's father drank away what money he did have in those years. I don't know, but it could help to explain why Bertha also took in laundry.

Nellie had left home by the time Kitty was born, working as nursemaid for a well to do family in the Totley area. Annie did the same for another family there, while Kitty was still very young. Perhaps Nellie recommended Annie to her employer.

The two sisters each had one day and night a week break from work, and a few holiday days each year. These were the only times they were able to go home and see their family.

So growing up Kitty was the only girl, and the baby, living in the family home with two older brothers.

Kitty was close to Tom, 4½ years her senior.

Kitty and Tom

During Kitty's early childhood Arthur Gee was courting her sister Annie. Arthur was very fond of little Kitty, for some reason nicknaming her "Jack' - or more commonly, "Our Jack" in the Yorkshire way. It's quite a coincidence that in later years Kitty's husband was named Jack.

As is the case with many younger sisters, Kitty wanted to be included in Annie and Arthur's activities. Arthur owned a motorbike and would sit Kitty on the seat, to her delight. I, like my cousin Brenda, think he probably also gave her short rides on it.

Annie was happy with that. With only one evening a week to spend with Arthur, she wasn't so happy when they wanted to go to the cinema on the High Street at Beighton Bottom.

Kitty begged to go with them. Annie refused, but Arthur? Kitty could wrap him round her little finger. "Oh, let her..." And so she went along, to Annie's disgust.

Silent films were still the order of the day, and it might well be that Nellie was playing the piano to create mood music for the film. I suppose she earned a bit of extra money that way. She'd keep glancing up at the screen to see what would be appropriate for any particular scene.

Nellie married Reginald (Reg) Cutts when Kitty was eight years old. Kitty and Annie were bridesmaids. Nellie's employers must have thought a lot of her, as the mother of the children she cared for loaned Nellie her wedding dress.

Annie married Arthur when Kitty was ten years old. Kitty was again a bridesmaid.

Not long after their marriage, Nellie and Reg moved down to Bletchley. Reg had obtained a post as manager of the Cooperative (Co-op) butcher's shop there.

Kitty spent a number of holidays with them until she left school, Easter 1934. Fourteen was then the legal school leaving age.

Reg and Nellie would go up to Beighton to visit both their families, with Reg riding his motorbike and Nellie in the sidecar. They also used the motorbike and sidecar for holidays, on these occasions with a suitcase strapped to the large back carrier.

When Reg and Nellie returned from Beighton to Bletchley Kitty often travelled with them, seated in a large toolbox on the back of the motorbike. It's hard to imagine such a thing happening nowadays.

Kitty loved those visits and her health was always better when she was at Bletchley, away from the coal mines, coal dust and ash.

What Kitty didn't love were the Christmas presents that she received from Nellie and Reg. When Kitty was old enough for school, Nellie always bought and sent black stockings as her gift. Kitty kept hoping for something better but it never materialised.

Many years later Kitty did tell Nellie of this disappointment. Nellie was filled with remorse, saying that she simply hadn't realised how Kitty would feel. Her only thought was that by sending the stockings as gifts she was helping out their mother.

Here is Reg's motorbike, Nellie in the sidecar.

Thanks to my friend Roger, I now know that the motorbike was a Brough Superior SS100, made at the Brough factory in Nottingham. The star adjuster on the forks at mudguard level, visible in the picture, is really the biggest clue. The side car also seems to be a Brough Superior, the Touring Sports.

Another view of bike and sidecar with Nellie onboard.

Looking at the registration number, and with information from the Sheffield City Council Archive, Reg would have bought the motorbike in the late 1920s.

Brough Superiors were individually made for their purchasers, so almost all were unique in some way.

They were known as the "Rolls Royce of Motorcycles." Only 383 SS100s were manufactured, from 1924 to 1940. They were very expensive.

Each bike had its parts assembled to check that they fit precisely. The motorbike was then taken apart and painted to customer specification. Every bike was individually tested to make sure it could do 100mph, as this model was guaranteed to reach that speed.

The bike also made a powerful noise. Reg, as a testosterone filled young man, removed the silencers from the exhaust pipes and replaced them with steel wool.

If a police officer was alerted by the engine noise, he might decide to check by pushing a stick down the exhaust. The stick would hit up against the steel wool. The officer, even if still suspicious, would find the bike's exhaust to be legal.

MOMENTOUS TIMES

All the family knew how much better Kitty's health was when staying in Bletchley. As she approached school leaving age, Nellie and Reg very generously offered her a home with them.

I don't know how difficult the decision was for her parents, only having been told that her father agreed to the move. Her mother just wasn't mentioned.

In those days it would have been the head of the household who made any major decisions. But in any event, I am sure that Bertha wanted what was best for Kitty, though it must have saddened her to have two daughters living so far away, one of them her "baby."

And though 115 miles might not seem such a huge distance now, it was to them. There were no motorways and not many people owned their own cars. I'm not sure when Reg bought his first car but nobody else in the family owned one.

If you went by train, you had to make two changes. In Bedford you even had to change stations, which meant getting from one side of the town to the other. At least at Crewe you only had to change platforms. But it was a very long journey.

As for keeping in touch, there were of course no internet or mobile phones. In fact nobody in the family had even a landline at the time, so all communication was by letter writing. Even though there was an excellent postal service, that meant a delay of at least two days before getting a reply.

When Nellie and Reg first moved down to Bletchley, they lodged in Bedford St with Mrs Castle before buying their house, 12 Cambridge St, "Lyndhurst."

This photograph was taken around 1960, the trees all well grown.

Ground Floor

As you entered the front door, the stairs led up on your right. The hallway went straight along to the kitchen door.

The kitchen was small and quite dark with just a little window at the side of the house, facing more or less east. It overlooked the small lawn behind the garage where there were two lovely lilac trees close to the next door house's fence. Behind the kitchen was a single story extension, with a coal shed and a second toilet. Both were accessed from outside.

The small kitchen table was under the window, with the door to the left and the cooker to the right of it - by the inside end wall of the kitchen. The sink was fitted to the back wall.

The left-hand sink draining board stayed in place but the right hand one could only be fitted when the kitchen door was closed because there was so little space between sink and door.

Opposite the table, on the wall between the kitchen and dining room, was a chimneybreast now containing an enclosed fire with a back boiler for heating water. In the alcove to the left of this was the dog's sleeping place.

The pantry led off from the right side of the hallway, against the outside wall next to the kitchen and under the stairs. There was no room for another door in the kitchen and very little for cabinets. It's a good thing there was a pantry and that there were cupboards in the living room where crockery could be kept.

The doors to the other two rooms were to the left of the hall. All the living was done, as was usual, in the back room. We might think of it as the dining room but it was living/diner then. For most people that was because heating two rooms would have cost too much. The kitchen fire warmed one wall there, too. The two big bedrooms had fireplaces that I don't think were ever used.

At Cambridge Street, another reason for living in the back room was that Nellie's piano for her teaching was in the front room. This was where she gave her lessons: late afternoons after school, early evenings and Saturday mornings.

It is a shame the living was done that way round, as the front room had a bay window and was very light. The living room, which faced north, only caught a bit of sunlight early in the morning.

The house had a lovely long rear garden, separated from the neighbours by low fences and backing onto the tennis courts of the Central Gardens, a beautiful small public park.

Around 1960: looking back at the house, garage to left.

You can see the shed behind the apple tree here. Just beyond are the coal barn/toilet extension, with bedroom 3 above. Kitty's bedroom is to the right of it in the photo, left in this image.

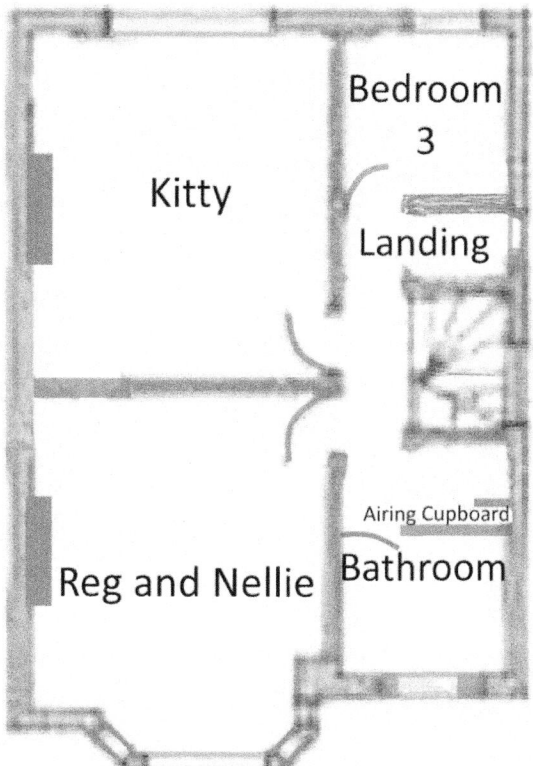

Upper Floor

The previous picture is the view from Kitty's bedroom window across to the tennis courts about 1960, with the fruit trees on the left well grown.

I'm not sure just when Reg and Nellie purchased the house but it would have been between 1928 and the early 1930s. They had most definitely bought it before Kitty went to live with them permanently in 1934. By then they had also bought a black Cocker Spaniel, "Laddie," a much loved addition to the family.

Kitty really felt at home in Bletchley. She loved living with Nellie and Reg, who made much of her. But I don't know if she expected to live with them for the next 14 years!

Reg was known for his wicked sense of humour. Whenever Kitty had an egg for breakfast, or egg and chips for supper, she carefully cut away and ate the white first. The yolk was her favourite part and she saved it until last, before sticking her fork into it. Then she'd dip toast or chips into the yolk, or let it run over fried bread.

She'd save it, that is, unless Reg got his fork to it, stabbing it before Kitty was ready. Sometimes he succeeded and sometimes Kitty saw the fork coming and was ready to stab his hand with her own fork!

I told you that Kitty was bright. Despite her problems at school, she had a good knowledge of basic maths and money management.

Her spelling was excellent and she was a stickler for the correct use of words. As an example, if anyone used the word "bit" when referring to liquid it really annoyed her. Someone might say, "I just take a bit of milk in my tea." And Kitty would fume, if not aloud, "It's a **drop** of milk, not a bit!"

You could take a bit of time over a job - or a bit of a break. You could have a bit of fun - but liquid was and is a drop. Perhaps that's where some of my own pedantry comes from.

In the early 1930s a printing company, The Premier Press, relocated from London and took over the stable block of Bletchley Park, which was situated opposite the then Bletchley Police Station.

Kitty easily gained employment there. I'm not sure of just what her job entailed. But I know that when she was visiting Bertha on the day of WWII National ID Card Registration, 29 September 1939, her occupation was given as print folder.

She met Renee, (known as Reen) who became her great friend. You see them here on one of the seaside holidays they took together. Almost inseparable, their friendship lasted for many years.

There were a number of native woodland areas around Bletchley, where both bluebells and primroses grew in profusion. In those days people would go out into the woods and gather as many as they wished. Every year they blossomed again in abundance.

Kitty's favourite flowers were bluebells, the delicate English variety with their sweet scent. The hardier, stronger Spanish variety had not yet invaded England and hybridised with the natives.

Bluebells had to be picked very carefully, breaking off the stems rather than pulling them right out of the ground, which would kill the plant. Kitty gathered armfuls.

Every year she, Nellie and Reg, went "primrosing." They bunched up the primroses and packed some in shoe boxes with moist moss, to send to relatives as a treat. Post never took more than a day to arrive, so they stayed fresh.

Kitty's sister Annie in particular, loved to get them. Kitty also took bunches to Jack's parents, who lived on Brooklands Road in Bletchley, just a short walk from Cambridge Street.

The primrosing tradition continued well into my childhood, with the whole family involved in picking, bunching and packing.

The Premier Press closed down early during WWII. Bletchley Printers, another printing company, had opened on the High Street side of the Central Gardens in competition a few years previously. When the Premier Press closed, the head of typesetting there joined Bletchley Printers as a director.

By a fortunate coincidence, the Tetley Tea company relocated to Osborne Street, Bletchley, from London at around the time the Premier Press closed its doors. The factory was located on the corner of Clifford Avenue, where Jack's brother Bob lived with his family. Kitty had no problem finding new employment there.

However, I get ahead of myself. Kitty hadn't been in Bletchley long before she and Renee made their way to the "Monkey Walk" on the Watling Street. This was a favourite haunt of the youth of the town on fine Sunday evenings.

The road was quiet in those days, with little car ownership. Boys walked along one side, the girls on the opposite side, eyeing up one another and doubtless calling out various comments. It was rather like an early version of a dating site.

Across the Watling Street from Bletchley itself was a worked out, and flooded, gravel pit. The gravel pit was now a small lake, set in an area of grassed over wasteland, with molehills scattered about.

The town's teenagers would also congregate there and, as the modern idiom goes, hang out together just chatting and larking around. Kitty and Renee often joined in with those groups.

Larking about? Kitty has two memories of that. One was of being thrown into the gravel pit. I don't know how funny she found it at the time, but she could laugh about it years later.

The other memory was not at all humorous. On one occasion when the youngsters were indulging in horseplay, Kitty was inadvertently clouted on the ear. It must have been a hard blow, because it ruptured her eardrum.

Kitty's ear became infected and antibiotics didn't come into general use until after WWII. So healing was slow and painful, and the opening never completely closed.

For the rest of her life Kitty had to be really careful not to get water into her ear, and certainly not allow anyone to try to clean it in any way. It saddened her that she could never learn to swim. She did try in later life but just couldn't keep the pool water out of her ear, despite the best protection she could find.

I don't know how often Kitty managed to get up to Beighton but I do know that on one trip, not too long after moving down to Bletchley, she took a cottage ware "biscuit barrel" as a gift to her mother. Although without it's wicker handle, it now sits in my own home.

Brenda, Annie's daughter, was born 13 January 1936. Kitty went up to Beighton soon after and met her new niece for the first time.

That same year, at sixteen years old, Kitty had her very first eye test and was issued with her first pair of glasses. A whole new world opened up to her!

When she walked into the house after being fitted with the glasses she looked around and suddenly said, "There's a fly on the wall!" Never before had she been able to see anything that small.

Something else that turned out to be momentous happened in 1936. Kitty and her future husband Jack Blane, then aged eighteen, began going out together.

Later that year Kitty's father died. She told the story of waking in the night to see him standing by her bed. And she was always adamant that it was true, he really had been there.

So 1936 was a very mixed year for Kitty emotionally.

In 1937 Charles, Fred and Mary's first son, was born. That was a happy occasion and a visit for Kitty.

Bertha found it hard to survive on her 10/- (ten shillings) a week widow's pension. It helped that William Harrison, known as "Uncle Billy," still boarded with her, having been with the family since at least 1921. He was very good with Bertha's grandchildren. Brenda loved him as the grandfather she had never known. She also took in another lodger for a few years to help with finances.

Brenda's brother Brian was born on New Year's Eve of 1938. Here's Kitty in early 1939 with him and Brenda.

Later in 1939 Jack was called up to do his six months' National Service in the British Army. By this time, he and Kitty were engaged.

When Jack actually enlisted, 13 September 1939, Britain was already at war with Germany. He was posted to an RAMC Casualty Clearing Station (3 CCS), remaining with that unit throughout the war.

Jack had three months' training before embarkation leave at Christmas, when Kitty could see him again after what then seemed a very long time. He left for France with the British Expeditionary Force on New Year's Eve.

I can only imagine how Kitty felt as the Germans advanced on France, not knowing where Jack was or how he was. And then came the evacuation from Dunkirk.

Was he one of those rescued? Was he injured? Was he dead? It must have been a dreadful wait until knowing that her fiancé was safely back in England. He was evacuated from the beach

Jack now spent time in various army camps around the country, from which he was able to get home leave.

9 October 1940 Kitty and Jack were married. The wedding took place in St Martin's Church, Fenny Stratford. The reception was held in the church hall.

The best man was Jack's brother Martin. Kitty's maids of honour were her sisters-in-law Edna, Tom's wife, and Mary, Fred's wife. Her sister Annie's four-year-old daughter Brenda was a bridesmaid. Mary's son three-year-old Charles was pageboy.

Poor little Charles started to become unwell on the day and was very unhappy during the ceremony.

The following photo is the only one of him with the wedding group, taken outside the church immediately after the ceremony. Then Annie took him back to Cambridge Street, while more pictures were taken at the church hall.

You can see that Charles isn't happy!

Edna missed the reception as she was looking after Charles, who was feeling really ill by then. It transpired that he had chickenpox. Brenda was also starting to feel unwell by the end of the day and she too came down with chickenpox, a few days later.

Bertha managed to get from Beighton to Bletchley with Annie and Edna for the wedding. I can only assume that the men, working in the coalmines, weren't allowed the time off. Bear in mind that this was wartime, with travel restrictions in place and the start of rationing.

On 8 January 1940, bacon, butter and sugar were rationed. Dried fruit was also soon rationed. Kitty, Nellie and members of Jack's family saved the rations necessary to make rich fruit cake layers, and the icing, for the wedding cake.

Kitty and Jack had planned to have a very brief honeymoon in Northampton.

Kitty all ready to leave for the honeymoon, wearing her favourite coat and hat, Laddie in the foreground, air raid shelter back right.

However, by evening a thick fog had set in. With the smoke from all the coal fires, it was a real pea souper. So they sadly but wisely cancelled the trip.

But Reg made sure the night was memorable. I told you he had a wicked sense of humour. He made their bed into an apple pie bed. (Look it up if you don't know!) After discovering this, they then had to remake the bed before they could get into it.

In 1941, Jack was for some months stationed at a camp known as "Snow Hill" in Sussex. It was close to the village of Anstye Cross, not far from the town of Haywards Heath.

Local people took in the troops. The Anstye Cross village constable and his wife, Eddie and Jo Voice, were one couple that did so. They lived in the police house with their young son, David.

Jack was billeted with Eddie and Jo and they soon became firm friends. When she could, and Jack had some time off, Kitty would take the train to Haywards Heath. There was always an army lorry at the station, meeting the London train to collect troops.

And the men on the lorry always gave Kitty a lift to Anstye Cross, where she would spend a weekend, or some holiday time, with Jack and the little family there.

Kitty too became great friends with Eddie and Jo. They all kept in touch and visited one another until Eddie and Jo died. Kitty and Jack then kept in touch with David until almost their own deaths.

I knew the couple as Uncle Eddie and Auntie Jo. And I'm still in touch with David. But I'm getting ahead of myself now.

The following picture was taken at Anstye Cross, when Jack was on leave in the summer of 1941. Jack is sitting with Kitty, Jo, David and the family dog.

In early 1941, Nellie and Reg took in two evacuee children from London: sisters Joan and Marjory (Marj) Hart. I think Joan may have been about ten years old and Marj six or seven. They stayed in Bletchley for over four years, which Joan later told me were the happiest years of her childhood.

Reg and Nellie, with no children of their own, really took Joan and Marj to their hearts. Reg even sourced two pet rabbits for them. Kitty was very fond of the girls too and Jack's family, of whom most still lived in Bletchley, also made much of them.

Reg with the young Marj and Joan, the rabbits and Laddie.

This picture from the Cambridge Street garden is from very early 1941, taken soon after the girls' arrival.

Joan and Marj's mother Ruth, and occasionally their father John, managed to visit by train from London. They brought welcome gifts, at least some of which (with hindsight) I imagine were probably purchased on the black market.

Everyone kept in touch after the war, we children knowing Ruth and John as Auntie and Uncle. We never did go to see them in London but they still came to Bletchley at least once a year.

From 1941 Kitty had another job, still at the Tetley Tea factory, but this was voluntary. Along with other staff she acted on some nights as a fire watcher. She said it was a lot of fun, as the young people chatted and joked around while at the same time keeping their eyes open.

Jack embarked for North Africa in December 1941. Neither he, Kitty, any of the other troops or civilians, knew at the time where his ship was heading. Again it was wondering and anxiety.

As the war went on, rationing began to bite more and Kitty made blouses from her wedding dress. Eggs weren't in short supply, as Jack's father and other family members kept chickens.

The local Baptist minister, Mr Richardson, lived at 14 Cambridge Street with his family, including his elderly father. They also had a chicken run at the bottom of their garden.

I don't think their chickens were too well cared for. They were poor scrawny looking, smelly creatures.

When they were cackling away, the older Mr Richardson would shout down the garden, "Shut up, you bare arsed buggers!"

Meat wasn't a problem at number 12 either, with Reg being a butcher. I don't doubt he managed to keep the family reasonably well supplied throughout the war. And I don't think anybody would have asked any questions!

But the war brought blackout and fear. A nationwide blackout was declared very early on in the war, to help prevent enemy aircraft from accurately pinpointing targets.

Don't forget: there was not even radar at that time, let alone GPS, for navigation. Blackout wardens patrolled at night to make sure no lights were showing.

Bedroom curtains were lined with blackout material. Everyone used this during WWII for all their curtains. Any traffic also had to have headlights shaded.

I really liked the blackout curtains. For many years I slept much better if my bedroom was totally dark.

There was fear that Bletchley, with its large rail junction, or the Sheffield area with its industry and coal mines, would be bombed.

Bletchley itself wasn't bombed, although one bomb did fall close to the main London to Scotland railway line in October 1940. It was a different matter in Beighton, as Sheffield was frequently targeted by Luftwaffe bombers.

Brenda remembers that when the air raid sirens sounded in Beighton, at any hour of the day or night, she and Brian were carried to the Anderson air raid shelter in the garden of Bertha's next door neighbour, Mr Mace.

Later, the family had a Morrison table shelter in their own house, in which they would sit until the all clear sounded. Several bombs landed in the area. Whether or not the colliery or Beighton gas works were the targets, any bomb would have caused wholesale destruction had there been a direct hit.

But once Jack had embarked at the end of that year, there was a greater fear for Kitty. Jack was away in the thick of the war. Kitty could never know whether the next message she'd receive would be a letter from him - or a telegram to say he'd been killed or was missing in action.

At that time, it was quite common for servicemen to give a love token to their sweethearts and wives, something to hold close as a reminder of their love and promise of return.

Jack gave Kitty two beautiful silk handkerchiefs with embroidery edging and an embroidered RAMC insignia. One was lavender blue and one red. Kitty treasured them for the rest of her life.

Although she put a brave face on it, I know that Kitty was very anxious for him. He'd survived the early stages of the war and Dunkirk but there was no telling what was coming next.

As it happened, Jack was in North Africa where he was involved in some of the bloodiest battles including Tobruk, Benghazi and El Alamein. All Kitty could know is what she heard on the radio or read in the newspapers.

Letters home from the troops were infrequent and heavily censored. But in 1942 she did receive an 8th Army Christmas card from Jack, with a personal greeting.

After North Africa and two week's rest in Malta, Jack's unit took part in the invasion of Sicily, moving up into Italy. He finally arrived back in England in January 1944.

Imagine being separated for a little over two years, knowing that your husband was always just behind the front line, hearing and reading of battles, hoping that none of the casualties was him.

The relief Kitty must have felt when Jack was back in the country would have been immense.

That January, stationed near Cambridge, Jack was given a sleeping out pass. His Aunt Alice lived in Cambridge and that's where Jack and Kitty stayed for his pass.

Following that came preparations for the D-Day invasion of Normandy. Everyone knew the invasion was coming but nobody knew exactly where or when.

In the Spring of 1944 Kitty discovered that she was pregnant. It was of course a pregnancy that was totally unplanned. I think that both Kitty and Jack had very mixed feelings.

There was joy at the thought of having their first child. There was anxiety that this child might never know its father.

Yet for Kitty there was also some small solace in knowing that whatever happened to Jack, she would still have this baby of his.

Jack embarked for Normandy on D- Day, 6 June. Kitty spent the next months of her pregnancy anxious and fearful, as the Allied armies progressed through Europe.

She would have heard news of the major battles, not knowing in which Jack was involved or just where he and his unit were. Letters were infrequent and not much could be said. I think of

Kitty waiting to hear from him, always hoping there would be another letter and not the dreaded telegram with news of his death.

Everything the troops wrote was censored. But at least with each letter that arrived, Kitty would know Jack was still safe and well.

Kitty resigned from her job that summer and from then on, she dedicated herself to the care of her home and family. I was the child that Kitty was expecting and I was born 10 October 1944.

Sometime before I was born, Laddie died. Reg bought a German Shepherd puppy, a breed known as Alsatian during the war. I think you can guess why.

Nellie was afraid of the breed, one having previously attacked Laddie. But she soon came to love the puppy. He was a really well trained and generally placid dog, very much a part of all our lives. Uncle's sense of humour? The Germans were the enemy. He named the dog Fritz.

When Kitty went into labour, Joan and Marj were sent off to stay with other relatives, whom of course they also knew very well. On their return, to find a brand new baby in the house, they were both somewhat upset not to have been there for my arrival!

Kitty had quite a long and difficult labour, at home in Cambridge Street. Eventually the doctor gave her a general anaesthetic and I was delivered just after midnight.

I was welcomed and loved but was a very fractious baby. I am sure that I picked up my mother's anxiety. She didn't know where Jack was but must have heard news of the war.

As it happened, at the time he must just about have finished 14 very gruelling days and nights, without any break, in the field hospital at Nijmegen. 3 Casualty Clearing Station returned there following the Battle of Arnhem.

Fearful for her husband, Kitty also felt constrained and anxious about having a baby in the house with Nellie and Reg. She worried that they would be upset by my crying, which probably only made us both worse.

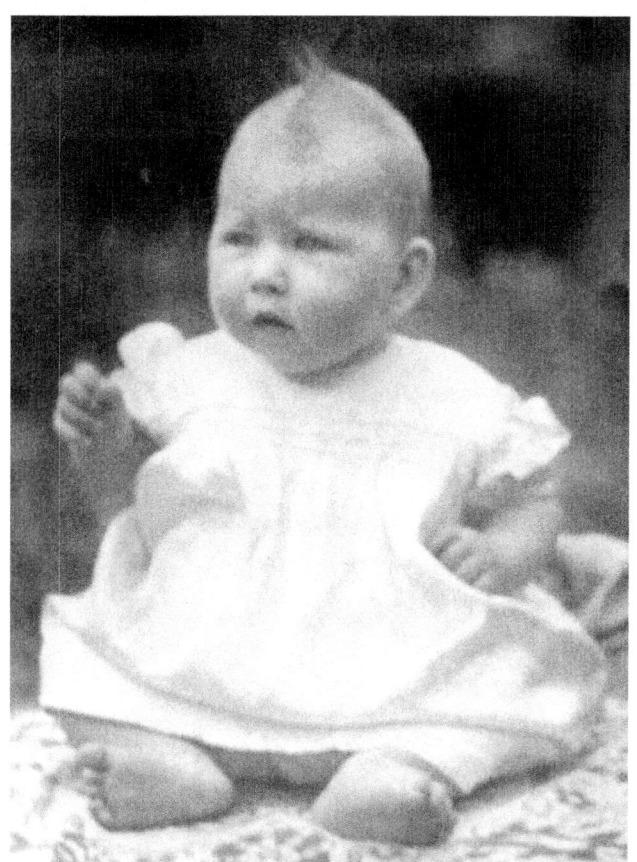

This is the first picture of me, taken in early 1945.

You can just see Kitty's shoulder on the right, as she held her hand behind me to keep me upright.

Kitty didn't breast-feed me, not only from embarrassment but also a sense that this would be rubbing Nellie's face in the fact that her sister and Reg were childless. It also meant that Nellie could share in my feeding, as well as caring for me in other ways. But I don't think Kitty need really have worried. Nellie and Reg both also very much loved this new little niece of theirs.

Her sense of guilt also led to Kitty feeling that she had to almost give me to Nellie. She would very often offer to do the housework, telling Nellie to take me out for a walk or play with me in the garden. Kitty never felt that I was completely her child.

Kitty and Nellie took me out together at times. And Kitty did also take me out on her own. These outings might be for shopping, visiting Renee, other friends and relatives, or walking Fritz to the gravel pit, where he could run free - and dig for moles!

Kitty's anxiety even led to her choice of name for me When asked why Jean, she said that it was because nobody on either side of the family had that name, so nobody could feel put out by the choice.

I was christened 29 October 1944 in St Margaret's Church, which faced Bletchley Road on the corner of Brooklands Road. It was next door to our doctors' Surgery.

The full title of the church was St Margaret's Mission Church, opened in 1866 by the Bishop of Oxford as a chapel of ease to St Martin's in Fenny Stratford, where Kitty and Jack were married.

There must have been large church attendances in those days, given a need to ease the burden on St Martin's. Though St

Martin's Church still stands, St Margaret's was demolished in 1962.

I imagine that my father and most of his siblings had been christened in St Margaret's as it was also the nearest church to Railway Terrace, where the family first lived in Bletchley. The younger family members, including Jack, were all born in the house on Brooklands Road, where Jack's parents still lived.

St Margaret's Church, where I was christened, in later years

My christening would have been another occasion for a family gathering - those who were not in the armed forces at the time. Among those present would have been my grandfather Blane, who as a train driver was in a reserved occupation.

Kitty never lost her sense of humour, despite all her anxieties. Bletchley was a lovely small market town, where most people were at least acquainted. When Kitty took me out in my pram, everyone she came across wanted to look at the new baby.

"Doesn't she look like her Dad?" was a frequent comment. What was Kitty's response? "I ordered her that way!" There could be no doubt about my paternity, no wondering whether or not I was, as the saying went, the milkman's child.

Although the war was in its later stages, the Luftwaffe was still attacking Britain. It was on Christmas Eve 1944, at 5.40am, that a V21 flying bomb (Doodlebug) exploded in Cow Lane, on the outskirts of Beighton. Thankfully, it didn't cause any major damage.

At the time, Kitty's brother Tom was serving overseas. His wife Edna was living with her mother-in-law Bertha in Robin Lane. The air raid siren had sounded and roused them, but Edna wouldn't go next door to the bomb shelter.

Bertha opened the kitchen door, either to just go herself or try to also get Edna to the bomb shelter. Edna was standing in the kitchen, in line with the open door, when the bomb exploded.

The blast from the explosion threw her across the room. Luckily she wasn't seriously injured, though both women were very shaken.

At Easter 1945, Jack somehow obtained a short home leave. Whether or not it was because he was a new father, I don't know.

By then the Allied forces were in Germany and the war drawing to a close. But however it came about, it was then that my father first met me.

After that leave, Kitty took me to Beighton to meet her mother. Bertha seems to have also been a bit of a home pharmacist. She gave me what Kitty always referred to as "Jolly Drops." Goodness knows what was in the mixture - quite possibly laudanum, in those days.

I did become much more content, with no more almost constant crying. While Kitty always put this down to the medicine, I think that having my father home on leave, seeing him safe, eased her own anxiety and correspondingly mine.

When VE day came, Kitty really knew that Jack would be coming back safe and sound. With that knowledge, she began to agonise over whether she should literally give me to Nellie and Reg, to raise as their own.

Had Jack been killed in the war, Kitty would have continued to live with her sister and brother-in-law, sharing me with them.

She thought about how she and Jack could have more children, whereas Reg and Nellie would always be childless - and they too loved me so much. However, thankfully she couldn't bring herself to do it.

I loved my aunt and uncle dearly but they weren't my parents. I don't know what my father would have had to say about it, either!

With the war in Europe over, Jack was back in England in December 1945. He had four weeks demob leave, so was home for Christmas for the first time since 1940.

In February 1946 he was finally demobbed from the army and

home for good, back to his old job at the nearby London Brick Company (LBC) Newton Longville brickworks.

There was a big post-war national house building programme, with local councils building new estates of homes for people to rent. Kitty and Jack applied for one of these council houses and were placed on a waiting list.

Kitty used to cycle quite a lot. She would go to look round the shops in Leighton Buzzard and Newport Pagnell. In the Spring, Kitty always bought a bunch of the first daffodils from Newport Pagnell for Nellie.

I often went along too, when old enough, strapped into a rear child seat as you see in the picture of us just setting off. There were no cycle helmets and rear child seats like this were the norm.

You can also see that the front area of the house looks quite different from the 1960s.

Once when she had me on board, Kitty's bicycle tyre had a puncture as she cycled through a village on the way home from Newport Pagnell. She was really worried, with no way of contacting anyone in Bletchley.

Don't forget, not only were there no mobile phones but Nellie and Reg didn't even have a landline. However, a Good Samaritan saw her plight and saved the day by mending the puncture for her.

Remember what I said about Kitty not being able to stand the taste of butter? Even before I was two years old, if the butter dish had been left out within my reach I dipped my fingers in to scoop out the butter and just eat it on its own. This gave Kitty the horrors as, not being able to stand butter herself, she even hated wiping my fingers and mouth.

On the other hand, Nellie would suck the butter off my fingers with every evidence of enjoyment, something that Kitty couldn't even bear to watch her doing. How to explain the different reactions people can have to something, whatever it may be?

Whenever Kitty or Nellie visited Beighton, Annie had the job of getting a bedroom ready in Bertha's house. When they went home, she put the room back to rights and washed the bed linen. I think she felt rather taken for granted, somewhat like the story of the prodigal son. Nonetheless, the three sisters remained close. I don't know how frequent these visits were but I think that the last time Kitty took me to visit my grandmother must have been in the late summer of 1946.

In the winter of 1946-47, when I was two, I wore a matching wool coat and leggings for going out in the cold. Apparently I hated having my leggings put on and would fight Kitty, going rigid and screaming. She would eventually get so frustrated that she would slap my legs to make me behave. Then she felt dreadful, with me in tears and Nellie wringing her hands. It can't have been easy for her. Me? That's something I simply don't remember.

What also can't have been easy for Kitty is that in January 1947 her mother died. Once again, I have two stories.

This is the one that Kitty told. Bertha went into hospital for a hysterectomy. Whilst still in hospital she died. Kitty didn't seem to know just what had caused her death.

However, when family members went to collect her belongings they found what seemed to be all her medication, the tablets, in her handbag. She had been secreting them instead of taking them, without any of the hospital staff realising it.

The story my cousin Brenda was told by her mother Annie is somewhat different. All Brenda knew about the reason for her grandmother's surgery is that it was to do with "women's problems."

The last time Brenda saw Bertha was from the hospital garden. Children weren't allowed to visit in those days and Brenda was left in the garden while the adults went to the ward. She remembers seeing her grandmother through a window and waving to her, receiving a wave back.

The next thing she remembers is being told by Annie that her grandmother had died. Later she heard that following the initial surgery Bertha had some kind of complications. She was rushed back to the operating theatre but didn't recover. Hence her death.

It wasn't considered right for children to attend funerals. But Brenda also remembers sitting by the window at school, taking her mock Eleven Plus exam, when she saw her grandmother's funeral procession pass by. That made quite an impact on her.

Tom and Edna owned a grocery shop/general store in Swallownest, a short distance from Beighton. They took Billy in to live with them after Bertha died. I think that shows how much he was appreciated by all the family.

With Joan and Marj having returned home, and Kitty and Jack waiting to move into a council house, Reg and Nellie applied to adopt a child.

Being an older couple, they were realistic enough not to expect to adopt a baby. Nellie was also giving piano lessons in the front room by now. With a baby to care for, she would have given up her teaching for quite some time - though I don't know that she would have minded that. They were cleared for adoption and now waited to be offered a child.

That summer Kitty and Jack had their first family holiday, taking me to the Isle of Wight. Although Jack's brother Don lived there, we stayed in a boarding house.

With no self-catering, boarding houses were where most families would stay for their holiday. They were fairly cheap and many were just ordinary large family homes, in which bedrooms would be let to holidaymakers in the summer season. All the booking and arrangements would usually be made by post.

Boarding house landladies were a standing joke, depicted as strict dragons on holiday postcards. There were rules to be observed.

Among these would be that after breakfast, where there would be little choice of food, you would have to leave the boarding house for the day by a set time. That would certainly be no later than 10.00am.

Then no matter the weather, you were often not allowed to return until early evening. You had an evening meal at the boarding house, with usually two choices on the menu: take it or leave it!

Our boarding house had a landlord, who was rather unpleasant - but in those days you didn't argue. With much food still on ration the landlord took our ration books, as was normal, so that he could feed us for the week. But apparently the evening meal was always just a basic salad with a bit of meat, cheese or tinned fish.

There was never a cooked meal; and Jack has never liked salad. The other thing the landlord insisted on was that I should eat earlier and be in bed before the evening meal. So by 6 o'clock every evening, that was the day over for me. But those annoyances couldn't stop us all enjoying our week by the sea.

At around the same time, Reg and Nellie were offered a boy of three to adopt. Kenneth Peter, who became simply my cousin Ken, was six months older than me. He came into the household in October 1947, when I was just three.

Poor Ken was most unhappy at first. Everything was completely alien to him and he didn't really know any of his new family. He was also, understandably, afraid of Fritz in the early days.

Ken missed the orphanage and his "nurse." He had no memories of his mother, who took him to the orphanage as a baby, visited him regularly for some time, and then simply disappeared from view. The orphanage staff and our family too, thought that she may have been killed in one of the last air raids of the war.

Kitty's kind heart was wrung by Ken's distress. And I didn't help! I most definitely resented this interloper, who now took so much of the attention that I had previously received.

Not only that, but I was expected to share my toys with him. Kitty felt for us both. And she was again "walking on eggshells" with Nellie and Reg.

On one occasion Kitty became very upset and was close to tears, when she overheard Reg say that it would be a good thing when "they" left, "with that little bugger" - me.

Reg must just have been really exasperated, as in my own memory he was nothing but kind to me throughout my childhood. And certainly, any rift with my parents was quickly mended.

It wasn't long after this outburst that Jack and Kitty were allocated their council house: 1 Whiteley Crescent, Far Bletchley. It was one of the first houses on a new council estate being built about 1½ miles from the Cambridge Street house. As a bonus, the location was much closer to Jack's work at the brickyard.

I'm not sure if Kitty could really believe it until they had the keys.

But yes, it was true. Easter 1948 saw us move into our new home.

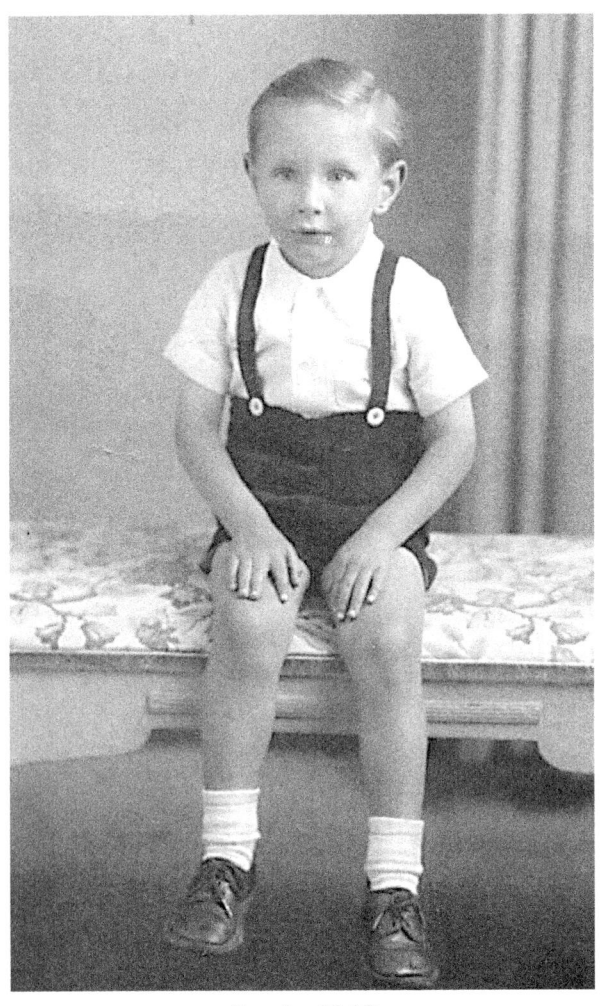

Ken in 1948

A HOME OF HER OWN

Kitty was thrilled with her first home, a brand new house. One unusual feature she really liked was that the living room fireplace backed onto the dining room, warming it too.

1 Whiteley Crescent today, with a solid door and double glazing

There was a brick shed close to the back door, visible in this picture. It contained another toilet and the coal barn.

You could see all the way through the house, along the hallway from front door to back, with the stairs going up on the left.

All the walls were painted with distemper when we moved in, I think to save money. The living room in all our houses would be decorated every two or three years, given how the accumulation of ash and smoke discoloured the walls and ceiling.

1 Whiteley Crescent, approximate floor plans

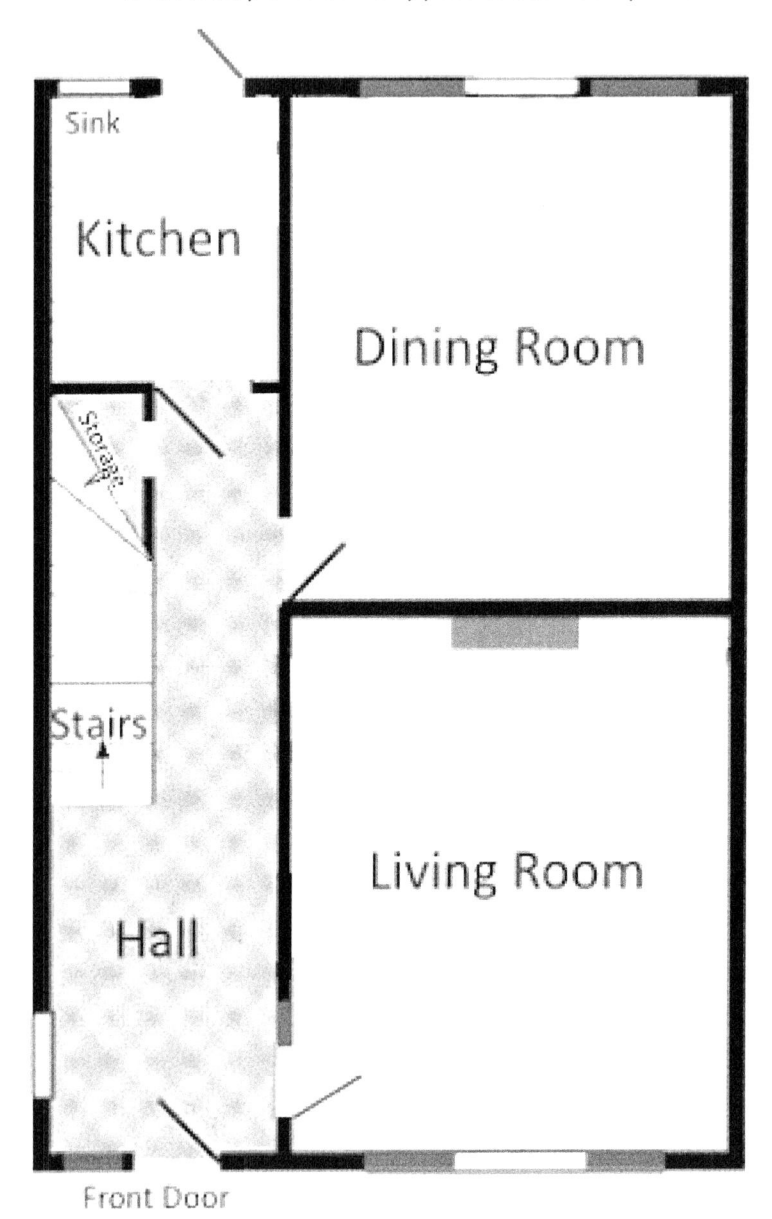

Ground Floor

Most houses had a storage area under the stairs, generally known as a "cubbyhole," a term used for any small enclosed space.

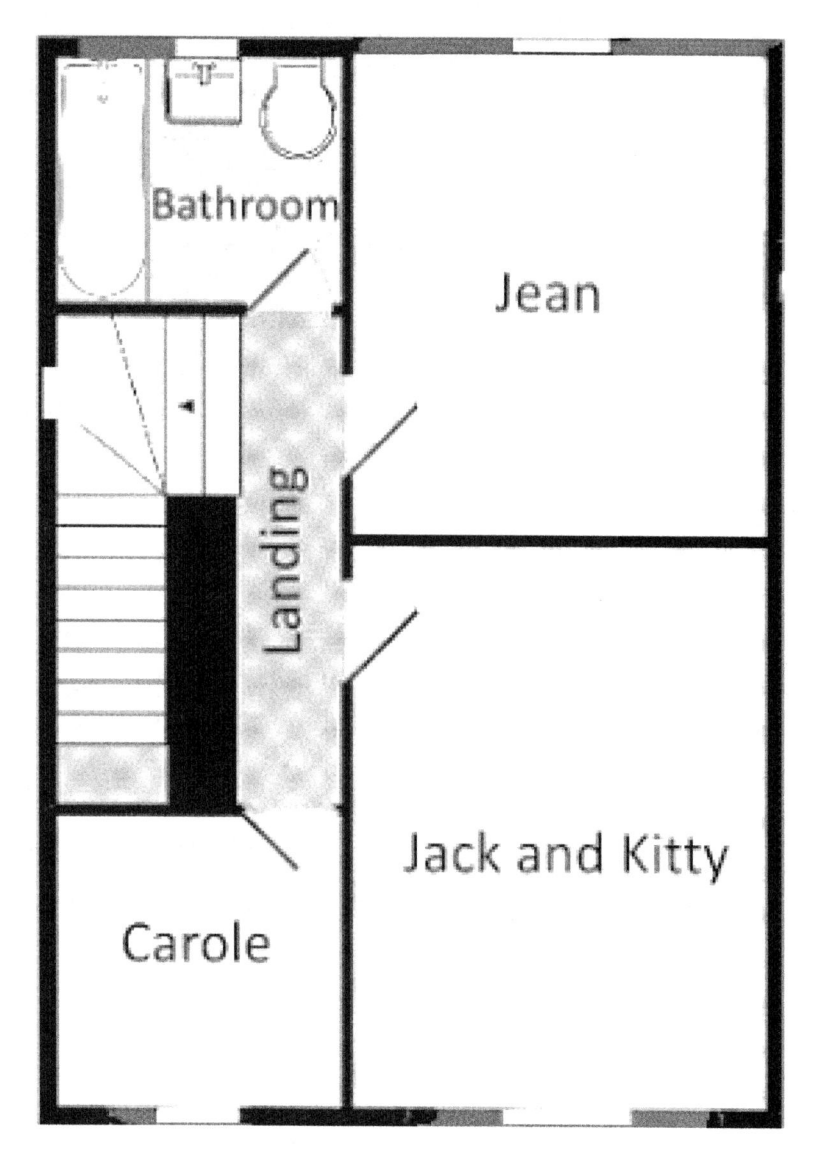

Upper Floor

The upper floor layout was simple, with an upstairs bathroom containing another toilet.

Being on the corner of Whiteley Crescent and Newton Road our garden was triangular in shape, the base toward the house. It was still big enough for Dad to grow some vegetables in, as well as having his allotment.

All the fences were quite low, (like picket fences but the posts joined by wire), so you could see and talk to any neighbour who was close enough. The fronts were open and had been seeded with grass that was starting to grow.

In all our houses, with no double-glazing and doors not fitting tightly, the draughts whipped through in the winter. So two big brass hooks were fitted at the top on the inside of the front door and the living room door.

In the winter a pole was placed across these, from which hung a heavy curtain. A "sausage" or "snake," a draught excluder made from a stuffed tube of material, was also laid at the base of the living room door.

Furnishing the house can't have been easy. Not only did Kitty and Jack not have much money but for some time after the war all you could buy was still mostly utility furniture. Coupons were needed for the purchases and everything had to be officially applied for, even the linoleum (lino) floor covering.

They bought two large utility armchairs, which lasted for many years, for the living room. These were square with wide arms, covered in a dark green fake leather, with similar coloured fabric seats.

The dining room suite: a table, four chairs and a sideboard, which again lasted many years, was also utility furniture. Their nicer bedroom suite wasn't. It consisted of one large and one small wardrobe and a dressing table, which they still had and used until moving into their care home in 2010.

I don't know where that bedroom suite came from. It may have been either a gift or bought second-hand, as was most of the rest of the furniture.

One item that puzzled me in later life was the piano. I'm not sure of its origin, though it may have come from Bertha's home, or why my parents kept it in the dining room. Neither of them played the piano. But it did mean that I had one to practise on when I started to have lessons from Nellie a few years later.

There was no fitted kitchen. The main furniture item in most kitchens was a freestanding kitchen cabinet, some six feet high. The top part was a storage cupboard with one or two shelves.

Below this a drop-down door, which served as a work surface, hid another storage area. And under this again were drawers and a bottom cupboard with another shelf.

A walk-in pantry (larder) was standard. In ordinary houses it was a very small walk-in room with shelves for storing bottles, jars, tins (cans) and packets.

One shelf, along an outside wall, was a thick marble or concrete slab for things such as butter, milk and cheese, that needed keeping cold. Beneath it was a meat safe, a cupboard with a wire mesh door, both for keeping the meat cool and keeping flies out.

The cooker was gas, as in the Cambridge Street house. Kitty always preferred gas to electric for both the oven and stove top.

In really hot weather the milk bottles stood in a bucket of cold water, in the pantry or a cooler place outside, to stop the milk from souring. Refrigerators were very uncommon and expensive, and would have been just a dream for Kitty for many more years.

Having no refrigerator meant all perishables needed to be bought fresh. Ice cream was a luxury, that could only be bought shortly before eating.

Whilst very happy with her new home, Kitty did miss Nellie. With no telephone, the only way to talk was to get together.

Kitty would take me on the bus to Bletchley one afternoon a week. She and I, with Nellie and Ken, visited the shops or the market held on land behind Reg's butcher shop, or just spent an hour or two at Cambridge Street, getting home in the late afternoon.

It was always a rush to catch the bus as before I started school I had to hear "Listen with Mother," a programme for children on the wireless (radio) at 1.45pm. I think the bus must have been at our stop on Newton Road shortly after 2.00pm, the time the programme ended.

I know now that Kitty always worried that we might not get to the bus stop on time. But being so soft hearted, she wouldn't stop me listening or get me out of the house before the programme ended. Nellie and Ken also visited us and quite often our two families got together over the weekend. We also visited Jack's parents and other members of his family.

But housework did keep Kitty busy. It wasn't easy in those days. There were no automatic washing machines, and no dryers. The whites (all cotton) were boil washed in a special washing boiler. To make the white clothes brighter, Kitty also added what was called a blue bag to the wash water.

All the clothes were rubbed on a scrubbing board with bar soap to get them clean. The clothes and linen were taken out of the hot water with long, wooden handled wash tongs and left until cool enough to handle.

After washing, and again after rinsing, everything was put through the two wooden rollers of a mangle, turned by hand, to wring out as much water as possible. Then it was hung out on the garden washing line, weather permitting. When the weather was bad it was all strung on a line across the kitchen, filling it with steam.

Kitty and Jack had only lino and small rugs on the floors. But every floor and any big carpet had to be swept with a brush. Tile and lino floors were scrubbed with a scrubbing brush. That was a hands and knees job. The small rugs were taken out and shaken every week.

Where people had larger rugs, these were taken out less frequently, hung over the clothesline and beaten with a carpet beater to get out all the dust and grime. Later Kitty had a manual carpet sweeper of the kind you can still buy today.

All heating was solid fuel, an open coal fire to warm at least the living room and a coke (hard, more efficient fuel made from coal) boiler in the kitchen for hot water. In winter the living room needed a thorough clean every day. Ash and coal dust settled everywhere, however careful you were.

The grate was emptied of ash first thing in the morning, after it had cooled down overnight. Then crumpled newspaper was placed on the grate, sticks layered on top, with a few pieces of coal placed on them. The paper was lit in several places, hopefully the fire caught and then more coal would be tipped on.

If the wind was in the wrong direction, and the fire wouldn't catch, you'd hold a sheet of newspaper across it to funnel air through the kindling up into the chimney. But be careful! If the draught dragged in the paper and it caught fire you had to let go of it pretty smartly.

Every house had a front doorstep and most a back one too, which would be scrubbed every week, usually on the same day as the drains were cleaned. The grates over the drains were thoroughly scoured as well.

Dustbins were metal and there were no bin liners. So the dustbin too needed a regular scouring. The dustbins were emptied on a weekly basis and although all waste went into them, they were seldom full by collection day.

There was far less disposable packaging and vegetable waste would go into the compost heap, or to feed the chickens mentioned earlier.

Speaking of compost heaps, Jack had one on the allotment that he tended many evenings after tea and, in the summer, quite often early in the morning. He also worked on it at the weekends but in the fishing season he was on the river bank most Sundays.

Jack worked at the brickworks' office 9.00am to 5.00 pm from

Monday to Friday. He had an hour's break at midday. And for most working people, midday was when they ate their main meal, dinner.

It wasn't that many years ago that most work had been manual or agricultural. The workers needed a good meal in the middle of the day to sustain them until whatever time they finished.

Dinner was always a main course and a dessert, known as pudding or afters. I don't know why pudding, because the steamed desserts were specifically known as pudding, as were milk puddings such as rice pudding and sago. We all called the latter frog's eggs because it was just like a cloud of frogspawn in the milk, only without the black "eye" in each "egg."

Monday dinner was leftover Sunday roast, often eaten with bubble and squeak (left over mashed potato and greens, mixed together and fried).

Sometimes the meat was hand minced and turned into shepherd's pie, with leftover mashed potato topping. Pudding would be an easy one, with it being washday.

Jack and Kitty's most common main course was meat, with potatoes and a seasonal vegetable. Kitty made her own gravy, for stews and casseroles as well. Once a week on a Friday she usually cooked fried fresh fish that she battered, and home-made chips.

Something Kitty loved, that I haven't seen for years, was cod roe. She bought both the hard and soft varieties. The hard, she battered and deep fried. Carole remembers spreading the soft on toast.

When Jack got home from work at the end of the day, it was teatime. Tea was usually bread and butter with jam, meat or fish paste from a jar, or perhaps cheese, in the week.

In the winter crumpets might be toasted on a toasting fork over the open fire or toast cooked in the same way. Whatever was eaten first would be followed by Kitty's homemade cake or jam tarts.

Kitty made all her own cakes - Victoria sponge with jam and buttercream, coffee and walnut cake, fruit cake and little fairy cakes that were smaller than cupcakes and much smaller than today's muffins.

She made jam tarts, mince tarts, scones, sometimes sausage rolls, and a variety of pies and tarts to have with custard for pudding. What else? Hot cross buns at Easter, bonfire toffee and parkin for Guy Fawkes Day, then Christmas cake and Christmas puddings later in November.

If she ran out of bread on a Sunday, with no shops open in those days other than a newsagent, Kitty made what she called milk rolls. Yeastless, they were a type of plain scone, like an American biscuit.

Then there were the puddings she made – all manner of suet and sponge steamed puddings, Yorkshire puddings... She'd make jelly (Jell-O) or trifle for a special tea.

But Kitty didn't stop there. She bottled fruit in season, made jams and chutneys, pickled onions, even preserved eggs in isinglass. With no battery hens, egg laying was on a go slow in the winter.

What Kitty didn't make were biscuits (cookies). Those she did buy, quite plain ones mostly and sold in paper bags by weight. A bag of broken biscuits would be even cheaper!

There was very little convenience food but Jack and Kitty always had plenty of fresh seasonal vegetables, meat from Reg, all Kitty's home baking and the preserves she made.

Bread and milk were delivered to the house. Milk was delivered to the doorstep in pint bottles daily from Monday to Saturday. It was full cream milk, as there was no semi-skimmed or skimmed (that I ever saw).

This milk was not homogenised as most is now but had a layer of cream on top. Mostly, the bottle would be shaken to mix the milk and cream. On a Sunday though, Kitty sometimes poured "top of the milk" on tinned fruit for tea.

The baker's van came round daily too in the week, with freshly baked uncut loaves and rolls. We didn't have sliced, packaged bread. There was just white bread and, though far less common, wholemeal bread. Loaf shaped wholemeal Hovis rolls were a special treat. There were also different shaped white loaves and bread rolls, both soft and crusty.

At Bletchley, the milk came from the Co-op dairy and the bread from their bakery. Kitty bought milk and bread checks (plastic tokens) at the Co-op shop.

She left milk tokens out with the empty bottles on the doorstep, for however many pints she wanted. The man who delivered the bread was paid with guess what? Yes, bread tokens.

Although Jack was on quite a low wage, Kitty was a good manager who made every penny count. Wages were paid in cash and Jack handed over all but a small amount of pocket money to Kitty. This money went into a cash tin that was divided into compartments for rent (£1 per week), utilities, coal, insurance, food etc.

Kitty was up early every morning. She had a wash, made a cup of early morning tea and in winter cleared the grate and lit a fire. Breakfast might be cereal and toast - porridge or cornflakes the cereal. But at the weekends especially it could be bacon or sausage and egg, or a boiled egg, with toast.

After breakfast Kitty did the dishes to clear them out of the way. She always did her washing, baking, all her housework, in the mornings, dressed in her old clothes and laddered stockings.

Of course, she also had me at home all day in those early days. There was no thought in our family then of any preschool care outside the home.

Throughout the morning Kitty listened to the wireless. She loved it, singing along to the old songs. Soon after Jack left on his bike for work, she started with "Housewives' Choice," at 9.00am every weekday, followed by "Workers' Playtime" later in the morning.

The latter came live from a work's canteen somewhere, supposedly in the workers' mid-morning coffee break, and was comedy and music. Kitty sang her way through her housework, her favourite singer being Bing Crosby.

After dinner Kitty made a pot of tea (no teabags then!) and when that had been drunk she washed, dried, and put away the dishes.

After that she had a thorough wash herself, having worked all morning.

Then she changed into her good clothes and stockings. As she put it, she changed out of her "disibles." I suspect this was a corruption of the French deshabille (state of undress), one of a number of such corrupted words brought back by those serving in France in two world wars.

Kitty's glasses would get marked and smudged, something I know very well! At frequent intervals throughout the day she washed them under the tap in the sink and dried them off.

Kitty used Pond's face cream as a moisturiser. The only makeup she wore was a light dusting of face powder.

In the afternoons Kitty might listen to "Woman's Hour" on the wireless and on a nice day go out for a walk with me. Most afternoons she would sit for a while with her knitting. She made all our warm wool jumpers (sweaters) and cardigans.

Kitty also used her Singer hand sewing machine to make me dresses and, in the early days, make window curtains. Although still rationed after the war, you could get more fabric for your coupons than you could pairs of ready-made curtains, even when you could find those to buy. And of course it was cheaper.

The living room curtains were changed twice a year, lightweight summer ones and heavier ones for winter. With the coal and ash dust, and smoke from Jack's cigarettes although he wasn't a heavy smoker, they needed it.

If any socks had a hole in the heel, a "spud," Kitty would darn them with a similar colour wool. The area with the hole was stretched over a wooden "mushroom," the wool woven back and forth across the hole with a large darning needle.

Men's jackets had the elbows patched with pieces of leather when they became very worn, to make them last longer too. Make do and mend was the watchword. It even stretched to sheets.

Worn cotton sheets were also mended on the Singer machine. The middle wore out before the sides, so a sheet was cut right down the centre and the two outer edges sewn together, to become the new middle. (Got that?)

What had now become the worn outer edges were then hemmed. This was known as "sides to middling." That was real make do and mend!

Kitty took "Woman's Weekly" magazine, still published at that time on thin paper like a newspaper, and all in black and white, no colour. It was the same with all magazines. Nellie took "Woman's Own," so they would swop magazines after reading them.

Kitty would sit and read her magazine in an afternoon and read me the little stories about the robin family that were included. This little family of robins lived in a home in the tree roots, as far as I recall - but at the time I didn't question it!

A mid-afternoon cup of tea hit the spot and later Kitty prepared the light evening meal ready for when Jack got home from work.

In the evenings, Kitty washed up the tea things and put them away, before getting me to bed.

Then, most evenings, Kitty and Jack listened to the wireless, mainly light-hearted programmes. It wouldn't have occurred to them to go out for an evening, leaving me with a babysitter. They didn't have the money, in any event.

As time went by Kitty made friends with some of her neighbours, in particular Mrs Smith. The Smith family lived next door on the corner of Newton Road. I had become friendly with Robert Smith, a boy of about my own age.

But let's go back to the early summer of 1948. Kitty and Jack always planned to have another child but wanted to wait until Jack's wages improved and they felt more able to afford two children. Would that ever have been the case?

That question became immaterial. Happily nesting in a home of her own, Kitty found that she was pregnant.

Although knowing money would be even tighter, both Kitty and Jack were happy and looked forward to the new baby. No telling in those days what the sex would be until birth. But that didn't bother either of them.

Jack had already booked a family holiday for that summer, a week in Great Yarmouth on the east coast. It turned out that this was to be our last family holiday, other than with relatives, for the next nine years.

Our boarding house this time had a friendly landlady, the rules were far less strict, and the food much better than the previous year's holiday.

It was a lovely week with good weather, a happy relaxed time for Kitty and Jack. I even had a donkey ride and from somewhere came a, rather large for a little girl, stuffed rabbit toy. As you see, I have my reading material too! Kitty looks amused.

It looks as though it may have been a bit cool that day.

Here we are enjoying a paddle in the sea. But we stayed at the tide line, no risk of Jack getting his trousers wet!

After such a welcome break, it was back to the workaday world. And once back at home, Kitty was busy making preparations for the new baby. Her baby was due in February, so would need to be kept warm and cosy through the last of winter.

Kitty knitted matinée jackets (look it up if you don't know!), warm wool leggings, jackets, hats and mittens for the baby, all in either white or yellow. She made a few long nightgowns, too. But without knowing the sex, as you couldn't then, there were no pink or blue colours.

For my birthday that year Jack and Kitty bought me a lovely big second-hand doll's pram. It was a wonderful gift and even second-hand I know it can't have been an easy purchase for them.

I think it was probably about that time that they also bought a second-hand pram for the new baby. Kitty and Jack weren't proud. They were happy with their purchases and never lived beyond their means.

In November, Kitty made her Christmas cake and Christmas puddings. As she mixed the puddings, even I had a stir to make a wish. Then the kitchen was filled with steam as the puddings cooked for hours in the washing boiler.

Some, as in many years to come, would be given to relatives. The pudding eaten on Christmas Day was one that Kitty had made the year before. That too, was a tradition. It would seem that like a good wine the puddings matured with keeping.

As Christmas approached, Jack strung multicoloured crêpe paper streamers across the ceiling, hanging paper bells and balls between them. String was pinned to the picture rail, which almost all houses had then, from which to hang the Christmas cards.

Jack bought the tree a week before Christmas, a real pine tree about six feet high. Nobody put up their tree early, which I think helped to keep Christmas very special.

Jack filled an old metal bucket with earth and placed it in an alcove by the chimney breast, before adding the tree and pressing the damp earth firmly around it. Kitty wrapped the bucket in red crêpe paper with a band of green, tied in a bow, around the middle.

Kitty had bought ornaments, mainly made of plaster, along with tinsel, a string of lights - and a fairy for the top of the tree. The lights had pastel coloured plastic shades, with scenes from Walt Disney's Cinderella.

They were bell shaped and quite large compared to most tree lights nowadays, brighter too and with fewer to a string. Those lights lasted for over twenty years, no built-in obsolescence! The whole effect seemed quite magical to Kitty. She loved it.

On Christmas Day, after opening my stocking and going downstairs, I discovered a lovely big red tricycle waiting for me. Again it was second-hand, but as with the pram I neither knew nor cared. I had learned to ride on Ken's tricycle and was thrilled to have one of my own.

Reg, Nellie and Ken came to us for Christmas Day that year, Kitty wanting to be in her own home and host her first Christmas there. Reg had provided the turkey and Nellie helped with the preparations.

Although Reg was by no means drunk, I suspect he may not have passed a breathalyser test as he drove home that evening!

On Boxing Day afternoon, we joined the rest of Jack's family at his parents' house in Brooklands Road. With no buses on Christmas Day or Boxing Day, Jack and Kitty walked and I rode my tricycle there. We had a happy few hours, including an early tea, before making our way home.

And so that memorable year ended.

THE FAMILY COMPLETES

Kitty hadn't even thought of getting a dog. However, the dog owned by a workmate of Jack's had died. This man ordered another and in the meantime was given a puppy. So here came that puppy, Bess, brought home in Jack's pocket.

And guess what? Kitty was too soft hearted to turn her away and soon grew to really love her. Bess was a small black mixed breed terrier, with a white patch on her chest.

She was a very placid dog, not given to barking, running, or making any kind of a fuss - other than when she saw a cat. If not on the lead, she then gave chase. But if the cat stopped and stood its ground, Bess would circle before turning away as much as to say that she really couldn't be bothered.

Birthdays and Christmas always saw family gatherings. On Kitty's 29th birthday in 1949, Nellie and Ken came over to share a birthday tea with us in Whiteley Crescent. I imagine that Reg was still working when they left home in the afternoon.

Kitty always had a light touch with baking, and had made a Victoria sponge that morning. She didn't know what had gone wrong when it turned out, in her words, "As flat as a fart!"

Reg arrived and despite the flat cake, everyone enjoyed the birthday meal before Reg drove Nellie and Ken back to Bletchley.

By this time, Kitty wasn't feeling too good and soon after they left realised that she was in labour.

Later that evening, Jack sent for the doctor and baby Carole was born in the early hours of the following day, 20 February. So one daughter was born the day after Kitty's wedding anniversary and one the day after her birthday.

When Nellie heard the news, she said that before she and Ken left Kitty should have told how she felt. Nellie would have taken me home with her for the night, so that my parents didn't have to worry about me waking or taking care of me in the morning.

Cambridge Street was still like a second home to me, so I'd have been happy to go. But it simply didn't occur to either Kitty or Jack to do that.

In any event I got to see the new baby soon after she was born, while it was still dark. I think something must have woken me for Jack to bring her in to show her to me. And I have a vague feeling that I heard the doctor leaving.

I don't remember what I was told about the baby, other than that the doctor would bring it - which as far as I was concerned, she did!

Kitty had not needed a general anaesthetic for this birth, being able to see and greet the baby as soon as she was born. And she didn't have to share this one with anybody other than Jack. Many years later I learned from something Kitty let slip that she felt with Carole's birth she now had a baby who was really her own.

What to call the new baby? I'd had a best friend in Cambridge Street - Carole, Mr Richardson's daughter who was born very close to the time Kitty had me. I thought that the new baby girl would be a playmate for me and wanted to call her Carole too.

I don't know whether or not Kitty and Jack had any strong views on a name but Carole was the choice. It wasn't long before I realised that whatever her name, she couldn't be a playmate for me! Here's Carole's baby picture.

Kitty felt her little family was complete.

She was very content and Carole was a contented baby. Our walks now were with Kitty pushing Carole in her pram and me walking alongside with mine.

Here we are!

Kitty did have some anxiety that summer. I came down with scarlet fever, and I think it was because Carole was so young that I was admitted to Northampton Hospital children's isolation ward. I was quite happy but Kitty fretted.

Visiting times were very strict in any event, but no visitor was allowed to even come into the same room as me. Reg and Nellie took Kitty to the hospital at the weekend, where she left treats for me and waved from the corridor through a window into the ward.

Reg and Nellie also picked me up from the hospital when I'd recovered and was no longer infectious. Kitty was so looking forward to having me home, thinking I would be overjoyed too. She was upset again when I arrived and at first didn't seem too happy to be back. But that didn't last.

I started school on my 5th birthday. After being taken by Jack on the first day, I just walked there and back with friends. Nobody in those days had any thought of that being at all risky.

Kitty initially felt a bit of a wrench but having Carole (seen in the previous picture) to care for soon detracted from that. Kitty is in the background in this photo, taken in 1950, and I'm at school. But we were all together after school and in the holidays.

Now Carole caused a rush for the bus to Bletchley. She too always wanted to hear the very last strains of music at the close of "Listen with Mother." And of course Kitty let her.

Poor Kitty, she had such a soft heart and I sorely tried her, with my friend Sandra who lived along Whiteley Crescent. To get home from school for dinner we started to frequently take a detour via a footpath that led straight out onto the Buckingham Road, near Chandler's grocery shop. There we crossed the road and went into Holne Chase Spinney (a little wood).

A pond in the spinney always seemed to have planks of wood across it, probably put there by the older children. Sandra and I would lose all sense of time as we played there.

Jack arrived home from work just after 12.30pm for his dinner, too often to be told by Kitty that I wasn't home yet - again. So off he went on his bike to find me. It upset Kitty, who hated it, knowing I was in trouble. They tried various punishments, including the only time I was ever spanked by Dad, until they found one that did work.

One day they left me to get home in my own time. I arrived about when I was due to walk back to school for the afternoon. Instead, I spent the time in my room and had to take a letter in to the head mistress the next day explaining my absence, not knowing that Jack had already been to see her. I felt mortified and embarrassed as I handed over the letter. That did cure me, which was a great relief to Kitty.

When Carole was a bit older, and I went to play with my friends, Kitty would sometimes send me out with Carole in her pushchair. Kitty had no qualms that I'd neglect Carole or that anything bad might happen.

One day, when there were no friends around, I decided to take Carole to visit our Aunt Nellie. I didn't even think to let Kitty know my plan before setting off.

I'm not sure how long it took me but I was quite proud of myself for making the journey with my little sister. When Nellie opened the door though, and saw me standing at the step with Carole in her pushchair, she was horrified. I don't remember seeing Ken there but he must have been in the house.

Nellie hastily got herself and Ken ready and walked us back to Whiteley Crescent. When we arrived, Kitty was very surprised to see us all. She hadn't realised that Carole and I were missing, still thinking that we were just outside somewhere in the crescent.

Now I have to say that Carole's memory is different to mine on this matter. Though she would have been no more than two years old, Carole always had it in mind that Kitty did miss us and walked down to Cambridge Street to find us, thinking that is where we would be.

In the summer of 1951, probably somewhere around that same time, Kitty's niece Brenda and her friend Margaret had a holiday at Whiteley Crescent, taking the train from Sheffield to Bletchley. Kitty was thrilled to have them with her and made much of them while they were there. I know that they enjoyed it too.

They loved a cycle ride. Jack took them to Bow Brickhill, riding through the woods. I don't know what they thought to the steep hill going through the village up to the woods!

Kitty was very fond of all Jack's family and they of her. But she loved going up to Beighton, staying with Annie and Arthur after Bertha died, and being able to visit the rest of her family.

After Carole was born all four of us would make the journey. This is the story as Kitty told it.

After walking to the station, we took the train from Bletchley (later from Stewartby) to Bedford. The main Euston line, through Bletchley, ran to the wrong London station for us. We needed the St Pancras line and that ran through Bedford.

At Bedford we came into the little St John's station, on the south side of the town and quite a way from the town centre. There was no through line then to the main station, Midland Road, on the other side of the town centre.

When Carole was very young her pram went on the train too. With a connection to catch, Jack dashed across Bedford through little side streets that are now non-existent, pushing the pram in front of him.

Kitty, Carole and I, with the luggage, rode across in a taxi. That part of the journey became easier when Carole no longer needed either pram or pushchair.

Even this train though did not go directly to Sheffield, the nearest main station to Beighton, and we had to change again en route. That could also be a bit fraught, time being rather tight.

The journey took much longer then than now and there were no refreshments sold on the train. Kitty packed up food and drinks to keep us going.

Toward the end of the journey, we were all looking out of the train window to catch sight of the crooked spire of the church in Chesterfield. Then we knew we were almost there. I'm sure both Kitty and Jack breathed a sigh of relief.

What you might expect to be the front living room of Annie and Arthur's detached house, 164 Manvers Road, was in fact a newspaper shop with a cosy home in the rest of the house. Arthur had the house designed and built with the integral shop, to replace the small wooden building of his father's business. The front apron was totally open, no wall or fence.

164 Manvers Road as it looks under new ownership, with a change of front door and shop window.

The shop has been transformed into a living room. You can just see the shape of the old shop door below the wall bracket. A low wall now separates the front apron from the footpath. You can also see that there's still a fish and chip shop next door!

Kitty would have been happy to live in Whiteley Crescent for the foreseeable future. But one fly appeared in the ointment, probably at around the time that I took Carole on that walk.

Reg, who was a very heavy smoker of strong untipped cigarettes and loved his fatty foods, suffered from stomach ulcers. There were always packets of Renny indigestion tablets lying about the house.

I really don't know if the link between lifestyle and his ulcers had been made then. But I do know that he had been rushed to hospital as an emergency and had surgery more than once to remove an ulcer.

Kitty worried. She felt cut off from Nellie. Nowadays, the physical distance between them seems very little. And communication is so easy. We have landline and mobile phones and most people drive a car. But although Reg did own a car, Nellie couldn't drive.

So Kitty began to think about moving back to Bletchley, with a council house exchange. Jack, who would do anything for his darling Kitty, put the wheels in motion.

BACK TO BLETCHLEY

A house on Western Road, number 106 and close to Nellie and Reg, was offered as an exchange for the family. Jack went to look at it, said he thought it was suitable although with only two bedrooms, and at Easter 1952 our family moved in.

The house some years later with new door and windows.

However, although Kitty was happy to be back in Bletchley, she was far from happy with the house. After Whiteley Crescent it was a real disappointment to her and she later said that she wouldn't have taken it had she seen inside it for herself.

It was an older terraced house, double fronted. The floor plans that follow are not altogether accurate but do show the layout.

Ground Floor

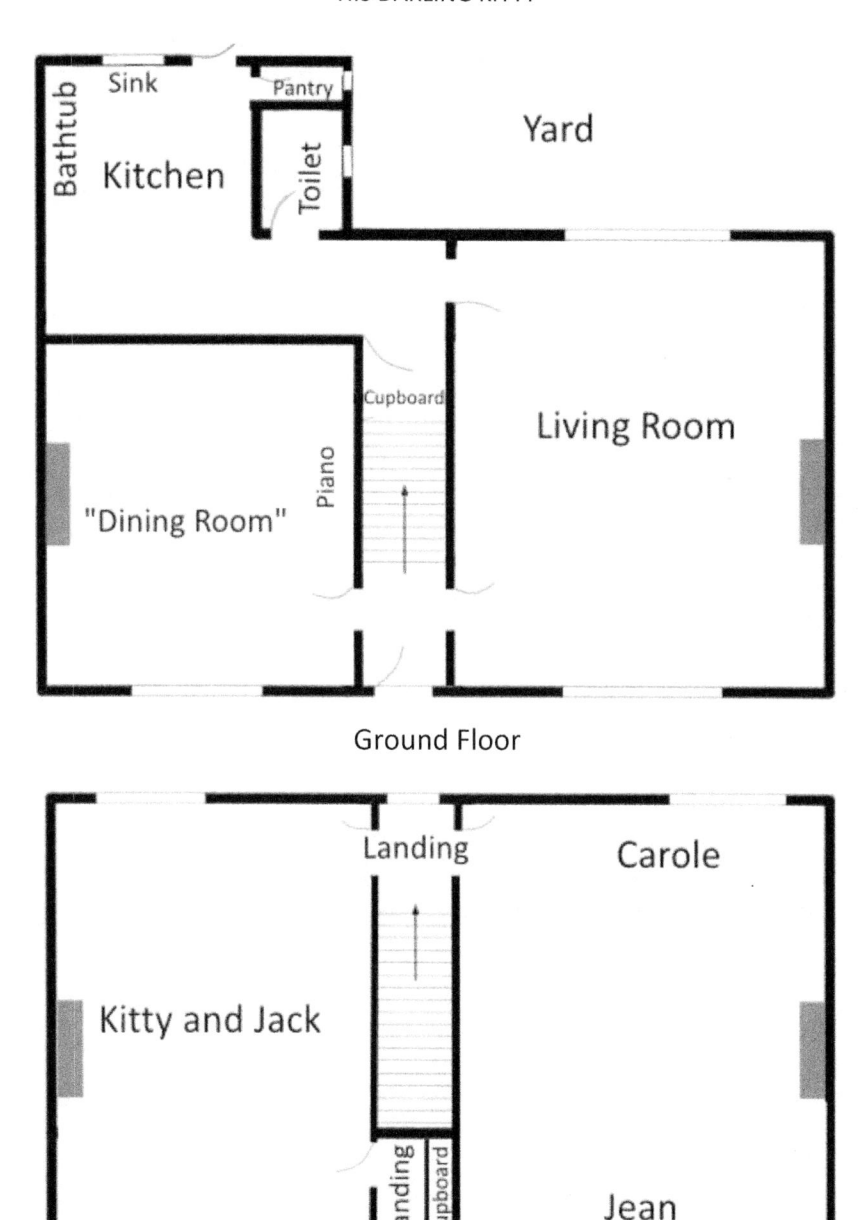

Upper floor, showing chimney breasts with no fireplaces

Downstairs there were two reception rooms and a kitchen. The only bathtub was in the kitchen, covered by a counter top that could be lifted out of the way. A gas geyser with a long tap could be swivelled over either the sink or bathtub, as needed. A toilet led just off the kitchen.

Under the stairs was the cubbyhole. In this instance the small space was used for storing items such as brooms, mops and buckets.

I have written "Dining Room" in inverted commas because really it was a spare reception room. Nobody used precious coal to heat an extra room when it wasn't needed. All our living was done in the living room.

The piano was now in the dining room here. When I started to have piano lessons from Nellie, that was where I practised. In the winter it felt very cold indeed in there.

Upstairs were the two bedrooms. Now Carole and I had to share.

Our house was the second from the right of a row of six. At the front of each house was a very small enclosed area, not really a garden.

At the back of each house was a small enclosed paved yard, beyond which a path ran behind the whole row. Long gardens beyond ran down to an area of waste ground, which led to the Bletchley-Bedford railway line. A shed stood on the left of our garden, close to the footpath.

Back garden fences were again low wooden picket style fences, and so we could see right across neighbouring gardens. Each garden was more or less allotment sized and Jack grew vegetables on ours, just as he did on the allotment he still worked. The only grass was a footpath down the garden, between vegetable plots.

I thought Kitty would have known what the houses were like, as she'd certainly have been on Western Road while living in Cambridge Street. But never having been inside one, I suppose she hadn't known quite what to expect. In any event, as always she made the best of things.

Here's Kitty at the front door, with me on the left and David Voice on the right.

David would have been 16 or 17 years old here and he had come to Bletchley for a short holiday.

This house was home for the next two years. And while the house may not have been ideal, the location was. As Western Road rounded a bend it became Cambridge Street, so just a short walk to Kitty's old home.

One entrance to the lovely small public park, the Central Gardens, was on the opposite side of Western Road to our house, on the way to Cambridge Street. A short walk through the Gardens led to Bletchley Road, with its shops and the Studio cinema.

Walking up Western Road in the opposite direction would bring you eventually to the Watling Street and Fenny Stratford railway station. But before that, along Victoria Road, were more shops.

Between Easter and the school summer holidays of 1952, I walked to the bus stop on Bletchley Road to catch the bus to the Buckingham Road end of Church Green Road, along which I walked to school. After school I did the trip in reverse.

I was only seven years old but Kitty trusted me and she had no fears for my safety. It was a far cry from today's England.

That summer holidays, we started going for picnics in Brickhill woods with Nellie and Ken. With sandwiches, cakes, and orange squash packed, we took the train to Bow Brickhill Halt, from where it was about a mile walk to the woods.

The latter part of the walk was up a steep hill. Carole was alright in her pushchair and I don't remember Ken and I being especially bothered. But on a very warm summer day, Kitty must have been out of breath well before we reached the woods, pushing Carole in front of her.

We continued to go on these picnics for the next few years. It was always cool in the woods, once we reached them. Kitty and Nellie would sit in the tree shade while we children played and explored.

On one visit, in a later year, Ken took home and planted a silver birch sapling he found in the woods. It eventually grew into a magnificent tree.

Back to 1952: after the school summer holidays, I just walked to Bletchley Road School. This was often with other children but again, Kitty had no fears that anything bad could happen to me.

She didn't even worry if I was an hour or so late getting home in the afternoon, having stayed to play at the rec. Bletchley was a small, community minded town, and felt very safe in those days.

Kitty's life continued in much the same pattern as previously but with the bonus of her sister, and all the shops, being only a short walk from her home. She and Nellie often went shopping together, usually just for groceries and perhaps knitting wool or other essentials. But it was doing it together that mattered to them.

One evening a week the sisters had a real treat. Jack and Reg babysat for them while they went to the Studio cinema. The films changed twice a week so there was no lack of something new to see, with a B movie before the main event.

What Kitty didn't enjoy were the Sundays when Jack went fishing all day with the angling club, often to a competition. She still cooked Sunday dinner - and plated up Jack's, covering it with a saucepan lid to heat up over a saucepan of simmering water at teatime. Being Kitty though, she didn't complain or nag Jack about it. And it was only during the fishing season.

There was always a family party for birthdays, and the two Christmases that Kitty lived in Bletchley alternated between Cambridge Street and Western Road.

Bonfire night saw Jack and Reg building a bonfire in one garden or the other. Kitty made her bonfire toffee and parkin, and supervised us children with our sparklers.

Coronation Day 1953 was special. Kitty made costumes from crêpe paper for Carole, Ken and me. And Ken won first prize in the fancy dress competition.

Here we are with Jack's cabbages growing behind us.

Looking along the gardens, you can see that Coronation Day or not, somebody had hung out their washing!

Nellie and Reg had purchased a television. We all crowded into their living room, neighbours too, to watch the coronation itself. It was a very special occasion.

Kitty did have her worries though, with Carole and I having childhood illnesses. I know that I was quite ill with measles and that was an anxious time. I remember the curtains being kept drawn shut to protect my eyes.

In the Spring of 1954, Kitty had a different worry over Carole. I don't know why I didn't go home from school with Carole, who was in her first term, that day. But Kitty was at Nellie's house and had told Carole to go there after school.

Carole didn't remember, went to our own house, and just sat on the doorstep feeling really miserable when she couldn't get in. Sometime later, Kitty realised that Carole was very late arriving and wondered what had happened. She hurried home, somewhat anxious as Carole was only five years old. She was relieved when she saw that Carole was there, although rather upset for her and for the worry caused.

Oh dear though, it was me who really upset my mother when I unthinkingly asked her who was the older, her or Auntie Nellie. I could tell she was unhappy with me as she asked, "Do I *look* older than Auntie Nellie?"

I realised I'd made a mistake there and hastily said no, that I just wondered. To me as a child they were simply two adults. But with seventeen years difference in age, I can understand Kitty feeling upset by the question.

While we lived in Western Road, Bess had a litter of five puppies.

Two were spoken for. Three just disappeared and I'm sure Kitty's heart was torn. She cared for Bess and the remaining two puppies until the puppies went to their new homes.

I have said that Jack's family were all very fond of Kitty. One of his nieces, Pauline, told me only recently that Kitty was her favourite auntie. She said that she loved being with Kitty, who was always warm and motherly towards her.

Pauline told everyone that Kitty was her favourite auntie. When asked why, she couldn't say. But she realised in later years that it was Kitty's warmth and love. Whenever she saw Pauline, Kitty would say "Come here," and give her a big cuddle.

When Pauline told her mother that Kitty was her favourite auntie, her mother said that she must love all her aunts equally. Pauline made no reply but said to herself that anyway, Auntie Kitty **was** her favourite auntie!

Other cousins of mine have also said how much they loved Kitty, and also loved her cooking! In fact, Kitty was well known throughout the family for the quality of her food.

Kitty would have made do with the house and been very happy to stay in Bletchley amongst family and friends. She enjoyed her life there, the freedom to walk to visit Nellie and members of Jack's family, and all the shops close to hand.

Fate once again intervened. This time it was promotion for Jack that beckoned. A few years previously he had been offered a promotion that would have taken him to Bristol. Kitty couldn't bear the thought of being so far away from everyone and everything she knew, so Jack refused the promotion.

This time, the promotion was to Social and Sports Club Secretary. It meant running Stewartby club, its social activities, and the brickworks sports sections - ten miles away by rail from Bletchley.

Stewartby was a small village, its only shop a Co-op grocery store with a post office. Kitty knew nobody there and to her it felt like isolation. She really didn't want to leave Bletchley.

Jack told her that if he refused this promotion he was unlikely to be offered another one anywhere. He added that there would almost certainly be no kind of promotion available at the small Newton Longville brickworks offices, where he was working in the personnel department.

When Jack also said the house in Stewartby that would be theirs was much better than the house in Western Road, and that the village would be a good place to bring up us children, Kitty very reluctantly agreed to go to see it.

It wasn't an auspicious start. The day was wet and it was quite a trek from the railway station at the bottom of the village, uphill to the house that would be their home.

The three-bedroom house on the corner of Wavell Close was spacious. The LBC agreed to decorate it throughout, Jack and Kitty only having to choose and buy any wallpaper they wanted.

Despite her feelings and misgivings, Kitty accepted the move without further complaint. And so was to begin the next and longest chapter of her life.

EARLY YEARS IN STEWARTBY

Kitty was 34 years old and had lived in six different houses in her life up to this point. She was to live at 199 Wavell Close, seen below, for the next forty-four years. But no thought of that was in her mind when she moved to Stewartby in August 1954.

Not a very good picture here but it shows the side gate and how the shed wall extended to the end of the garden, making it really private.

Here's a view from Stewartby Way, with the bushes trimmed.

The lower window front left is the living room of 199, with Jack and Kitty's bedroom window above. The front door and windows to the right are 200 Stewartby Way. The bushes and street lamp are long gone.

This house and garden were very different to the one in Western Road. To start with the garden, being on a corner, was very small. But unlike the one at Whitely Crescent, it was squared off.

The house itself was larger and was one of just four in the village of the same design. Three were for what I suppose we'd call middle management and one for the village constable.

The living room faced south, lovely and light, whereas the kitchen always felt quite dark. But it was better that way round than the other. The kitchen only looked out on our small garden and the house wall beyond. The living room looked out across Stewartby Way to the allotments, one of which Jack had taken on, so still providing fresh vegetables for his family.

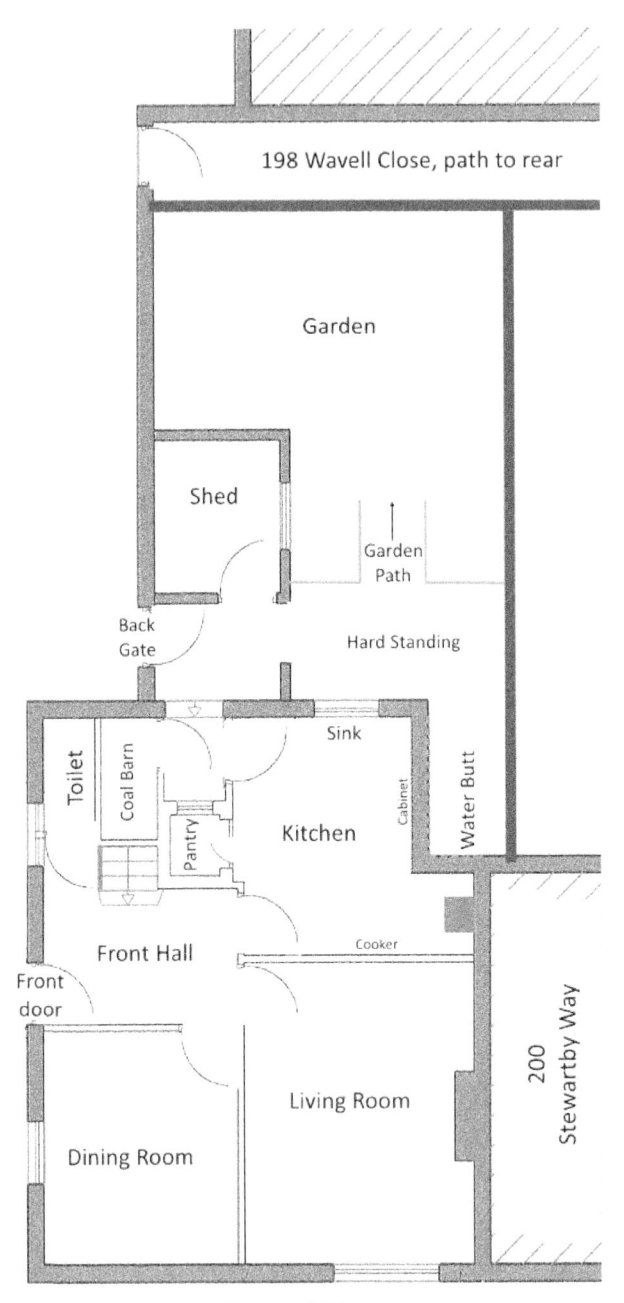

Ground Floor

There was a short, six feet high balustrade along the bottom few stairs in front of the toilet wall. There it joined the main wall reaching to the top of the upper floor.

Upper Floor

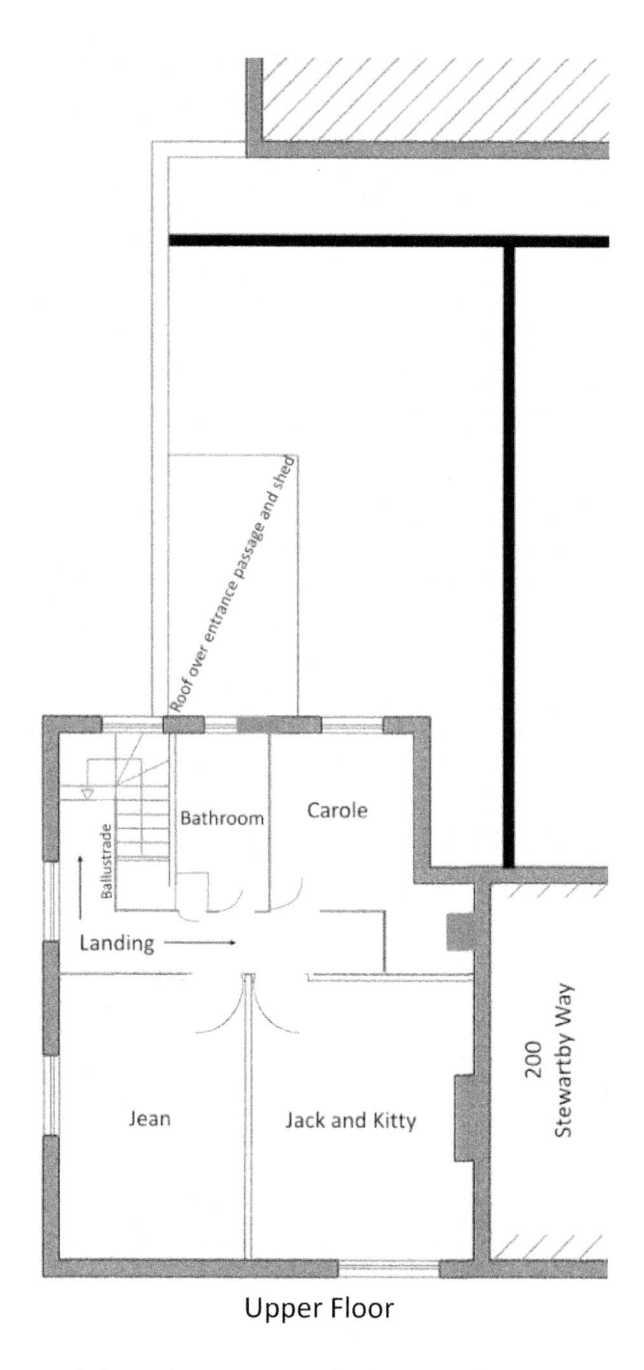

At the turn of the stairs, against the back wall, was a half landing with a window. Along the inner side of the landing, above the hall, ran another balustrade, this one about four feet high. Being so open made it very light both upstairs and down.

The balustrade ran to the edge of the airing cupboard, which was inset into the small bathroom. The hot water tank was heated by the kitchen boiler.

There was no mains gas supply laid on to the village, only mains electricity, as far as power went. That meant Kitty had to start using an electric cooker, which she really disliked. The hot plates on the old-fashioned cookers then in use were solid. They took an age to heat up and cool down, far less responsive than gas.

The chimney of the living room fire ran up the side of Jack and Kitty's bedroom, adding a little warmth in winter. The chimney of the kitchen boiler ran through the short L of Carole's bedroom, doing the same. I wasn't so lucky and my bedroom also had two outside walls.

This time Kitty loved the house but hated the location. To get to any shops other than the Co-op meant a bus ride to Bedford. There were a few shops in Ampthill, in the other direction from Stewartby and closer, but it was still a bus trip away. The train went to Bletchley but that would be a journey arranged in advance.

There is a description of the village, as of Hackenthorpe, Beighton and Bletchley, at the back of this book. You will also find maps to help you visualise the locations.

The village was very small and to Kitty it felt quite remote. It was the furthest she had ever lived from family members. Bear in mind that Jack and Kitty still had no telephone, leaving Kitty feeling quite cut off. It was not only Nellie and Reg she missed but also Jack's family and her Bletchley friends, especially Renee.

But these feelings were eased a little for her. Reg drove to Bedford every Monday afternoon to pick up dog meat from a supplier there for his butcher's shop. Now Nellie went with him on all his trips and they made the slight detour to Stewartby, staying for a cup of tea with Kitty each week.

Our garden had chain link fences to the back and the side. But 200 Stewartby Way, our adjoining next door neighbour, had a privet hedge on the far side of their garden that extended across the back, too. That again made for more privacy.

Kitty soon got to know Mrs Holden, who lived at 200, and they became good friends. Mrs Holden had three children living at home. Richard was my age, Jenny Carole's, and Lana (pronounced Laina and short for Milana) was two when we moved in.

The other occupant of the house we knew as "Croz," a Yugoslav who, like so many East Europeans, had fled his homeland after WWII. He was a lovely, gentle, man and they all soon became much more than neighbours.

One thing though, that rather annoyed Kitty (though not too seriously), was when Mrs Holden told her that their hallway and stairs were lovely and warm in the winter. Our chimney breast was against the party wall so we were heating that area of their house rather than another of our own. Our kitchen boiler flu also gave some heat to next door's kitchen and a bedroom!

Kitty's routine for most of the week was much as it had been previously. The difference was that she couldn't just walk round to see her sister or to visit the shops. She did sometimes take the bus into Bedford but of course that was nowhere near the same. And there were no more visits to the cinema with Nellie.

However, travelling to Bletchley for the day by train on a Thursday also became a regular habit for Kitty. She saw Carole and I off to school, after sitting a pan of stew to simmer on the stove for our dinner. Then she walked down to the station. She loved her day, visiting the shops and market with Nellie, having dinner at Cambridge Street, sometimes seeing Renee.

She knew that Jack would take care of our dinner back in Stewartby. Pudding would be something cold, perhaps a milk jelly, so no problem. Mrs Holden was at home for when we came out of school. And Kitty arrived back in time to get the tea.

It wasn't long before Kitty got to know people in our square (as the Close was known), and others in the village. You couldn't help but meet people in the Co-op. With her warm, friendly nature, and the twinkle in her eye, Kitty soon became accepted and well liked within the village.

The Co-op was a busy shop, being the only one in the village. Most people bought their weekly groceries there, delivered to their homes. Kitty had an order book, in which she wrote her shopping list.

The pages were carboned so that when the groceries were delivered Kitty had a copy, along with the prices of the goods and of course a total. She would then go down to the Co-op to make her payment.

Being a member of the Co-operative Society meant that the shoppers were effectively shareholders. Everyone had a dividend number. On paying for goods you were given a small ticket as a receipt, again from a carboned book, with the amount paid and your dividend number. Every year each member received a dividend payout, the "divi." Kitty among others found it very helpful as Christmas approached.

Kitty's sense of mischief also came through. She teased the young baker who delivered the freshest of bread in his van. He also delivered currant buns, or sticky buns as we called them, once a week. They were often warm from the oven and in the school holidays Kitty would give Carole and I one each with our weak, milky, morning coffee.

Mrs Holden and Kitty became firm friends, chatting over the garden fence. Mrs Holden reminds me now of Les Dawson in his comedy sketch. She almost always wore a crossover overall and when she laughed, she heaved all over. Our two families got on really well.

Kitty started having her hair done in the village, by Hazel Brightman who lived in Churchill Close and with whom she then also became friends. It saved Kitty having to take the bus into Bedford to a hairdresser and was of course cheaper.

But she did go into Bedford to buy her corsets from a small specialist shop. These had suspenders (garters) to hold up her stockings, and came just up to her waist. They were made of a satiny brocaded material in a pink, so-called flesh colour, though I've never seen any flesh that looked remotely like it.

With a long row of small hooks and eyes up the side, those corsets must have been very fiddly to fasten. I'm sure Kitty was glad when "roll-ons" became available.

Neither Carole nor I have many clear memories of our mother during this time. She was just ever present, other of course than on a Thursday! The other weekdays she saw us off to school and was in the kitchen with our dinner ready at midday.

When we came home from school in the afternoon, Mum would be sitting in the living room with her knitting or a magazine, Bess under her legs. A cup of tea kept us going until 5 o'clock, when Dad came home from work.

I know now how we took her and her loving care for granted. Some years later a friend from the village, one of a family of four girls, told me how she and her sisters always thought of Kitty as a "real Mum." She was warm and welcoming, kind to all the children, in a word I suppose, "motherly."

Kitty continued to knit all our jumpers and cardigans but no longer made dresses for us, though she would "let down" a dress as we grew, inserting a contrasting panel to lengthen it.

Jack was still fishing with the LBC Angling Club though now the Stewartby branch. And Kitty continued to hate the Sundays when he was gone all day. She didn't like the few months before Christmas either, when Jack spent most evenings at the Club working. He organised all the Christmas activities.

First of all, there were Christmas parties for pre-school and primary age children, held in the village hall. The brick company paid for everything but Jack did all of the organising. There were several parties, as children of not only the Stewartby workers but those at other nearby smaller brickworks, had to be catered for and travel arrangements made.

For the older children, Jack organised New Year coach trips to a pantomime or ice show. And he also ordered the Christmas trees for the Club and village hall, purchasing ours at the same time.

What else? Whist drives and raffles were held at the club, with all kinds of festive prizes. Again, Jack did the organising and the purchasing. He was also present each evening to ensure the smooth running of things. Proceeds from these events went towards gifts for the pensioners and widows of the company, with the LBC contributing a large part.

Again, it was Jack who did all the practical work. Each pensioner or widow household received a supply of coal and a chicken. The men also had a bottle of whisky and the women a box of chocolates. Jack delivered the smaller gifts personally.

I think you can see why Kitty would get rather fed up! She wasn't ever one for socialising much, outside of a small circle of family and friends.

On one or two occasions just before Christmas she did go to a dinner with Jack, but other than that she was a real homebody. She enjoyed nothing better than a quiet evening at home with Jack, as you see her in the next picture.

Kitty sits on one of Auntie May's rag rugs with Bess, Jack in his chair. (Auntie May features in this chapter a little later.)

But Kitty always loved Christmas itself. As Reg had a car he, Nellie and Ken, spent every Christmas at Stewartby now, from Christmas Eve until Boxing Day. Here's a picture from 1959 that remains a favourite of mine

Left to right: Reg, Jack, Nellie and Kitty, with Carole and Ken sitting in front.

Roast turkey and roast pork with all the trimmings, homemade Christmas pudding and Christmas cake, sausage rolls, mince pies, trifle and more, Kitty did herself proud. She loved seeing how much everyone enjoyed the results of all her work. And it was a lot of work.

Kitty and Jack lay the table for Christmas tea - see the twinkle in her eye!

In the evening there were snacks, nuts and chocolates along with hot sausage rolls, as we played fun card games around the table. I think it was almost my mother's idea of heaven.

On Maundy Thursdays Nellie and Ken came over for the day, as we all gathered in the kitchen while Kitty made hot cross buns.

Fortunately there was room around the big kitchen table. While the hot cross buns cooked we had a cup of coffee, as we enjoyed the wonderful aroma.

We were all allowed one bun after they had cooled a little from the oven. They were the best I've ever eaten. When Nellie and Ken left, they took hot cross buns with them. We had the buns heated for breakfast on Good Friday and there were always some left to eat later.

Thinking of family visits, Brenda's husband Keith drove her and Annie down to Stewartby every Easter Monday, once Arthur had bought a car. Hot cross buns anyone? There were always enough left to heat and enjoy with morning coffee that day!

We also had relatives staying at various times. Her sister Annie and husband Arthur, my cousin Brenda, Fred and Mary, were among them. Kitty was always welcoming.

Reg's widowed sister-in- law Mary, known as Auntie May, came down from her home near Sheffield every year. She stayed with us and also with Reg and Nellie. Auntie May's eyesight was really poor and the lenses in her glasses were very thick.

When we had fresh peas from Jack's allotment for dinner, May insisted on shelling them. Then one of us carefully picked them over for the maggots that poor May wouldn't have seen.

But she was very kind, met Carole and I from school, and taught us some old children's songs that we still recall. She also made rag rugs, one of which we always had lying in front of the living room hearth as you have seen.

On Jack's side of the family, his brother Don and sister-in-law Ruby stayed with us, as did Don's son Gary and his wife Anne.

Eddie and Jo, with whom Jack had been billeted at Anstye Cross, were counted as family. We all enjoyed their visits, especially when they came to stay just before Christmas.

The next picture was taken on one of these visits. I think you can tell that it was around the Christmas period!

1959 Left to right: Kitty, Jo, Eddie, Jack. Carole front.

Kitty loved the company, seeing and making all her visitors and guests welcome. But at times she did rather tire of spending so much time in the kitchen while they were there!

Along with other parents, mostly mothers, Kitty attended school plays and carol services while Carole and I were still at the village primary school. She also helped with costumes and props. These weren't very sophisticated but the children and teachers were more than happy with them.

Jack built a bonfire on his allotment for Guy Fawkes' Night. Mrs Holden's family joined ours around it, to watch the fireworks Jack set off and wave our sparklers about.

Kitty still made parkin and bonfire toffee. But Lana remembers taking a sandwich out to the bonfire one year. When Kitty saw it she asked, "Bad hand?" Lana remained puzzled over that until I researched it while writing this book.

I discovered that it was an old expression, usually expanded to "Got a bad hand?" There were two explanations. One is that a jam sandwich made with white bread could look like a bandaged wound. The other is that a thick sandwich might be so heavy that holding it would pain your hand! Take your pick as to which, if either (or both) is true.

In the late summer we sometimes went on blackberrying expeditions, to Ampthill Park or even just along the footpath by the railway embankment. Kitty made blackberry and apple pies and blackberry and apple jam from our gatherings, both delicious.

Soon after we moved to Stewartby the first of the Sir Malcolm

Stewart Trust bungalows were built, along from the houses on the Crescent. They provided free housing for the brick company's pensioners and widows. Later, Carter's Farm and the allotments disappeared when more bungalows were built. That completely changed the outlook from our front window and there were no more bonfires on the allotments.

These were the days when doctors did still make house calls. A doctor from our local practice visited when any family member was seriously ill, and when Jack was laid up with a slipped disc.

One of these doctors, a Scotsman known to everyone simply as "Dr Mac" was really memorable. "Wye aye, Mrs Blane" he'd say to Kitty, before going on to diagnosis an illness or prescribe medication.

I don't know how it started that he would be offered a whisky at the end of each visit but it became a tradition, not only at our house but others. "Just a wee dram," was Dr Mac's response. I suspect that at first he was simply offered a drink, with the speaker thinking of tea or coffee.

However that came about, years later he was arrested for driving while intoxicated - to nobody's surprise.

MOVING ON

During our second year in Stewartby I took and passed the Eleven Plus examination. Children who passed that went on to grammar school, but Bedford did not have its own grammar school then.

The Harpur Trust ran four private schools in Bedford, two being boys' schools. The other two were girls' schools, Bedford High School for Girls and The Dame Alice Harpur School.

The local council paid the trust for a free place at one of these schools for any pupil who passed the Eleven Plus. The exam application had to state which of the schools was your first choice to attend, of the two boys' or girls' schools.

Kitty and Jack knew nothing about the schools. My friend Margaret said that she would choose Bedford High School if she passed so my parents agreed to put that down as my first choice.

We didn't know at the time that the other girls' school had a grant from the council for a set number of funded scholarship pupils a year. Bedford High School was fully independent and didn't have to take us, even though we were still funded by the council. It required another test before accepting me.

I don't know which of us was the more nervous the day Kitty took me for that test. I was glad to have her with me. And in the event I did pass, so starting my secondary education.

My parents never complained but I know that they didn't find it easy having to pay for school uniform items. Bear in mind that the state schools didn't require uniforms at that time. And the uniforms for the private schools could only be purchased at certain shops, which were far from cheap.

Fortunately we were given some of the items that I needed, including a satchel and a tennis racket. Perhaps the biggest help to my parents was an outgrown winter coat. Those coats were very expensive!

In September 1956 I started at Bedford High School. Now Kitty had to get me out of the door by 8.10 in the morning, to make sure I caught the bus to Bedford. She just had Carole still at the village school.

For the first term I had school dinners, so Kitty cooked at midday for the rest of the family and we all had tea together when Jack and I came home. But I didn't like the school dinners and they had to be paid for, so Kitty started packing me up sandwiches. Now it was my turn to have a plated dinner when I got home, heated over a saucepan of simmering water, while the others ate their tea.

About the time I turned thirteen my parents rented our first TV. Black and white, with two channels and of course no remote control, it was a nevertheless a real novelty for us.

We may have had to wait for it to warm up, sometimes had to correct horizontal or vertical hold, and a few other hiccups, but that didn't matter.

That same year is the only time I remember my mother being really ill, until much later in her life. She had a bad case of influenza and could hardly get out of bed.

I was recovering from a sinus head cold, which had left me with a blocked nose. I remember well one dinner I cooked when Kitty simply could not do anything. I fried pork chops.

Unfortunately, the scent of the raw meat somehow just stuck in my nostrils and I couldn't smell anything else or believe the chops were cooked. By the time Dad and Carole got home for dinner those chops were so hard and tough they could probably have been used to sole our shoes!

Kitty continued to budget carefully, thrifty as ever, still keeping money for the different expenses separated in the compartments of the tin box. We never went without and although Christmas and birthday presents weren't expensive, they were always thoughtful.

Kitty and Jack did manage to save enough for us to have a lovely family holiday by the sea at Broadstairs, in 1958. We went with Nellie and Ken, Reg staying behind to work and care for the dogs. Fritz was failing by now.

Kitty loved that week. She was with her adored husband, her daughters, her beloved sister and Ken. There was no cooking, housework or washing to be done. And the weather was perfect. She couldn't ask for more.

Or could she? We stayed in a boarding house with a lovely landlady, Mrs Mugford. Mrs Mugford owned a parrot that sat on a perch in the dining room. Kitty, along with the rest of us, enjoyed his antics.

Carole passed the Eleven Plus in 1960, to the other Harpur Trust girls' school in Bedford, Dame Alice. So now she too left home earlier. For her first year, we caught the morning bus together.

Kitty didn't speak of how she felt about us both being gone all day. But with hindsight, and knowing her feelings, I think that she would have missed us coming home at dinner time and mid-afternoon.

Having both of us at these schools must have stretched finances even more, with uniforms to buy as we grew - and as the High School changed its summer uniform. Thankfully the council paid for our bus passes and books.

After leaving school in the Summer of 1961, I started work in Bedford. I could have stayed on to do my A levels, as encouraged by the school, but there was no history of even grammar school in our family. I knew it would be more expense for my parents and wanted to start paying my way - be independent, as I saw it.

However I now caused Kitty real worry, starting that December. I'd had a "grumbling appendix" for some time but was then really laid low with appendicitis. I stayed mostly in bed, eating very little and only drinking water. But it was February before I had an appendectomy.

And it was only then that the surgeon discovered I was pregnant. I'd been going out with my boyfriend for over a year, first love, but the news was a shock to me.

The worst thing was telling my parents, knowing how upset they would be. It did shock and upset them both, Kitty very much. My boyfriend was in the US Air Force and soon to be returned to the

USA after finishing his tour of duty in England. I was upset enough about that!

I learned later that Jack thought it might be best if I had the baby adopted, especially bearing in mind the attitudes of the time. It was far from acceptable to have a baby "out of wedlock."

Kitty was uncertain about the idea of adoption but Nellie was firm in saying, "No." I think seeing how being abandoned by his mother had affected Ken was what made her so adamant. In any event, I wouldn't have given up my baby no matter the difficulties. And I'm sure Kitty was glad of the decision, though not wanting to have to face other people with the news.

What I am eternally grateful for is what I took for granted then. Both my parents loved me and would have supported me whatever I decided. I never doubted that I and my baby had a home with them. But it wasn't an easy time for my mother.

That Easter Monday, when our Beighton relatives came to visit, my cousin Brenda and her husband Keith offered to take me back with them, to stay until my baby was born.

Kitty didn't really want to let me go but we all thought it would be best if I wasn't in the village to be stared at and gossiped about while pregnant. I was quite happy to think of coming back with my baby.

But the rest of the family had to face the village while I was away. I know Kitty in particular felt quite ashamed, anxious and upset. Yet villagers were not unkind. Even before the baby was born, Kitty was offered a second-hand Silver Cross pram, which she and

Jack bought for a very reasonable price.

Mrs Holden in particular was a real source of comfort to my mother. Her youngest, Lana, was born a few years after Mrs Holden was widowed and was the daughter of Croz.

When Mrs Holden was pregnant with Lana some self-righteous person reported her to Social Services as being unfit to care for a child. The Social Worker who called on her could see that was patently untrue.

The fuss died down and I never heard any comment. I don't think as children Lana's Dad was ever mentioned. I only learned it was Croz when I was an adult, by some casual comment about him and Lana, perhaps that she'd called to see Kitty while visiting her Dad. It wasn't derogatory or critical, simply assumed that I knew.

Back to Kitty now. She did come up to Beighton for a visit that

Summer, staying with Annie and Arthur. The previous picture was taken in Annie and Arthur's back garden.

From front left you see me, Kitty, Brenda with two-year old Timothy, and Annie. At the back is Sylvia, my cousin Brian's first wife

Carl was born 10 August 1961. I was in hospital for 8 days after the birth, as was quite normal then. The day after my discharge, a Sunday, was when Reg drove Nellie and Kitty up to take me home.

I don't really know why it was so fast, though I'm sure Kitty wanted to see her new grandson as soon as possible. I suppose Reg didn't want to have to take a day off work and nobody wanted to wait until the following Sunday.

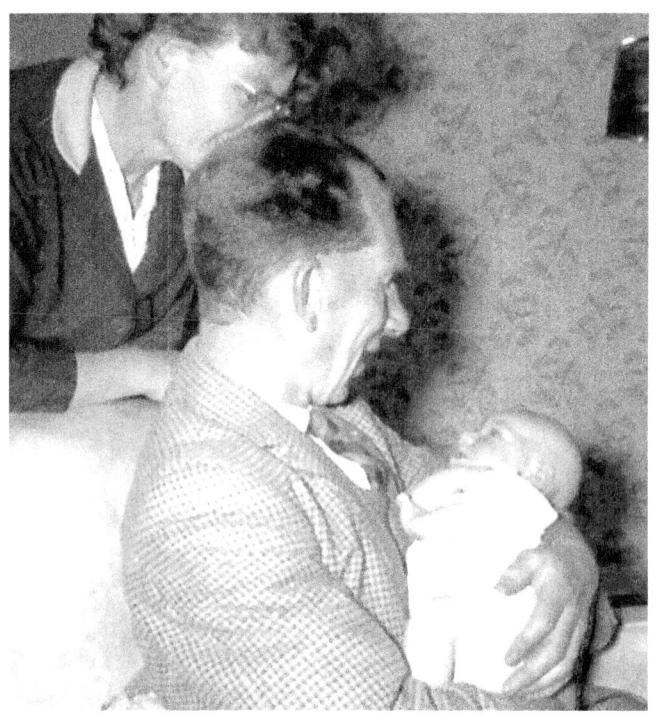

Kitty and Jack both quickly fell in love with their first grandchild.

Carole too was besotted with her little nephew, as I think you can see in the next picture. Nellie and Reg also loved him on sight. Jack's parents, all his and Kitty's family, accepted and loved this little baby. And then there were the Holden family members too, taking him to their hearts.

Kitty's anxieties were completely laid to rest. Carl and I were readily accepted in the village and he was made much of when we took him out in his pram.

My parents thought it would be best for me to go back out to work. At the time, I didn't know anything about possible benefits and didn't want to be a burden on them - though I didn't really want to leave Carl either. I did go out to work and Kitty gladly looked after Carl, bringing echoes of my own infancy.

But 1963 brought great sadness. Jack had a phone call at work to say that Reg had died - suddenly and unexpectedly, from a massive heart attack. Nellie learned that the cause was severe atherosclerosis. She hadn't known Reg had the condition and didn't think he knew either. His death came as a complete shock.

Nellie was utterly grief-stricken. Ken too, was badly affected. Kitty felt not only grief but helpless and frustrated at living so far away, unable to be of much comfort.

Everyone slowly began to recover and 19 December 1964 I married Ray. He too was a US airman but with plans to leave the USAF and stay in England after finishing his four years conscription. Fate conspired against this and he was deployed to Glasgow Air Force Base, Montana, leaving in May 1965.

We had been living in Bedford but Carl and I now returned to Stewartby, waiting to join Ray once he was allocated a house.

In the previous picture, Carl is with Croz and Mrs Holden in the back garden of 200. You can see the rear of 198 Wavell Close behind them.

In August the time came for Carl and I to leave. As I think back now, I can really imagine how Kitty must have felt. She was losing us both, not knowing if she would ever see us again. And I was pregnant with her second grandchild.

Yet my lovely, loving mother, uttered no word of complaint or protest, never suggested that she wanted us to stay. She waved us off at the airport before breaking down.

We wrote weekly and Kitty sent "care packages" for all of us, including Winn following his birth. Kitty and Jack still had no home telephone but, in any event, calls would have been far too expensive for either of us.

Then fate took another turn. Ray re-enlisted and at the beginning of July 1967 was deployed to Clark Air Force Base in the Philippines. Again we had to wait for approved housing. So I took my sons back to England, for however long that would take. Carl started school and Kitty had another little boy, too, to dote on.

Carole was engaged to be married to Mervyn (Merv) Hulatt, who worked at the brickworks. They had planned to marry later in 1968, until we learned that I would be leaving with the boys for the Philippines in mid-March.

They brought their wedding forward and it was a wonderful day for us all. I think Kitty enjoyed it probably more than anyone, having all her family there, with relatives from both sides celebrating with Carole and Merv.

Before the ceremony: Kitty holds Winn with Fred, Ken and Mary standing alongside her.

You can see in the next picture that as at Kitty and Jack's wedding, the page boy doesn't look happy. And just like Charles, Carl was coming down with chickenpox!

But then came another parting, more heartache. Kitty was so glad that she still had Carole at home. Carole and Merv lived with Kitty and Jack until they moved into a home of their own.

That move came later the same year but Carole and Merv were not very far away. They had a caravan on a site in Clapham, just North of Bedford. So Kitty, gratefully, could still see Carole quite frequently.

However, now Kitty had an empty nest. She missed us all but with Jack by her side she didn't give way to sadness.

She and Jack lived at 199 Wavell Close for another 32 years.

A DIFFERENT TACK

I could continue Kitty's story chronologically. But I fear that would just turn into a succession of events and you, dear reader, might find it rather boring. So I am taking a different tack here.

I don't feel that I have at all adequately described my mother. And she remains elusive to me, words slipping from my grasp. She brightened any gathering, putting others at ease and seemingly at ease with all those around her, however she truly felt.

There was never any malice in Kitty, though she might occasionally make a slightly barbed comment. She seldom complained about the real pain her arthritis caused her either, and then only within the family. "It's no use complaining; folk get fed up with hearing you." That was her philosophy. She'd also quote her mother: "I look well so I must be well." Another saying, spoken somewhat ironically, was "Mustn't Grumble!"

Children responded to her evident love for them. She also endeared them to her with the childlike playfulness in her nature, which she kept until dementia started to take its cruel grip.

Two instances of this playfulness come immediately to mind. The first is from the early 1970s. Kitty and Jack were spending a holiday with us on Crete. We quite often went to a small cove with a beach we had all to ourselves, to enjoy the sea, sun and sand.

On this occasion we took a space hopper with us for the boys. What did Kitty do? She hoiked herself up onto it and started to bounce. It wasn't long before she tipped off but her enjoyment and laughter were infectious. I think you can get the idea from the following pictures!

Action shot, just before Kitty came off

Oops!

Carole reminded me of another occasion. Kitty was visiting her in Clapham, where my young nieces were playing a skipping game. Despite by now suffering quite badly with arthritis of the spine, Kitty enthusiastically joined in - to the delight of the girls.

I'm getting ahead of myself but I'll come back to the timeline later. While Kitty loved children, and they responded to that love, she was completely besotted by babies. There was nothing she liked better than to cuddle and coo to a little one.

Kitty's wit wasn't always obvious. But it was definitely there with the glint in her eye and her mischievous humour. She could also be light heartedly slightly flirtatious at times, but never in a way that anyone could take seriously.

She'd always find an excuse to make somebody smile when she could. Here's a picture one of the Holden children took of Kitty as she was getting the washing off the line. It looks as though there's ice on the ground but Kitty doesn't seem to notice the cold.

It appears Jack's underpants are a little large for Kitty!

When we were growing up, and when her young grandchildren and great grandchildren were around, Kitty didn't swear at all. Even "Bloody' and "Damn" were out of bounds.

Fred's wife Mary however, liberally sprinkled "Bloody" (pronounced in her Yorkshire accent as you'd say "could") throughout her conversation. But she was so lovely, always cheerful, always fun, and so very welcoming, that nobody complained. It was just looked on as her way.

Even in later life, the strongest word Kitty ever used was "Bugger," it too pronounced in her Yorkshire accent, an accent she never lost. If something really frustrated her, she might say, "Bugger it" or, "It's a bugger."

I know that in the USA the word bugger became dissociated from its original meaning long ago. But I remember the first time I heard it there, when I was just twenty years old.

A child was being cheeky and his father affectionately called him, "You little bugger." I was quite shocked but I did get used to it. I'm not sure what Kitty would have said.

As Carole and I grew into adults, our mother also showed a slightly bawdy side to her nature, making me think now of some of Shakespeare's characters. The Nurse in Romeo and Juliet comes to mind.

When Carole and Merv were living at Stewartby before moving into a home of their own, Merv wore overalls for work and these were very baggy, hanging down below his crotch - long before that became a fashion! Kitty would grab a piece of the loose fabric, whilst asking Merv, "Have you got enough ball room?"

She did enjoy a mild double entendre or innuendo, of the kind you'd hear from "The Two Ronnies" or perhaps Dick Emery.

But Kitty had a barbed wit too, as I said. She privately called one woman in Wavell Close, a real gossip who knew it all, "News of the World" after the tabloid newspaper. Mrs Holden said you should just ask that one if you wanted to know what time you got home last night! Another woman, who always seemed to have a cigarette hanging off her lower lip, Kitty named "Fag Ash Lil." But she would never have used those terms in public.

Much later, it seemed that somehow the talk always turned to bowels over the meal table. At one point when this was going on, Kitty said jokingly, "It's not a meal without a bit of shit, is it?"

Again in later life, when taking medication for arthritis and gastric problems, Kitty had been known to say, "I might as well shove it up my arse for all the good it does!"

We still say it today, for the same reasons. And always when we say it, we smile as we think of Kitty. That reminds me of another of her sayings, this of a blunt knife: "You could ride bare arsed to London on that."

She was also always happy to enjoy other people's jokes on her.

Lana Holden remembers when she and Richard put stockings over their heads, crept along the house wall and tapped on our living room window, popping up to scare Kitty as she looked out. Kitty found it hilarious.

Yet there was a somewhat contradictory side to Kitty, in that she found any talk of actual sexual matters very embarrassing. She never spoke of any of the sexual organs by their correct name and hardly referred to them at all.

The first time I heard her use a word for penis was with Carl, when he was a baby and she spoke of his "winkle!" Female sexual organs were just "down below" and there might be vague talk of what were euphemistically called women's troubles.

Any straightforward mention or image of sexual activity mortified Kitty. She couldn't even bear to watch a nature programme where mating scenes were shown.

When I was eleven years old, I was in bed ill when Kitty made a trip into Bedford. On her return, she gave me a book with a plain blue cover and said that she thought I was ready to learn about "this" now. The book was on human reproduction (with diagrams), written for my age group.

I did read it and found it quite interesting - but at the same time I was very disappointed, having thought when handed it that I was getting a story book in my favourite series! But I suppose that Kitty felt it was time that I knew about such things, although she couldn't broach them herself. And we didn't have sex education lessons at school. In fact, I never heard of anything about such lessons as I was growing up.

As younger children we picked up bits and pieces of information, or more often misinformation, from the older ones, so did need something to put us straight. At least this meant that I now had some real knowledge that I could pass on and we girls could talk about amongst ourselves.

I was almost too embarrassed to tell Kitty when I started my first period. Fortunately it was either a weekend or in the school holidays that I woke up to it. When I did tell her, she just handed me a sanitary towel (pad) and belt to use.

Carole in her turn was given the book and had the same reaction from Kitty as I did when she started her periods. Of course, we followed Kitty's lead and said nothing about our experiences until many years later.

The sanitary towels were bulky, stuffed with an absorbent material that looked like kapok. Loops at each end wrapped over the belt hooks. (Things are so much simpler now!) I was a bit bewildered but, following her lead, I didn't say anything. I worked out how to use them, though still wondering if I had it right.

Both Carole and I remember being sent down to the Co-op in Stewartby to buy sanitary towels for Kitty. We were the ones embarrassed by having to ask, then carrying the packet home in a plain brown paper bag.

In a very different vein, Carole has reminded me that after Kitty took her first airplane flight, she had a taste for trying different forms of travel - always with Jack. On a visit to Canada, they rode in a seaplane. Other forms of transport she tried and enjoyed were a hovercraft and hydrofoil. She and Jack took a cruise to the Canary Islands.

What Kitty really wanted to do, after they started building airships again at Cardington, was to go for a ride in one of those, gliding high over the local countryside. Jack's brother Bob bought them tickets in 1990, as a Golden Wedding anniversary gift. Kitty enjoyed it so much that they later went up for another trip. Here they are in the next photo, ready for their first flight. It more than fulfilled Kitty's dream.

"Fed up t' t'back 'air" (fed up to the back hair), was one of Kitty's sayings, as in fed up to the back teeth or fed up to the eyeballs, in other words really sick and tired of something, sated with it as in having over-eaten.

In Edwardian times a woman's back hair was gathered up into a chignon or twist. So you were filled almost to the top with whatever you were "fed up" with.

Kitty also spoke of gathering up her tremanklements - her bits and pieces, anything left lying about. It was only later in life that I discovered the old Yorkshire word tranklement, meaning ornaments, trinkets, bits of things. So my mother's word was a corruption, perhaps hers or perhaps her own mother's - but maybe also an indication of how language changes.

Another word Kitty used was "aggled." By it she meant irritated, most often in the physical sense. When she developed arthritis in her neck, anything tight fitting would aggle her. Very different to the meaning of haggle, she hadn't simply dropped the H.

We remember, and still use too, Kitty's malapropisms. Once she said that she'd have to wear a "fornicator" to a wedding. Err: a fascinator?! Rather than a sliver of cake, she'd ask for a slither.

Another was probably the word furrucking. By it she meant ferreting about looking for something - in a handbag, a sewing box, whatever. Like a ferret sent down a rabbit hole? It's a rummage search really, rather as I like to use the term fossicking, originally meaning prospecting for anything from gold to fossils.

Kitty didn't use the common phrase that she hadn't lost her marbles yet, instead: "My marbles are still rolling the right way!"

There weren't many things Kitty hated but though she loved most birds, she did hate starlings, how they bullied the smaller birds. Her name for them was "Little Hitlers." The birds she loved most were robins: the birds themselves, pictures, ornaments, and Jack's stuffed toys. Kitty sometimes wryly quoted what one of her grandchildren said of her. "She loves robins."

Blackbirds were another favourite. At Wavell Close, one nested in the forsythia growing up the side of the shed. The nest wasn't far from the ground and Kitty fretted that a cat would reach it and kill the nestlings once they had hatched. She kept a watchful eye when in the kitchen, and thankfully the nestlings survived to fledge and leave the nest.

Kitty's care, loving kindness and patience were clearly shown in her attitude to my bed wetting. We had moved to Stewartby before I was consistently dry all night. Kitty had no automatic washer and it must have been a real chore for her to have to keep washing my sheets, especially in the winter. But I never heard one word of accusation, disapproval, or complaint, was never made to feel bad or guilty about it.

Yes, above all Kitty was loving and caring. She would do anything for anybody, and not look for praise or credit.

Mrs Holden died very suddenly and tragically when Lana was just seventeen years old. It was a dreadful time for everyone. What did Kitty do in a practical way for Lana? Every morning she went next door and made Lana her breakfast before Lana went to work. In some ways a small thing, Lana has always remembered it with gratitude.

But neither Carole nor I, nor I suspect anyone else other than Lana's family and Jack, knew of it. Kitty told nobody. And I only learned about it very recently from Lana herself.

Never confrontational, Kitty hated to upset anyone. As an example, one of my aunts wanted to learn to play the piano so Kitty loaned her ours. The aunt never did learn to play it - and in the end sold it! That really got Kitty's goat. But she didn't say anything to the aunt, even though she hadn't wanted to lose the piano. Nor did Kitty get back her lovely big copper jam making pan. I think the aunt ended up hanging that on her kitchen wall.

Was Kitty perfect? Of course she wasn't. But you would be hard pressed to find anyone with a bad word to say of her. She stole their hearts of everyone who knew her.

BESS

I've written of how Bess joined our family, and a little more. But she was such a big part of Kitty's life in particular that I thought I'd add to the story.

Bess was always an extremely good natured, placid dog. She never growled, bared her teeth, or snapped at anyone. Chasing a cat was the most unfriendly thing that she ever did.

Although I remember Fritz at Cambridge Street before we moved, I don't remember the arrival of Bess at Whiteley Crescent. She is just always there in my memory. And of course, she has always been there in Carole's.

Bess's rounded figure wasn't caused by over-eating or lack of exercise, it was just "our Bess." She had her one meal a day, a saucer of morning tea, a drop of cocoa and her evening plain biscuit, no other kind of treats in between.

As for exercise, Bess was always walked at least four times a day. The normal routine was that Jack took her for a walk before going to work. She had another walk just after dinner and Kitty might take her mid-afternoon.

A walk after tea, followed by a short one before bedtime, completed the day. Mind you, these were as the name states, walks. She didn't go in for over-exertion.

Bess loved the fire. She would lie in front of it, as close as she could get, until her stomach became almost too hot for your hand to touch. It didn't faze her at all.

Mice occasionally made their way into the kitchen pantry. Kitty was terrified of them and if she saw one, she climbed straight up onto a chair. More often, mice would be in the shed. When Bess picked up the scent of one, she would become as excited as we ever saw her. She seemed almost desperate to get at it.

One day, Jack managed to catch one of these mice. Bess was circling, sniffing, trying to get at it. Jack held it in his closed hands, As Bess was pushing her nose right up against them, Jack opened his hands.

I don't know who was most scared, the mouse or Bess! The mouse shot away as fast as it could - and Bess shot backwards at about the same speed. Jack didn't try that experiment again.

Bess was almost always to be found in the same room as Kitty. And in the afternoons when Kitty was knitting or reading a magazine, Bess would be lying in front of the chair under Kitty's legs.

She wasn't a demonstrative dog, in the sense of barking a greeting, licking or climbing onto somebody's lap. In any event, all three would have been greatly discouraged. But it was clear to see where Bess's main affection lay.

At night, Bess slept in the kitchen. Her bed was an old rug in a low wooden crate. I don't know what the crate had originally held. But it was big enough for Bess to turn around in and she certainly seemed comfortable enough.

Bess was only allowed upstairs once, that I recall. Jack was confined to bed with, I think, a slipped disc. Kitty let Bess go upstairs to keep him company when she went out. I don't remember Bess going upstairs the one time that Kitty was ill in bed.

Fritz and Bess got along really well. When our family went away, Bess would go to stay with Nellie and Reg. When they went away, Fritz came to stay with us.

Kitty really loved that little dog, as did we all. As Bess got older, her muzzle greyed and she slowed down even more. But she seemed quite content and had no serious health problems.

The way that the end came, when Bess must have been fourteen years old, was a real shock.

Kitty went downstairs one morning and Bess got up to greet her. But Bess had obviously had a sudden, catastrophic, sight loss. She blundered straight into a table leg and started to shake, moved and just walked straight into another obstruction.

Bess was clearly terrified and Kitty, in tears, called Jack downstairs. Hearing the anguish in Kitty's voice, Jack hurried down before he'd finished dressing. He too found it hard to see Bess in such a state, as did Carole and I when we heard the commotion and went to see what the trouble was.

Kitty loved Bess so much and just couldn't let her suffer. Bess was too old to learn how to live with her sight loss, was so visibly distressed, that both Kitty and Jack felt there was only one decision to be made. Bess was put down that day, as the kindest thing they could do for her.

We were all very upset, I think Kitty and Carole most of all. A lot of tears were shed and for a long time it felt really strange without Bess's constant presence. Kitty, who had spent almost all her time with Bess close by, felt it most keenly. Of course, in time we got used to it but her absence left a gap.

Kitty and Jack never did get another dog.

BACK TO KITTY'S LIFE

Soon after I moved to America, Kitty and Jack joined the Bedford Transatlantic Brides and Parents Association (TBPA) and attended their monthly social events. Bob and Lou Chapman from the village, whose daughter now lived in the USA, were also members. They and my parents soon became firm friends.

From then on, the two couples would get together some evenings to play cards and they also started taking holidays together. They enjoyed one another's company for many years.

1974: On holiday with Bob and Lou Chapman

Friendly with everyone, Kitty also became a really good friend to another villager, Kath Harris.

1969 brought more mixed feelings for Kitty. I was living in the Philippines, the due date for my third pregnancy the end of August. It wasn't until I went into labour 25 July that the doctors discovered I was expecting twins, even though I had suspected and suggested it earlier. But there were no scans back then.

Kathryn and Kevin were born just before midnight. Kathryn survived to become a healthy baby. But Kevin died less than three days after his birth, from hyaline membrane syndrome.

I had to let Kitty and Jack know the news by air letter, as they still had no phone. The post was waiting on the doormat for Kitty when she went downstairs first thing in the morning.

Crying, she went back up to the bedroom where Jack was getting dressed. Somehow through her tears she managed to say, "Jean's got a little girl but the little boy died."

Bearing in mind that they hadn't known I was expecting twins, Jack's horrified reaction of "Winn's died?" was absolutely logical.

Kitty managed to explain, handing him the letter. So there was joy for Kitty in knowing she now had a precious little granddaughter, and sorrow at the loss of Kevin.

Later that year Mrs Holden's death, from a sudden severe stroke, came like a bolt from the blue. It was a very sad time for her family and for Kitty and Jack. Kitty was bereft. Mrs Holden had been far more than a neighbour to her.

It was made worse when, very soon after, the brick company asked Croz to move with Lana from 200 to 173, a two-bedroom terraced house on the opposite side of Wavell Close to Kitty and Jack. The company wanted the three-bedroom house for a family. Croz was just grateful to have a home but Kitty felt it to be really unfair. She thought the company could have waited.

Jack and Kitty kept in contact with Croz, and Lana visited both households, later with her daughter Charlotte. But with the loss of their friendly neighbours, Kitty and Jack erected a six-foot fence between their garden and 200 Stewartby Way. Kitty never had such a warm friendship with a neighbour again.

It was in 1971 that Kitty first left the shores of Britain, also taking her first ever flight, to travel with Jack for a three-week holiday stay with us in Crete. Two further such holidays followed before we moved back to England.

Kitty and Jack met a number of our friends when they visited. One couple, Jan and Chris Jones, were assigned to England later. They both remember Kitty very fondly, the memory of her warmth, as with everyone who came close to her. I remain in touch with them today. The space hopper event took place in 1973.

My parents by now finally had a telephone. They could keep in touch with family and friends, even on special occasions such as Christmas, calling us in Crete.

In the autumn of 1971 Carole and Merv purchased an older, semi-detached house on Clapham High Street. It needed some renovation but was basically sound and Merv set to work with a will.

Behind the house was a lovely long garden, with a lawn and

vegetable patch. A gate set into the high back fence opened on to the village playing field.

Carole was expecting her first child that November and Kitty began to visit Clapham once a week, taking two buses to get there. Jack had his dinner at the brickworks' canteen those days.

Kitty was thrilled when Dawn was born, 24 November. She had a grandchild she could visit frequently, cuddle and love. She was also pleased that she could help out Carole.

Jack started to join Kitty in going to Clapham on a Saturday, still taking the two buses, so Kitty was in her element.

But by now, Kitty was suffering from arthritis in her spine. Her doctor prescribed indomethacin, which was the strongest anti-inflammatory. But she had no monitoring.

When she began to complain about stomach pains, Kitty was told she just had indigestion and was prescribed something for that. Indigestion?

A few years after starting to take the indomethacin my parents were on holiday in Eastbourne, on the South coast of England. One night, Kitty began to feel very ill and nauseous.

She managed to get into the bathroom before vomiting bright red blood. Both of them were horrified and an ambulance was called right away.

It was found that Kitty had developed a stomach ulcer from taking the indomethacin continuously for so long. The ulcer had burst, causing the bleeding.

Such problems were even then known side effects of the drug, and Kitty should have been monitored. The indomethacin had helped greatly with her pain - but at what cost?

Now Kitty could no longer take any anti-inflammatory drugs and suffered not only from her arthritis but from digestive tract problems too, for the rest of her life. Co-codamol (paracetamol and codeine) was the strongest painkiller she was prescribed.

Kitty wore a surgical corset to support her back. This was of some help but she was in a degree of pain from her arthritis almost the whole time. Yet nobody she met would guess how she felt, as she maintained her cheerful face.

ALL HER FAMILY REUNITED

In 1974 we returned to England from Crete. Ray was deployed to RAF Chicksands again and we were home. For the first few months, until allocated base housing, we stayed at Stewartby with my parents.

Kitty loved having the three children there and they loved it too. Carl caught up with friends and both he and Winn enjoyed exploring the area.

When we moved onto the base Kitty had another family to visit. Once more, she took two buses to get there, this time taking a bus from Bedford in the opposite direction to Clapham.

Nothing would stop Kitty in her tracks.

At Hallowe'en 1974, Annie had come down from Beighton. She and Nellie, Kitty and Jack, came over to the base.

Carole and Dawn were there too. Ken and Merv did the driving.

Though Kitty just may have flown in on her broomstick?

She just had to dress up and give us all a laugh!

Carl and Winn went trick or treating with their friends and we had fun going round with the girls. Kitty enjoyed having her sisters with her and a good time was had by all.

Christmas 1974 was a real family affair, with everyone staying at our house on base. I'm still not sure how we found sleeping places for everyone with our family of five, my parents, Carole's family of three, my Aunt Nellie and cousin Ken.

But somehow we did, and had a wonderful time. Kitty was in her element with all her family around her, much fun, laughter and silliness.

I'm not sure what Kitty was doing here but Carole is wiping tears of laughter from her eyes!

Then Carole's second daughter Claire was born, 4 June 1975, another baby to love and cherish. Kathryn and I were at the house with Kitty to welcome her into the family when Merv brought mother and baby home from the hospital.

A month or so before Claire's birth, Ray, our three children and I, had moved into a house we purchased in Clifton, a few miles beyond the base. Kitty still came over on the bus for regular visits.

That year Kitty was determined to hold a family Christmas at Stewartby. She wanted everyone around her in her own home. We all arrived on Christmas Eve. But what was that smell?

Ken had driven over with Nellie and unfortunately stepped in some dog mess on his way in from the car. The hall floor and carpet had to be practically disinfected!

We were a full house, sleeping in the bedrooms and the dining room, Kitty and Jack on the living room floor. It was fun but somewhat chaotic!

And although Kitty enjoyed it, those few days were a lot of work. It was the last time we were to have Christmas with my parents at Stewartby.

Carole and I then alternated having family over for Christmas for a few years. Eventually we'd have our parents, Nellie and Ken, for either Christmas Day or Boxing Day. For as long as possible we made sure of a family Christmas.

The following picture was taken in 1984. Kitty and Jack, having spent Christmas Day with Carole and her family, were with my family on Boxing Day. Kathryn looks a bit startled at having her picture taken!

But now I take us back a little. Kitty developed polyps in her nose and for some years she, who was such a good cook and loved to share a meal with loved ones, could barely breath through her nose and had almost no sense of taste or smell.

Eventually she had surgery to remove the polyps. She was thrilled as her taste came back and she could once again enjoy her food.

When I had to have a minor operation myself, at Lakenheath, who stayed at the house for a few nights to look after children and cook while I was there and for a few days after I came home? I think you can guess. Of course, it was my lovely mother, Kitty.

There were some sad times during these years. Bob Chapman died of a sudden heart attack and Kath Harris' husband also died.

For as long as Lou lived, and until Kath moved into residential care, Kitty regularly visited both them and others living alone. She kept them company, made them tea. She didn't make a big thing of it. To her, it was just what you did when people needed you.

On a happier note, every summer we held family barbecues in our garden. As you might imagine, Kitty delighted in these. With loved ones around her, a chance to share jokes and fun in a happy atmosphere, she was in her element.

In this picture our friend Alistair is pouring Kitty a glass of punch. I don't know what Kitty was saying, but it's making Carole smile!

Never really a drinker, Kitty did enjoy this weak punch. She would also have an occasional small glass of sweet sherry or a port and lemon at Christmas. Carole has reminded me of how Kitty sometimes looked at a glass of red wine and said, "I wish I liked that. It's such a lovely colour."

Talking of colour reminds me of how, when she was turning grey, Kitty coloured her hair for some years. Carole used a henna dye on her own hair and Kitty decided to try it. Oh dear! Her hair turned a bright carrot red.

None of us knows just how many times Kitty's hair was rinsed, by both herself and Carole, to try to tone down the colour. But it didn't work. She had to wait until she could colour it again before she lost that brightness!

But she was Kitty, and even she could see the funny side of it once she got over her shock.

Seeing Alistair also reminds me of another occasion. Kitty and Jack were at our house one day when Carl's car needed attention. Alistair had come round to take a look and do what he could to try to fix it.

After checking out the car, he realised that the engine needed lifting. With that, he told us that he was just popping back to get a block and tackle.

Kitty hadn't quite caught the whole of what he said. She responded, "Where's that pub? I didn't know there was one called the Block and Tackle."

She enjoyed the joke as much as the rest of us, when we put her right. Alistair did collect his block and tackle. And he did manage to make the necessary repairs, with Carl helping under instruction.

There was no escaping though, that the arthritis in Kitty's back was becoming worse. And as her neck and fingers too became more arthritic, Kitty gradually became able to do less. But she would continue to do as much as she could for as long as she could.

She and Jack took a walk every evening in the good weather, often round the lake that had formed in the big old knothole just beyond the Bletchley to Bedford railway line at the bottom of the village. The area around it had been landscaped and it made for a pleasant walk.

I now went to visit Kitty, rather than her coming to us. My children were older and I had started working as a nurse. Being on shifts meant that I could always find a day and time to visit and to take Kitty to see Nellie every two weeks, as well.

Nellie became very frail, following a nasty dose of flu and having developed heart problems. The front (music) room became her bedroom. Lovely and light, Nellie could also sit looking out of the window at the happenings in the road, which was used for driving lessons so there was plenty to see on most days.

Ken had the wall between the kitchen and outside toilet knocked through. With a door put in and a heater in the toilet, Nellie didn't have to go upstairs on her own.

She only went up when a carer came and helped her up the stairs for a proper bath. On other days she had a strip wash.

Ken was living at home and although he worked, it was his loving care that enabled Nellie to stay in her own home.

Kitty and Nellie remained very close and the following picture shows them in the front room at Cambridge Street. A wardrobe now stood in the alcove next to the chimney breast.

Nellie had beautiful silver white hair. She had covered it with a wig for years, because her hair was thinning. But you can see how lovely it looked, once she was persuaded to stop wearing the wig. Kitty here is her usual cheery, smiling self.

Jack had retired from running Stewartby Club for the brick company in 1981. Having become friendly with Bob Rinsard, who supplied gaming machines to the club, Jack agreed to work part time for him at his office in Kempston until full retirement in 1983.

He cycled to the office and on his working days both he and Kitty ate their main meal when he returned home at what would have been tea time.

Kitty wasn't too happy about that but it wasn't worth cooking a meal just for herself at midday, saving Jack's for later. And after all, it would only be two years before they could go back to their accustomed ways.

When Hanson sold off the brick company houses Jack and Kitty couldn't afford to buy theirs, even at a heavily discounted price as sitting tenants. What to do?

If a private company purchased it, they would have to pay market rent, much higher than the subsidised rent they'd paid up to then. But neither Carole nor I could afford even the small mortgage required for the purchase.

Then Bob Rinsard came up with an offer. He would "loan" Kitty and Jack the money to buy the house. That way it would be a legal purchase.

They would pay him the weekly amount they'd been paying in rent to the brick company, for as long as they lived there. He would take care of all outside maintenance and repairs.

When both Kitty and Jack finally left the house, Bob would take it in lieu of repayment. That suited both sides. My parents were very relieved at this resolution, as were Carole and I.

I'm not sure that Bob realised just how many more years Kitty and Jack would be living there! But he kept to his word.

In 1984 we had a wonderful family narrowboat holiday. In the following picture you can see six of us, ready to cruise slowly along the Grand Union Canal. Merv and I are on the bank.

My children were the only family members missing. Carl and Winn were too old to want to join us on a family holiday. Kathryn was in Europe on a school trip.

We had hired the longest narrowboat available, with eight people having to live on it for a week. For most of the week the weather was fine but even the rain didn't bother us when we did have it.

We all had a great time. Kitty absolutely loved that holiday, having us all together, and Jack really enjoyed it too. He took a turn in "piloting" the boat from time to time.

After Jack's retirement, he and Kitty generally rode the bus into Bedford one morning a week. Kitty might do some shopping and they would go to a Wetherspoon's gastro-pub, The Pilgrim's Progress, for their dinner.

Kitty developed arthritis in her knees, even to the point that one night when she went downstairs to the toilet, she had to call Jack to help her stand up after using it. Carole and I were really concerned by this and explored possible alternative treatments.

We persuaded Kitty to try acupuncture, paying for it as a birthday gift to her. Wonderfully, it worked. And Kitty never had problems with her knees again. But sadly, it didn't help with her spine and neck.

Her neck - as her arthritis progressed, even the slightest pressure on the back of it was uncomfortable.

Kitty would pull collars and necklines away from the back of her neck, saying they "aggled" her, one of her unique expressions as already noted. (One original meaning of the word was a confused state!)

When Winn graduated from Alconbury High School Kitty, Kathryn, Nellie, Ken, and I went up to Peterborough Cathedral for the ceremony. Kitty loved to be included in all the family events and was proud of all her grandchildren.

Carl graduated from university in 1984. Ray and I took Kitty and Jack to his graduation ceremony. It was a lovely summer day and there was a light buffet and drinks table in the outside garden area afterwards.

Kitty was so proud of Carl and enjoyed the day thoroughly, her playfulness as evident as always, as you see in the following picture.

In 1985 I split up with Ray. Kitty, though saddened was as ever nothing but supportive.

The following year was Kathryn's graduation from high school, again a trip to Peterborough cathedral and a celebratory family meal.

But Kitty was devastated when, 6 July 1987, Nellie died. Ken came home from work that day to find her lying on the kitchen floor. She too had died of a heart attack.

I took Kathryn and Kitty to her funeral, which was heartbreaking. Only a few family members were present and Kitty really broke down at the graveside. Poor Ken was now on his own in the Cambridge Street house. It was so very sad.

When I moved to Lincoln in 1988, Kitty and Jack started to come up to visit. I drove to Stewartby and brought them back in the car. They loved the city and Kitty felt very much at home there.

It wasn't long after this that sadness hit when Carole's marriage broke up. She was devastated, not only with the physical break up, as bad as that was.

Dawn had left home. But the break up also meant that Carole and Claire, who was still at school, lost the home they both loved. Merv had over-mortgaged the house to try to keep his business going. Unfortunately, he had quite simply over stretched himself.

Kitty's heart ached for Carole's plight and for Claire. All she could do was to support Carole as much as possible, wishing that she could make things right for her while knowing that she couldn't.

Carole lived in a succession of flats, of various kinds and in varying conditions. She struggled greatly over those years, before finally moving into her little flat (apartment) in Russell Court, the sheltered accommodation where she still happily lives. Kitty too was happy and very relieved that Carole now had a forever home.

But that was for the future.

Back to those earlier years, when happier news followed. Kitty's first great grandchild, Luke, was born in 1991, a cause for much celebration and joy for Kitty. Ten more great grandchildren were to follow, from Ryan in 1993 to Orin in 2005. Each was also welcomed with great love and made much of.

Later in that year though, came sadness. Two of Kitty's remaining siblings died. Annie had been living in a residential care home for some time, following a stroke, and had been joined there by Arthur.

Tom had developed dementia to the point where poor Edna was no longer able to care for him. He too had been in a residential care home where he died in December that year.

With the deaths of Annie and Tom, now just Kitty and Fred were left.

The following year, my partner John came into my life. He got on well with both my parents and he and Kitty soon became very fond of one another. Now we both collected my parents for their visits to Lincoln.

Kitty and Jack also had two really special holidays in the following years. Thanks to Jack's brother Don and his son Rex, they were flown to Vancouver, Canada, and given a wonderful time by the family there.

On the second holiday they were joined by Jack's sister-in-law Daisy, following the death of her husband Bernard. Taken to so many lovely places, and having such a happy time with family, they treasured their memories and were always grateful.

Family and friends in Canada were also left with special memories of Kitty and Jack. Kitty, as ever, endeared herself to all she met.

Kitty, Don and Daisy

But while they were away in 1996, Kitty's brother Fred died. Carole and I both agreed that we wouldn't let our mother know until after her holiday. There was nothing Kitty could do and we didn't want to spoil her happiness.

When Kitty and Jack returned home, I was able to tell my mother that I had been to Fred's funeral on her behalf and that we'd also ordered flowers for Fred from her and Jack.

Again, happier memories were to come!

Dawn and Dave married in their village church, just a few miles from Lincoln, on a lovely July day in 1998. The reception was held at a city hotel and went on into the evening. Kitty and Jack were staying with us for a few days and after the reception the four of us took a taxi home.

None of us was drunk but we were in high spirits. Kitty indeed had only taken a sip of champagne to toast the bride and groom. But oh my, that taxi journey home!

It was Kitty who began to sing and we all joined in. She started with "Chase me Charlie," beginning with the verse "Auntie Mary had a canary..."

We sang "Daisy, Daisy" and several more of the old songs. It was great fun. Though not a long journey, we were stopped at the level crossing for a while. I don't know what the taxi driver thought!

As with all of us, there were occasions when Kitty felt frustrated and annoyed with herself over minor incidents. At such times we might hear, "I could bite my own arse!"

As Kitty became less able to do housework, even to hang washing on the line, Jack began to take over. Though Kitty still did the cooking, the stairs became a struggle for her too.

The house in Wavell Close wasn't easy for Jack to keep up as he got older, his strength and his sight beginning to fail.

Kitty didn't want to leave the house that had been her home for so many years. But eventually Jack persuaded her that they really needed to apply for one of the Trust bungalows.

In 1998, they moved into 2 Sir Malcolm Stewart Homes, just before Jack's 80th birthday. It was also the year Jack's brother Don was over from Canada and threw a big family party, enjoyed by all, as he himself turned 90 years old.

2 Sir Malcolm Stewart Homes was one of the earliest bungalows. It had a long, wide hallway running along the front of the house from the spacious kitchen to an equally spacious living room.

It was not quite detached, sharing a roof with the adjoining bungalow, number 1. Yet the properties didn't share a wall. Rather, they were linked properties, with the roof covering a narrow passageway that ran between the two.

Facing the back door

Look beyond the end front window. You can just see the covered passage separating the bungalows.

BUNGALOW LIVING

2 Sir Malcolm Stewart Homes from the front

Once moved in, Kitty loved the bungalow. She no longer had to struggle with stairs and finally had the bay windows she had always wanted, at the rear of both the living room and kitchen.

The front windows had an outlook over the green in the centre of the village, and the back windows over the tranquil grassy area between their row of bungalows and the one to the rear.

The coal barn to the right of the little inner porch was now a storage shed, where Kitty and Jack also housed a small chest freezer. The larger barn to the left housed their washer and dryer, along with some household items.

The kitchen was really a big country kitchen. The dining table stood in the bay window and Kitty had a couch opposite the back door, where she'd sit in the good weather with the door open.

HIS DARLING KITTY

Number 1

Passage

Living Room

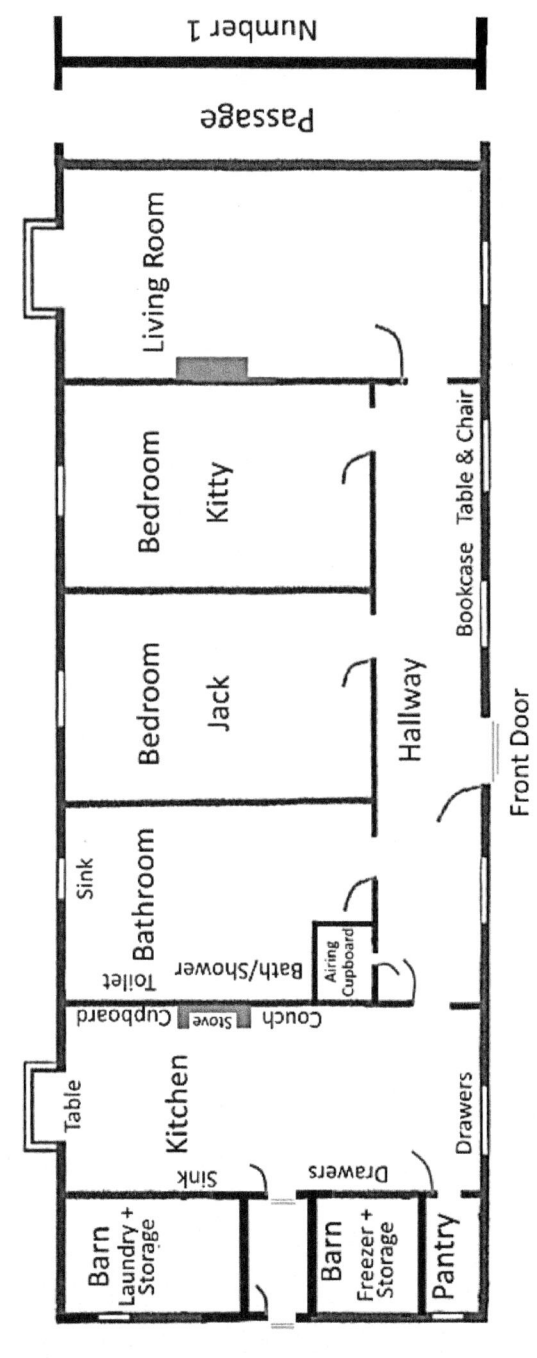

Bedroom Kitty

Bedroom Jack

Hallway

Bookcase | Table & Chair

Front Door

Bathroom
Sink
Toilet | Bath/Shower | Airing Cupboard

Couch | Stove | Cupboard

Kitchen
Table
Sink | Drawers
Drawers

Barn
Laundry + Storage

Barn
Freezer + Storage

Pantry

Very Approximate Floor Plan

The old solid fuel boiler had been removed from the chimney breast. The space left was big enough for the cooker. In the alcove to the left of it stood a big built-in cupboard.

In the corner next to the barn at the front of the house, was a pantry. It had shelving along the sides but no cold shelf. Instead, their refrigerator stood at the back.

There was a big old bath, toilet and sink in the bathroom. The toilet still had an overhead cistern. Kitty took the china pull that had been a gift from Winn to attach to the chain. She and Jack also took the wooden toilet seat and lid from Wavell Close! That seat was much kinder to the bottom than the modern plastic ones.

In the living room, the grate had been blocked off and Kitty stood a fire screen in front of it. The hearth held her collection of stuffed animals that Jack had made. He gave her one of each as he made them, from elephant to mouse.

With no longer having a boiler or open fire, heating in the bungalow now came from electric storage heaters. Although not the most efficient form of heating, they did keep everywhere nice and warm.

You know that the brickworks and village houses had been taken over by Hanson, who sold off the houses and other facilities and no longer maintained the grounds. But all internal and external maintenance of the bungalows and their surrounding grounds was taken care of by the Trust.

The house had been freshly painted before my parents moved in, and Kitty enjoyed choosing carpet and curtains for all the rooms.

With Jack's good company pension and their state pensions, a rent-free home, Kitty and Jack didn't have to worry about money now.

Although they were still by no means rich, they could live comfortably and not having extravagant tastes, they could buy the things they wanted.

Marion, David Voice's wife, had been welcomed into our family. She recalls Jack saying with a smile that he was the poorest man in the village, as Kitty spent all his money. Nobody believed that!

Carole and I were glad, though, that our parents didn't have to scrimp in their old age. When Jack said that his will would read, "Being of sound mind I spent it," we both said that sounded good to us.

One thing that Kitty wanted was a replacement for the lovely china cabinet that had been a wedding present. It had stood in their dining room at Wavell close, so it was seldom really noticed.

I had always loved it, with the redolent wood scent it still released when the doors were opened. But Kitty longed for something different. She had a number of ornaments, including quite a collection of beautiful miniature pottery houses, and wanted to display these to best advantage.

Now that she had a living room where she could do just that, Jack bought his darling Kitty the display cabinet with a mirrored back that she had chosen.

Ebonised, it was bigger than the old china cabinet. The doors were each a sheer pane of glass, with no leading. With the mirror behind, Kitty could see both front and back of her treasured ornaments.

I was very happy when Kitty gave me the old china cabinet and still treasure it to this day. It was with relief that I found the old, thin leaded glass doors intact when it arrived in New Zealand. Now the cottage ware biscuit barrel stands on top of it

But I digress.

The Co-op had been sold to a private owner. There was far less choice of goods, much poorer service, and no grocery delivery. But Kitty and Jack didn't need to take a taxi into Kempston for groceries. The Trust owned a minibus that took the bungalow residents shopping once a week.

The warden was on hand for any problems, with emergency pull cords in each bungalow. The warden would also collect prescriptions and generally keep an eye on residents.

All of this was at no cost to the residents of the bungalows. The pensioners and widows of the brick company had Sir Malcolm Stewart to thank for his generosity in setting up the Trust.

Don had been over from Canada in the past for big family celebrations held in the function room of Stewartby Club. But this time he had booked a hotel in Milton Keynes to celebrate his 90th birthday, and as it happened Jack's 80th, just after Kitty and Jack moved into the bungalow.

John and I drove Kitty, Jack and Carole over. All we had to pay for were the rooms he'd booked for us (bed and breakfast) at a special rate, for the night of the party. He provided pre-dinner drinks, the meal, and bottles of wine on every table.

We met a number of relatives from the younger generations of Don's family for the first time, and became reacquainted with other family members we hadn't seen for a good while. Everyone thoroughly enjoyed the evening.

It made for quite a start to Kitty and Jack's life in the bungalow.

The year 2000 was another momentous one. There were of course the Millennium celebrations. But far more important to Kitty were family ones.

We came together for a party lunch for Kitty's 80th birthday. Here she is with Jack

Then two more great grandchildren were born, Shannon in June and Loren in July.

October brought Kitty and Jack's 60th wedding anniversary, their Diamond. Kitty was really delighted to receive the Queen's congratulations card - and thrilled with the big celebration for family and friends we held in Stewartby Club. The next chapter speaks of that.

But Kitty 's arthritis started to make the hour or so drive to Lincoln too painful. She also struggled with our steep stairs. So, sadly and reluctantly, she and Jack no longer visited us. Instead we, or sometimes just I, drove down to Stewartby at regular intervals to see them and Carole.

We went out for lunch to the nearby Chequers pub/restaurant on the road to Ampthill, or as time passed more often to the Red Lion in Elstow. Occasionally we went to The Dog and Badger in Maulden. Kitty and Jack really enjoyed these outings.

Sadly, my parents were beginning to really show their age. But it was still Kitty's delight to welcome family visitors - and to cook for them - for as long as she could. The word hospitable might have been coined for her.

She would never mention any pain or discomfort she was suffering, rather always showing a cheerful face. With that twinkle in her eye, she chatted and joked with everyone. And if she did show a twinge of pain, she'd make light of it. Arthritis? "That bloody old Arthur!"

Kitty's steamed suet steak and kidney pudding was legendary

among family members as far afield as Don in Vancouver. John won't let me forget that he never did get to taste it!

Visitors from Canada: Jack's nephew Rex and his wife Kathryn. There was no steak and kidney pudding on this occasion either, but we all had a lovely time.

While Kitty still did the cooking, Jack began to take care of not only the housework but also the washing. They bought a tumble dryer, which made life a bit easier for him.

Sadly, as Kitty's arthritis deteriorated, so did Jack's eyesight. He was diagnosed with wet macular degeneration, with only laser treatment available then to slightly slow the progress.

WEDDING ANNIVERSARIES

I well remember my parents' later big wedding anniversaries. We had a family meal in a very nice nearby village pub for their Golden Wedding, their 50th anniversary.

But it was their 60th and 65th, the two Diamonds, that were the big celebrations. These were both held in the function room at Stewartby Club. And they were real cause for celebration.

In early 2000, the invitations went out to family near and far. Sadly there were too many no longer with us, but those who were and who could, joined us for a wonderful party.

Joan, Reg and Nellie's wartime evacuee with her husband Doug, and David and Marion, were among those included. There were a few old friends and with the children there were over thirty of us present.

You might know how much Kitty enjoyed it. Winn had come over from America. Kitty had all her grandchildren and great grandchildren around her, which was such a joy to her.

She met Carl's second son Loren, just 3 months old, for the first time. Katheryn, Jack's youngest niece, had brought an even newer baby with her. This event was too important to miss!

Kathryn's baby daughter Shannon was the same age as Loren, and Dawn's son Toby less than 18 months old. What a treat for Kitty to have them all together. Another real treat was to have Ken there with his partner Joan, whom we had never met.

We had lost touch with Ken some years previously. But when it came to this occasion, and knowing how much Kitty especially regretted having no contact, I decided to see what I could do.

I didn't know where Ken was living but took a chance and wrote to him at the Cambridge Street address. I am so glad that I did. He was, and still is, living there with Joan. Ken responded to me and there they were.

Kitty's eyes lit up to see Ken and we were all very happy to welcome Joan too into the family. We have thankfully never lost touch since.

There was so much love in the room for this lovely couple, who still cared so very much for one another, their own love undimmed.

The next big anniversary was Kitty and Jack's 65th in 2005. Once again, the invitations went out. Once again there was a great response. And once again it was held in the Club function room.

Kitty was sad that Carl and his family were missing this time. He had returned from Wales to work in the USA, and was unable to be with us. However, there were thankfully other grandchildren and great grandchildren to enjoy the fun, and for Kitty to enjoy. Winn had also managed to come over for the celebration.

Dawn had added twins Oli and Kitty (yes, another Kitty!), to her family three years previously. Kathryn now had two-year-old Caitlin, Claire two-year-old William and a new baby, Orin.

This anniversary celebration was easily as joyous the last; children were playing and running around on the sports field.

The sun again shone down on us all.

And as before, Kitty and Jack were surrounded by the love of family and friends.

Kitty and Jack's own love for one another was as strong as ever. And this celebration was a testament to their love.

Such a happy picture!

The final big anniversary party for Kitty and Jack was in 2010, after seventy years of marriage. But that belongs in a future chapter.

FINAL YEARS IN THE BUNGALOW

For some years things had run along quite contentedly. Jack's eyesight continued to slowly deteriorate but they managed well. And John remarked, "Your mum is still as sharp as a tack!"

She still had her sense of humour, too. Here she is in 2005 "trying on" Carole's cycle helmet. It's also amusing Jack.

Jack now didn't bother watching television, only listening to the news. Earphones on, he listened to audiobooks and his music.

What did Kitty enjoying watching on TV? You might not think that among her favourite programmes were snooker tournaments and rugby games - until you read Claire's tribute, which follows later.

Kitty was really quite knowledgeable but joked that she watched the rugby for the men's big thighs. She couldn't stand the commentators, and the scores appeared on the screen, so she just muted the sound.

What Kitty never watched, were any of the TV soaps. She enjoyed documentaries, especially the nature ones, and some of the old comedy sitcoms, anything that amused her. She didn't watch the television for hours at a time though.

She continued to read magazines and the occasional book. And for as long as possible, Kitty continued to knit. As her arthritis progressed she began to use ever bigger knitting needles, until the time came when she couldn't manage even the largest wooden ones. This was a real deprivation for poor Kitty.

We still had family gatherings, especially for Kitty and Jack's birthdays and Christmas meals, now in a pub. Both Kitty and Jack were very happy when we could all get together. Kitty positively blossomed on these occasions.

Kitty's hairdresser, Hazel Brightman, had by now retired. But she still kept doing Kitty's hair. However, as time went by Kitty began to need a walking frame.

She could no longer walk down the village. So Hazel's husband Terry drove Hazel from their home in Churchill Close to the bungalow. Hazel wouldn't let Kitty down.

My parents both found it increasingly difficult to use the bath, with its overhead shower. We managed to contact a non-profit organisation that took out the bath and fitted a wet-room style shower, with hand rail, at no cost. This was a real boon.

We hadn't really noticed small changes that were signs of dementia in Kitty. But following minor surgery she developed a urinary tract infection and became very confused. Once in hospital they discovered that she had very low sodium levels, too.

It took some time for her worst symptoms to resolve. But as she did begin to recover, poor Kitty took out her dentures one evening and - rather than putting them in her "chopper pot" as she called it, wrapped them in a paper tissue and placed them under her pillow.

She didn't think about them when she got up the next morning. In fact, it wasn't until after the staff had remade her bed that she looked for her "choppers." They had gone.

Kitty was very annoyed indeed, rather than upset, that anyone should have thrown them away. "They" ought to have known what was wrapped in the tissue. We pointed out that as far as the nurse knew, they had only picked up something in a tissue that could have been quite nasty. Kitty's chopper pot sat on her locker and they would have assumed her dentures were inside.

It was from this time on that we started to recognise the symptoms of dementia. We saw our poor mother become ever more forgetful and confused.

Then came the evening when she called me in a panic. "Jean, tell me the news is a repeat and that I'm not going mad." She was referring to the TV news.

I was puzzled and said the news was live, asking her what was wrong. Kitty was quite emphatic that it was a repeat, adding that my news must be different.

We learned that one symptom of Kitty's dementia was déjà vécu, or persistent déjà vu. As time passed, she became certain that every programme on TV was a repeat. That wasn't so bad as many really were, and she could still enjoy them. But she would look at the start of a programme and say "Repeat-o, they're all repeat-o."

What was really sad for her was that in her mind she had previously read every book, magazine or newspaper she picked up. To her, it wasn't worth reading them again and that was one of her real pleasures taken from her.

She started to believe that she had seen or read everything three times previously. It was all really sad at the time but "Three times" has now affectionately passed into family sayings, along with "Repeat-o."

An assessment and CT scan showed that Kitty had vascular dementia, not Alzheimer's. We would notice that every so often she would become quiet and rather vacant for a day or two, then show signs of deterioration. It appeared that she had intermittent trans-ischaemic attacks, taking her on a downward spiral.

My father had been diagnosed with prostate cancer a few years previously. It was already in his bones by the time it was discovered. Hormone treatment was the only option and although he became frailer, this did keep the cancer controlled.

Kitty's use of the stove was becoming a safety concern. So Carole and I organised frozen microwavable meals to be delivered to my parents on a weekly basis. Carole visited every Sunday and cooked dinner for them all. She checked both food and cleaning supplies, made a shopping list, asked what frozen meals they wanted and then let me know. I took it from there, placing all the orders online.

Time went by and Carole started visiting twice a week. I spoke to my parents on the phone most evenings, did what was needful that I could long distance, by phone and on the pc. Carole had the harder task, being the one always there in person, which I appreciate to this day.

I drove down once a month, John sometimes with me, taking Kitty, Jack and Carole out for Sunday lunch.

Kitty now really felt the cold, the temperature in the bungalow always high. Carole kept a tee shirt there to change into, and even so she wasn't always cool enough. Even in summer, with the oven on for Sunday dinner, Kitty would complain if she was sitting in the kitchen and Carole had the back door open.

Kitty had regularly visited and helped her elderly friends while they still lived. Now that she herself needed visits to brighten and comfort her there was nobody left who knew her well enough.

Our gentle mother became ever more confused and now sometimes quite verbally aggressive towards Jack. To the end of his life, he would say that this wasn't Kitty but the illness. She remained his "darling" always.

Jack now found caring for the bungalow too difficult and employed a weekly cleaner. Then carers started to come in to Kitty twice a day, morning and evening.

Kitty hated having the carers and they weren't very consistent either. But at least they gave some relief. However, even with Carole's help Jack was beginning to feel unable to cope with Kitty.

Our poor mother began to feel ever more distressed. In lay terms, I think it was partly that the signals in her brain had become muddled. She'd suffered bad abdominal pain for years, following the burst duodenal ulcer.

Now it seemed that this had become translated in her mind to a very urgent need to defecate and she began to sit on the toilet for lengthy periods of time more and more frequently.

There was just one toilet in the bungalow, in the bathroom. When Jack was using it Kitty would start to harangue him, saying that she needed the toilet and he didn't care about her. Life became very difficult for them both.

Almost every day, Kitty thought one of the beds needed changing and she wouldn't be gainsaid. So Jack was changing and washing bed linen almost constantly.

He heated up their frozen meals in the microwave, using raised stick-on buttons to gauge the timing. It took four minutes to heat up one meal. Jack heated up both at the same time, so told Kitty he was setting it for eight minutes. She was insistent that if one meal took four minutes, two took only half that time. It caused real argument.

The final straw for Jack came when Kitty was arguing with him about this and he got so frustrated that he struck the microwave door with his fist. This horrified him and he became afraid that in the heat of the moment he might strike out at his darling Kitty.

Jack was now ready to move into residential care. Kitty wasn't at all happy with the idea but she didn't refuse. It was what Jack wanted.

Determined that Kitty and Jack should not be separated Carole, John and I visited a number of care homes in Bedford. They were of varying sizes and standards but we settled on Salvete, a small private care home a few minutes' walk from where Carole lived. It had been recommended by one of Carole's friends and I don't think we could have done better.

I started writing emails and telephoning. With help from an excellent organisation, 'Residents and Relatives,' I presented our case and pressed for action.

We would not be fobbed off by the local council or Social Services. Our local councillor even came on board and wrote to Social Services on Kitty and Jack's behalf. I think his intervention gave the final push needed for the council to agree funding for the care home, in what was an unusually short period of time.

ENDINGS

My parents moved into Salvete care home in Bedford, close to Russell Court where Carole still lives, in October 2010. It was just a month after Jack had asked for residential care. And what did he say? He couldn't understand why it took so long!

Kitty and Jack each had their own room, opposite one another on the upper floor, with their own beds and other items from home. Kitty had her belovèd display cabinet with all her ornaments, her fluffy toys, and her favourite pictures.

But while Jack was delighted and relieved to be in Salvete, Kitty felt very differently. She'd never have agreed if Jack hadn't insisted.

Carole and I had the difficult job of emptying the bungalow ready for the next resident. We even had to take up the carpets, despite their excellent condition. So much had to go, to be taken away by a clearance firm, once we had chosen items to take to Salvete and a few personal items to keep for ourselves and our families.

It felt as though we were dismantling a lifetime. We kept coming across items that called up memories and feelings. And we hugged and cried together more than once over those long two days.

I'm not sure how we got the job done but we did. Once the house was cleared, we paid the two women who had recently started working for our parents to thoroughly clean it. Returning the keys to the warden was the final ending to this era.

Only a week after the move, it was Kitty and Jack's 70th wedding anniversary, their Platinum. Another card from the Queen and one last anniversary party, this time at the Chequers where as I said, we had enjoyed many family meals.

Many of those who had been guests at previous anniversaries came, though not all were able to. Kitty was pleased to see everyone gathered there but she couldn't rest or settle for very long.

She had to keep being walked to the toilet and didn't really want to leave it. Nonetheless, in between times Kitty did manage to forget herself enough to enjoy the occasion. But we knew there would be no more such celebrations.

Carole visited Kitty and Jack very regularly, initially every day and always, unless she was ill, at least twice a week. She was still the one at the coal face, and for that I shall ever be grateful.

For some time after the move to Salvete, whenever John and I visited them we, with Carole, took Kitty and Jack for a family lunch at the local Toby Carvery. Again, it could be difficult to persuade Kitty away from the toilets but she did enjoy the food.

John teased Kitty by saying that he should always wait to see what she ordered before choosing his own meal, as hers was always better.

Kitty had a phone in her room and I called at least once a week and went down to Bedford every month, by train unless John was with me. Carole booked me the guest room at Russell Court for these visits.

For a while, Kitty would sit in her recliner in the lounge next to Jack for an hour or so at a time. Jack always held her hand, trying to show her how much he cared for her and calling her, as ever, his darling.

Jack's physical health slowly deteriorated but Kitty's deteriorating mental health was more distressing. She started to believe that Jack was seeing another woman. This really upset her and also made her angry. We did eventually manage to convince her that Jack was "down the Club," rather than seeing some woman.

Even more upsetting for her in the longer term was Kitty's firmly held belief that a little girl came into her room and interfered with her belongings, getting into her display cabinet. This little girl also messed around with her treasured cuckoo clock. Had she broken it? Our poor mother's distress was palpable.

Carole and I didn't try to tell her that she was mistaken about the intruder. What would have been the point? She was adamant, convinced that she had seen this child. Whether it was nightmare or hallucination, it was very real to Kitty. So instead we reassured her that her possessions were intact and that we'd told "them" that the little girl must be kept out.

What about her bowels? Kitty was always heading to one bathroom or another with her walking frame. There she would sit until, in effect, forced to move. But as soon as she could she was off again.

So although not ideal, we bought a commode with a soft seat for her room. At least then she wasn't sitting alone in a cheerless bathroom or small toilet.

Kitty could occasionally be persuaded to sit in her recliner, brought from home and now from the residents' lounge to her room. She could very reluctantly be cajoled downstairs, to sit in the lounge for a while, to the dining room for breakfast and dinner, and to the hairdresser. The hairdresser also went to her room to massage her neck, arms and hands, lower legs and feet for her. That was something Kitty loved.

It was a good thing that Carole had made sure there was insurance for Kitty's hearing aid. It was lost - once somehow dropped down the gap between the lift and floor, and had various "maintenance" issues.

The staff used the saline spray we bought to clean Kitty's good ear, which stopped the wax build up from which she'd suffered. We also kept her stocked with hearing aid batteries!

Carole made sure that Salvete always had a supply of dripping for Kitty, and the apple juice that she liked to drink with a meal. Kitty loved cut flowers and liked carnations because they lasted a long time. Every three weeks I ordered her a fresh bunch from a company that delivered by post.

She enjoyed a game of dominoes and really liked it when John came down with me. He always cheered her up when he had a game with her. It was the same with Billy, Carole's partner. Kitty enjoyed their attention. Billy came with us to the Toby Carvery too, the last few months we were able to take Kitty and Jack.

So there were times when Kitty could be happy, when she saw her grandchildren, was taken out, or something else raised her spirits. Then she could forget her bowels for a while. But despite all our and the staff's best efforts, these times became fewer and farther between. Even going out for a meal became too much for Kitty to cope with.

In 2012, Jack started keeping to his room and towards the end of the year, to his bed. He wasn't unhappy, and his face always lit up to see any of us.

Kitty would go across to his room to see him for a little while every evening. But it was hard for her to understand why he wasn't up and about during the day.

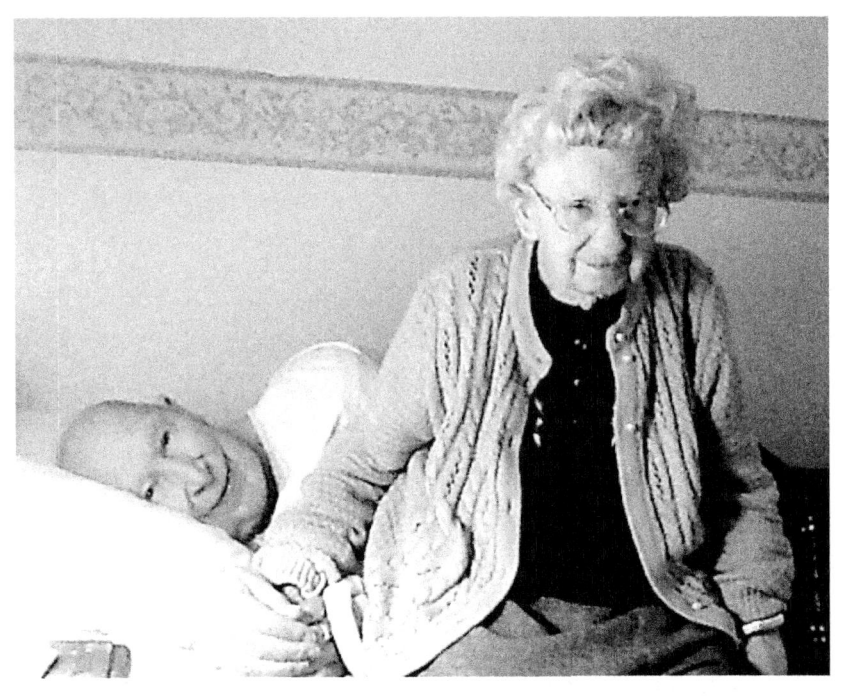

The last picture I have of Jack with his darling Kitty

Then came the sad day, 8 December 2012, that Jack died, thankfully in his own bed at Salvete. Carole and I were both able to be with him for his last hours, going in to Mum to see and comfort her as well. But poor Kitty was simply bewildered.

When we realised Jack was dead and told the staff, Maria a kitchen helper wheeled Kitty into his room and before we knew what was happening tried to get her to touch and kiss Jack. Poor Kitty was both bewildered and horrified. We gently asked Maria to leave and soothed our poor mother, trying to comfort her.

Brought by the staff at Salvete to Jack's funeral, our poor mother looked so small and frail, bewildered and upset by turn. We had a family gathering in the lounge at Russell Court after the funeral and Kitty did brighten for a time, with loved ones and those who loved her, around her.

But now Kitty was on her own, as she had never been before. She really found Jack's death hard to take in and for a good part of the time didn't realise that he had died. But she had enough of her old self left that the reality could still hit her. Then she was not only dreadfully upset but also felt guilty for not having remembered.

Although we all did our best, the last two years of Kitty's life were largely unhappy. I made sure she always had the carnations she loved and called her more often than before. Carole visited very frequently and did what she could in person.

We felt so sorry for her, frustrated that we could not do more, could not help her as her cruel dementia progressed. The times any of us could make her smile, lift her spirits, were real highlights.

Both Kitty and Jack had end of life instructions in place. Neither wanted more than palliative care as the end approached. Their documents were lodged at Salvete and everyone was aware of their wishes.

Kitty was hospitalised twice during these two years and received really good care the first time. But I bitterly regret not refusing permission for her to be admitted to hospital on the second occasion. Had I been able to travel to Bedford that day I could have kept her at Salvete.

However, Carole was too ill to be able to go to Salvete. I couldn't get to Bedford until the next day, so I very reluctantly agreed for Kitty to go to hospital. But the care this time was appalling.

I made my way to Bedford the following day and stayed awhile until Carole was feeling better. We both spoke repeatedly to a number of nurses on the ward and were always promised that messages would be passed on but nothing changed.

They seemed to have no clue about dementia or Kitty's own needs. She was distressed throughout her stay. Carole and I both also felt not only distressed but frustrated. Kitty was in a very sad state when she was discharged back to Salvete.

The one good thing that came out of this dreadful time is that the hospital responded to our complaints. Carole had a meeting with hospital and Social Service authorities. The need for improvements and what those should be was recorded. Implementation was promised and we hope it did take place.

A few months later Kitty was again physically unwell, and not eating or drinking. The doctor again thought that she should be hospitalised. This time I refused and of course they also had a copy of her end of life wishes and the doctor it was who this time reluctantly agreed.

Unfortunately, Carole was ill this time too but I was able to get straight down to Bedford. Mum was in bed and not very responsive. But the next morning? She had perked right up!

Kitty became frailer, both physically and mentally. But her eyes and smile would still light up when she saw one of her much-loved children or grandchildren, even great grandchildren, who visited.

When I moved to New Zealand towards the end of August 2014, Carole didn't want Kitty to be upset by being told. I respected Carole's wishes, knowing that I could call and that Kitty by now wouldn't really know when I'd last visited.

Hearing my voice on the phone she often said, "I thought we spoke this morning." Or I'd walk into her room and she'd say, "I wasn't expecting to see you again so soon," thinking I had only been there a day or two previously. And that was when in fact I hadn't seen her for perhaps four weeks.

I'd made sure Kitty's flowers would continue to be delivered but was waiting for our broadband connection to call her.

However, fate took another, very unhappy, twist.

John and I moved into our new home in Christchurch 6 September 2014 (5 September in the UK), just two weeks after arriving in the country. The next morning around 10.30am, Kathryn and Peter were banging on the door. Kathryn came in, grabbed me in a hug and sobbed that Nan had died.

Carole had called Kathryn because we had neither phone nor internet connected yet. She said that Kitty died sometime after

9pm, (UK time). Kitty had been unwell and having some trouble breathing in the evening, after one of her better days.

Staff were calling out the ambulance when Kitty fell asleep/into a coma, and died shortly after. Carole was called and hurried round distraught. She became even more upset when she wasn't allowed into Kitty's room until the doctor had certified death from natural causes. She finally saw Kitty and the truth really sank in and hit her hard.

It came as a shock but we know it was a mercy for our lovely Mum. She had been getting much worse and ever more unhappy over the past months, with fewer relatively good days.

Hurrying round to Kathryn's house, I called Carole on Skype from there. Kitty had died about an hour before Carole phoned. We cried, I felt guilty, I felt helpless. I was so far away.

Until we had our own connection, over which there was of course some confusion and delay, I walked round to Kathryn's house every day to Skype call Carole as we supported one another. I still felt guilty and helpless at being so far away.

It was so frustrating that we did not get phone or internet access at our own house for another fortnight, due to confusion on the part of the supplier. Thank goodness we lived just a short walk from Kathryn's home.

Before leaving England, I'd told Carole that when Kitty died I would go back to Bedford. I wanted to be there to support Carole however I could. But, and with more guilt, I simply couldn't face the journey so soon after arriving and not even settled into our home yet. I felt overwhelmed and knew nothing I did could help Mum. I simply did my best to provide long distance support to Carole, even though it felt nowhere near enough.

Fortunately, Carole understood and I did my best to support her long distance through the procedures, everything that we had already done for Jack. Her two daughters, Dawn and Claire, gave her both support and help.

Carole consulted me over Kitty's funeral arrangements and, although happy to go along with whatever she suggested, I remain very grateful for her thoughtfulness.

BLANE
Kitty

Formerly of Stewartby

Passed peacefully away in Salvete Care Home on 6th September 2014, aged 94 years.
Cherished wife of the late Jack. Much loved and greatly missed by all her family and many friends.
The funeral service will take place at Norse Road Crematorium Chapel on Wednesday 1st October at 2.30pm.
Family flowers only, donations welcome, made payable to Dementia UK
c/o Clarabut & Plumbe,
11, Kingsway,
Bedford MK42 9BJ.

I had gone to bed a few hours before Mum's funeral took place but found myself wide awake just before it was due to start, which was at 2.30pm 1 October in the UK, 3.30am on the 2nd here in New Zealand. There was no video link but I went into the living room and sat in my chair in the quiet darkness, with just a reading lamp on. As I read slowly through the order of service, I felt at one with those who were physically present, and gained a sense of peace.

The recessional was "Where the Blue of the Night Meets the Gold of the Day (someone waits for me)" sung by her favourite, Bing Crosby. Thinking of it now still brings tears to my eyes.

After the funeral Carole organised refreshments for a small gathering in the common room at Russell Court. Sadly, numbers of both family and friends have dwindled over the years. Of those still with us, few were able to attend Kitty's funeral.

David and Marion Voice were among those who did attend. You know that David had been considered family ever since Jack was billeted with his parents in WWII, Marion after their marriage.

They made the trip to Bedford this last time for a very different occasion and to support Carole. Unable nowadays to make such a journey, they were very glad they could say a final farewell to Kitty, whom they too loved so much.

Here they are with Carole.

Then came the final goodbye.

Carole scattered Kitty's ashes in a local ancient woodland that Kitty knew well, among the bluebells she so loved. Now living on opposite sides of the world, Carole and I each said our goodbyes.

Yet our darling Mum - Jack's darling Kitty - lives on forever in our hearts in so many ways. We cherish our shared memories.

Kitty's bluebell wood themed scatter tube with funeral flowers.

The ancient woodland at Clapham, that Kitty knew so well, where Carole scattered her ashes.

FAMILY TRIBUTES AND MEMORIES

Claire wrote her tribute very recently. The others are as they were read out at Kitty's funeral by the celebrant. All speak for themselves.

CLAIRE

If I could give you an ornament of my Nan, it would be a glittery snow-storm scene set inside a Christmas bauble, hanging on a Christmas tree, surrounded by tinsel and lights.

She would be sitting in her rocking chair in her comfy dark red trousers with her slippers on, ankles crossed, slightly back from the fireplace, next to her glass cabinet full of her collections of Lilliput Lane houses, ceramic thimbles, glass Beagles chasing a glass fox, and various other little trinkets, watching something on the TV like rugby, Morecambe & Wise, Dusty Bin, Frank Bruno or Barry McGuigan boxing, Big Daddy and Giant Haystacks wrestling, Last of the Summer Wine, and she would be laughing.

Nan was a huge influence in my life in early childhood. I would go and stay with her in Stewartby in the school holidays, sometimes with my older sister Dawn, sometimes on my own. She would be cooking dinner in the kitchen, to be ready when Grandad came home for lunch, while I mucked about doing nothing in particular.

Sometimes I'd walk down to the bottom of the square, Wavell Close, pass under the arch in the far corner and go into the wheat field to watch the trains pass by. Sometimes I'd stay outside the front door and stare into the moss which grew in the cracks of the broken brick pavement and imagine a microscopic world living in the moss.

When I grew bored of my intrinsic entertainment, Nan would give me something to look at, like her box of beads which consisted of necklaces she didn't wear anymore, costume jewellery of pearlescent beads, shiny and colourful; or her old headscarves, colourful fabric which was so thin it was barely there. Nan loved bright colours.

There would be old comic annuals to look at too, like Dandy and Beano. Then I'd wander into the kitchen to see what Nan was doing. If she'd made a meat pie, she might be making a jam pasty with the leftover pastry.

The kitchen was dark with a table in the middle and a pantry that I found fascinating. There would always be a bottle of Golden Lemonade in there, and mint cordial, which I found disgusting - but I would take a little sip of in secret, just to check it still tasted awful.

The garden was tiny and full of flowers and Nan would hang the washing out there in the sunshine.

After lunch, Grandad would help Nan tidy up and then rest his back by lying on the floor, before going back out to work. Then Nan and I would go for a long walk. She always had sweets in her pocket and would wait until I was fed up of walking before she said in her Yorkshire accent, "Do you want a sweet?" She would produce a humbug with a toffee centre from her pocket, which kept me going until we got back. Sometimes after lunch, instead of going for a walk, she'd visit Aunty Lou and take me with her. She would sit and chat with Aunt Lou for what felt like hours, putting the world to rights.

Tea would always be something cold, like sandwiches or pork pie. The ice cream van would come in the summer and we'd get an ice cream. The children from across the square, Natalia and Bubblo, would come and sit on the doorstep and Nan would give them an ice cream too. Nan loved children, and she was kind to them all.

In the evening, Nan would retire to bed at about 8pm. She needed to rest her back and all the rest of her aches and pains. She would drink tonic water to help with her indigestion. She had a small TV in her room, and we would get into bed with her with our supper biscuits and lemonade, and watch snooker, wrestling or boxing with her until it was our bedtime.

When it was time for bed, Nan would kiss me and Dawn good night and tuck the sheets in tightly all around us, which we immediately untucked as soon as she'd switched the light off and closed the door. We had stone hot-water bottles to warm the bed as there was no central heating, and we slept in the same bed. During the night we would wake up as a stone hot-water bottle thudded to the floor.

I remember waking up one morning and reaching for the curtain to tug it open. Well, not only did it open, the whole curtain rail fell down! Dawn and I were in hysterics. Hearing us laughing Nan came in to see what was going on, and when she saw what had happened, she burst out laughing too, and we all laughed and laughed uncontrollably for what seemed like ages.

That sums up Nan completely; she laughed about things, nothing was a bother, nothing was too much trouble, and nothing really mattered. As long as everyone was happy, everything was fine. It was when we weren't happy that she got fed up with us!

In school term time, Nan visited us at home at least twice a week. She'd get the bus from Stewartby to Bedford, and then Bedford to Clapham where we lived. She'd keep us entertained while Mum did the housework. When we were poorly in bed with high temperatures, Nan would bring us comics, fresh fruit like grapes, satsumas, dark red apples, and Lucozade - because that was the health drink of the day!

Our house had a bay window in the living room and we could see Nan walking up the street from the bus stop. One day, I caught sight of her and she had red hair. She liked Mum's Henna hair colour and fancied a change from her grey, but oh dear, Mum's natural hair colour wasn't grey, so when used on Nan's hair it came up much brighter! I cried when I saw her, I couldn't understand what had happened to my Nanny's familiar hair!

Nan and Grandad would stay overnight on Christmas Eve, and we would stay up late playing the card game Newmarket, betting with Nan's hoard of buttons, drinking pop and eating nuts, cheesy bits and hot sausage rolls.

Nan loved Christmas morning, she would get us to take our stockings to her and open them with her. She then helped Mum cook a full English breakfast, before the grand present opening. After that she helped cook the Christmas dinner, which was followed by a walk, sweets and after dinner snooze in the afternoon. This was followed by a cold tea! It consisted of three courses even though we never had a starter course, as we weren't that posh. Our Christmas tea main course of salad, cold meats and bread and butter, was followed by Christmas cake and mince pies, followed by trifle - or was it the other way round? My memory has faded - anyway, everything would be home-made right down to the jam and pastries, apart from the pickles that were shop bought.

In the summer, on my birthday, Nan and Grandad would come

over and sit in the garden, sunbathing in the afternoon sun. They were there when I got home from school, and would give me my presents before tea, staying a while until it was time to catch their bus.

It all sounds pretty simple, and it was, and perhaps that's why we felt so much love and security growing up. Everything was certain and straight forward, with its own routine. Nan did the housework and prepared the day's food in the morning, exercised in the afternoon, and rested in the evening.

She had her set days for washing sheets, colours, and whites, a set day for going to town, a set day for visiting her sister in Bletchley, and her friends, set days for visiting us at home, and set times for meals. Everything was clockwork, and everything worked: with bright colours, ice cream and lots of laughter and love.

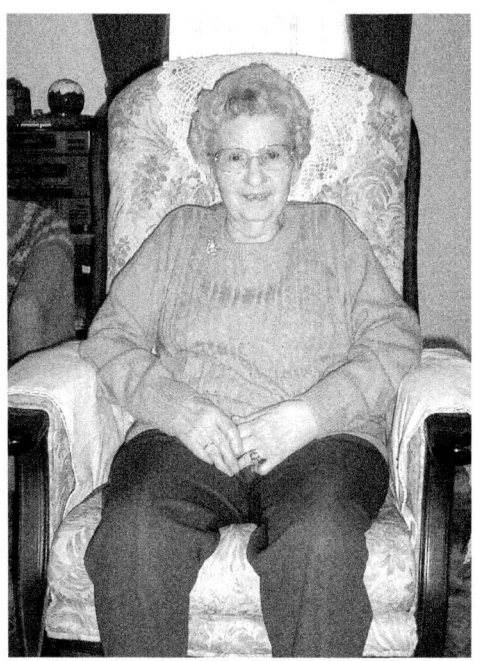

Here is Kitty in her dark red trousers. The china cabinet is to her left where she could just turn her head to see her treasures.

JEAN, KITTY'S ELDEST DAUGHTER

Mum

I am so sorry that I can't be there with you to say a final goodbye to Mum and to celebrate her life. You are the ones, especially of course Carole, who with me knew Mum and Dad the best and share memories.

Mum was the youngest of her family, so small and weak looking when she was born that her father said to just let the poor little bugger "dee." (die). Mum had other ideas! Small and sickly as a child she may have been but always full of life and love - and made of much tougher stuff than to give up at the first, or any, hurdle.

Mum and Dad - always together, a devoted couple, with Mum being Dad's "darling" to the end. We, certainly I, took them for granted when growing up. It was simply a given that they would both always be there for us, for me, come what may.

All Mum ever wanted was to be a wife and mother, to love and care for her own little family. And that she did. Mum was a true homemaker. The very term might have been created for her.

We made hot cross buns with Mum, stirred the Christmas puddings, sat by the fire as she did her knitting, so many warm memories, so much love. She was overjoyed with each new grandchild who came along and then with her great grandchildren. What I didn't realise, again accepting it as the norm, is how precious was her devotion to us all.

I think everyone who knew Mum felt her warmth and good nature, her kindness. And most would never know how much she suffered with her arthritis, as she made no display of her pain. She liked a joke and had a ready wit. "Sharp as a tack" is how John described her, only a few years ago.

I remember her as a younger woman loving to listen to, and sing along with, the radio's Light Programme - Housewives' Choice, Workers' Playtime and more - as she did her housework.

I can string together so many memories of light and love and laughter, joy and sorrow, fulfilment and yes, frustration too. But I find it impossible to put into words what Mum meant, still means, to me: my gratitude, my love for her.

My heart is filled with both thankfulness and grief.

Sitting on the hearth with Carole

CAROLE, HER YOUNGER DAUGHTER

My Mum

I like to think of my Mum as a 'proper' mum. She was always there for us and it was so comforting returning from school, to find her at home, ready with a cup of tea. Everything we ate was homemade; no shop-bought cakes or pastries, and her steak and kidney puddings were legendary!

Mum sang as she went round doing her housework; she'd always sung along with the other girls at the factory where she worked before becoming a housewife. She loved the 'Light Programme' on the 'wireless' and Dad rigged up a speaker in the kitchen so she wouldn't be without her music while she did the chores.

She was selfless, and never happier than when doing things for her family and friends. When I left work and had my two girls, she used to come and visit at least once a week (even though it meant catching two buses to get there!)

In later years, Mum used to go round to some of her friends' homes to keep them company and get their tea ready, even though she was in constant pain with arthritis.

No words can really express my gratitude for having had such a lovely, kind and caring Mum. She'll stay in my heart forever.

CARL, KITTY'S ELDEST GRANDSON

In Nan's Care

We always knew, whenever there,
That we were all in Nan's care.

That twinkle in her eye, that ready smile,
Her generous touch, and oh her laughter!

We couldn't feel more loved, more cherished,
More blessed in truth, ever after.

We'll always know, and always share,
The way we were, in Nan's care.

DAWN, HER GRANDDAUGHTER

Memories of Nan

A KitKat passed through the school fence every Tuesday
Crunching through autumn leaves on our walks along Carriage Drive
Endless washing of bright red hair when the 'tint' went wrong
Fish and chips on a Saturday
Ice cream sandwiches from the ice cream van
"Quick! Into the hall or you'll miss the cuckoo!" when the cuckoo clock was about to strike
Leaping onto a chair at the merest hint of a mouse
A bowl full of humbugs and mint imperials in the hall
Visits to the Rippingales, 'Auntie' Lou and 'Uncle' Bob, Mrs Harris and other friends around the village
A whole village of Lilliput Lane houses
Delicious homemade food, and always a pudding after dinner
Trifles topped with jelly babies
Sweets were often "Yuck! Too sweet!"
Pork dripping and Dream Topping replaced butter and cream
Wonderful Christmases were full of fun and laughter, fairy lights, robins and tinsel
'Cheating' at dominoes or games of Newmarket with a twinkle in her eye
The big button in the button tin that she got wedged in her mouth as a child
Always there; always loving and laughing

KATHRYN, HER GRANDDAUGHTER

What do you say about one of the most important figures in our lives?
Nan was an outstanding wife, mother, nan and great-nan.
It is a blessing knowing that she is now with Grandad.
I do hope that they are walking hand in hand and making up for the small time that they were apart.
Her wit and unfailing love and devotion to her family were unsurpassable. Going round to Nan and Grandad's and having dinner will always be the best of memories.
Also spending time with Nan and the boys whilst waiting for Grandad to get home from the club were such good fun.
We all send our love to you all. You will be in our thoughts.

GRANDSON WINN AND HIS WIFE SYLVIA

We both loved Nan, and we cherish the times we had with her and Jack.

JEAN FLANNERY

IN MEMORIAM

OUR BELOVED MUM

Now the final goodbye has been said
After Mum at last became free
Of dementia that dreadfully tightened its grip
And would not let her mind be.

Needing to live in the care home,
Hating it more when Dad died.
Bewildered and not understanding,
No matter how hard we tried.

Seeing her leaving us while still alive,
Becoming more and more frail,
Breaking our hearts and hers too,
Her very life becoming a jail.

Her younger days were as with Dad,
Always so ready to give.
Her loving arms, her loving heart,
With us will always live.

For what remain are our memories
Of laughter and love - and tears.
And though we don't have her presence
We shall cherish these down the years.

PICTURE GALLERY

PEOPLE

Bertha Annie Wallis

Women of the farm

Frederick Wallis, Kitty's uncle

1928 Wedding of Nellie and Reg
Kitty is the smallest bridesmaid: Annie next to her, far left.

Leaving on Honeymoon

1930 Wedding of Annie and Arthur
Kitty bridesmaid in front, Fred and Mary back left

1934 Wedding of Fred and Mary

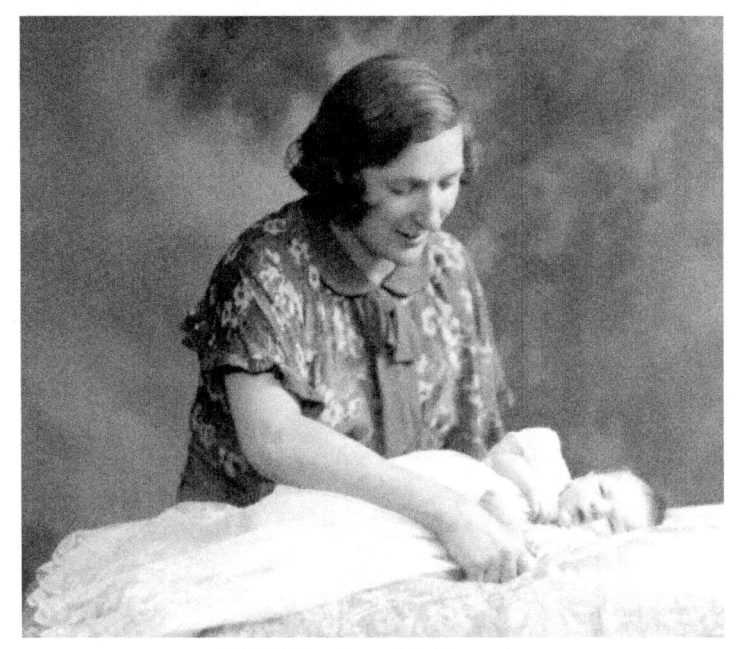

1936 Annie with Brenda

Spring 1936 Kitty in the bluebell woods

Reg with his two "girls"

Kitty and Renee on holiday

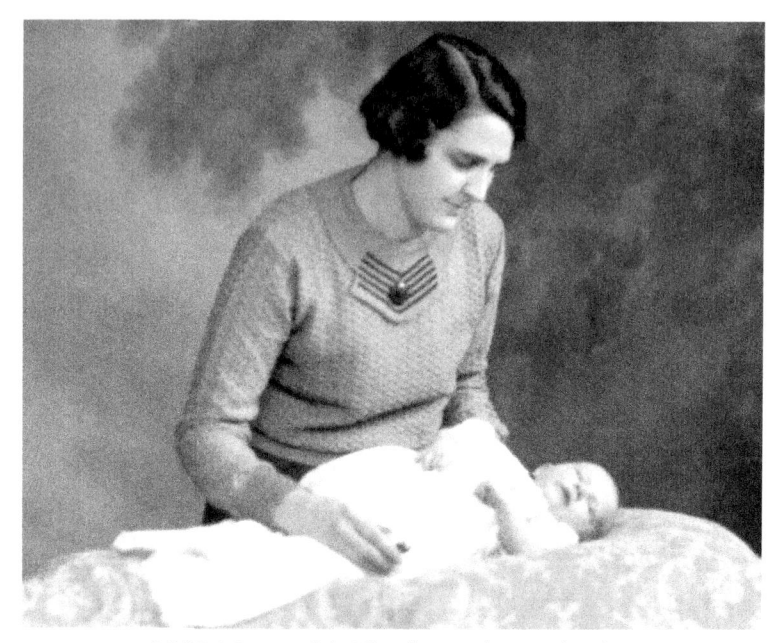

1937 Mary with Kitty's nephew Charles

Jack and Tom

7 October 1939 New Soldier Jack
One for Kitty

Early 1940 Tom and Edna's Wedding
Brenda is the small bridesmaid. Mary lower left, Fred upper right

Family Group
Back, Left to Right: Nellie, Reg, Jack's Father
Front Left of couple is Jack's Mother; Right is Kitty's Mother

9 October 1940
The Newly Weds

Tom's Wife Edna, Jack, Kitty, Fred's Wife Mary
Front: Kitty's Niece Brenda

Far Left: Jack's Brother Martin
Far Right: His Brother Bernard

Striding Out
Kitty in her favourite coat and hat

1941 Anstye Cross: Jack and Kitty with young David

1944 Joan and Marj with their mother Ruth

1945 Easter: Jack, his mother, Kitty holding me, Jack's father

1945 Annie visits Bletchley: holding me in front of "Lyndhurst"

1946 Brenda holds me; Kitty, Bertha. This perhaps our last visit

1947 The Isle of Wight

1948 Great Yarmouth

1949 February: In front or our new home, with new baby Carole

1950 Some guard dog!

1950 Enjoying summer

I give Carole a ride in my doll's pram, Whiteley Crescent garden

1951 Late Summer: Kitty and Carole, with Newton Road behind

1953, 28 August: at the back garden fence, 106 Western Road

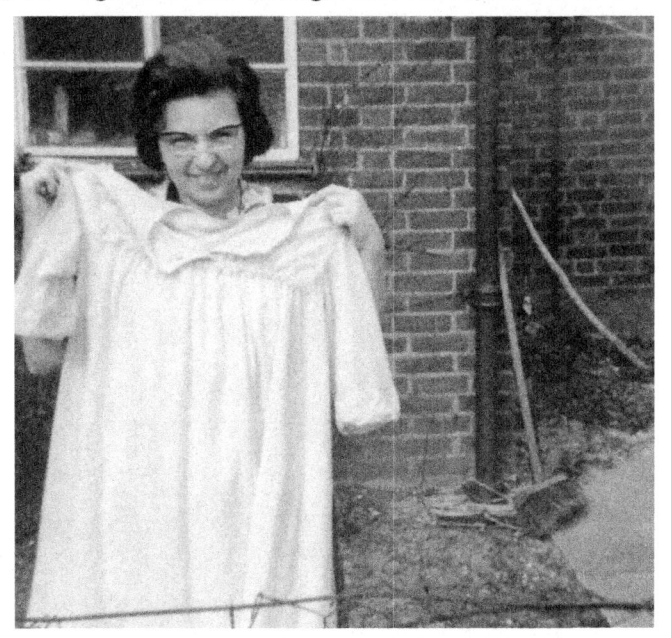

Larking about, early years at Stewartby

1957, 31 August: Brenda marries Keith, with me far left

1958, Broadstairs
Kitty and Jack play Jokari, while Carole and Ken watch

Late 1950s, footpath to the Ampthill road: Carole, Kitty and Bess

About 1960

1960 Wavell Close: Fred's son Charles and his fiancée Carol visit

1960s, Lou Chapman, Kitty, Mr and Mrs Scott, Jack
The Scotts, more good friends, ran a hostel at Kempston Hardwick for East European refugee Stewartby brickyard workers.

1962 Christmas with Carl

1965 Cutting the Silver Wedding Anniversary Cake

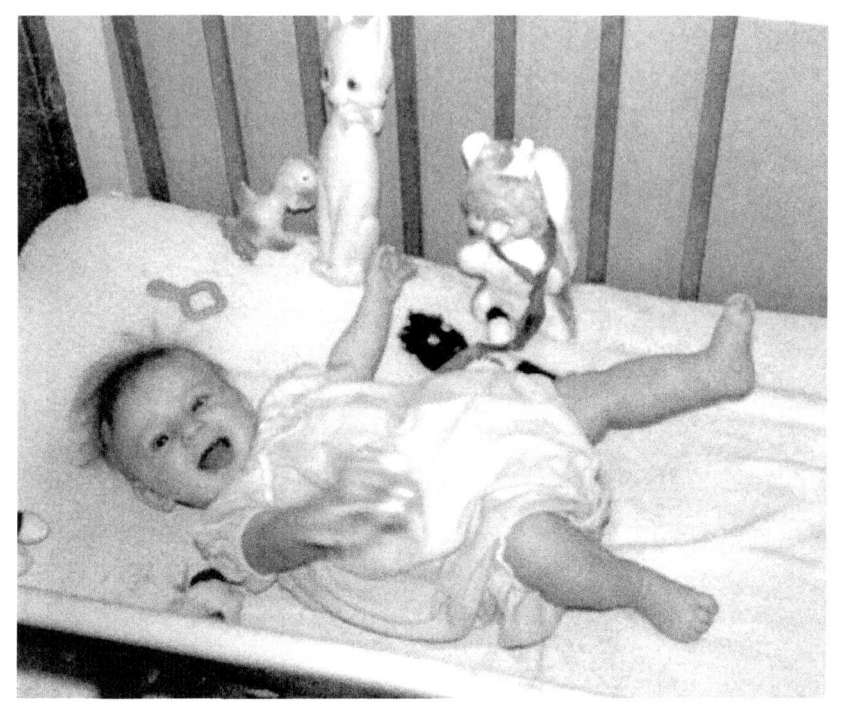

1966 Kitty's second grandson, Winn - born 3 November 1965
When Kitty saw him a year later, his hair had turned blond.

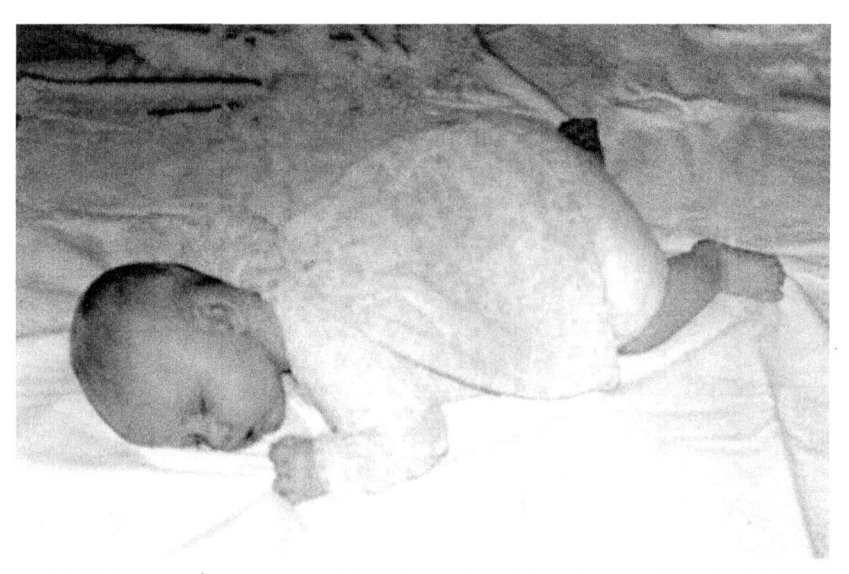

1969 Now a baby granddaughter for Kitty, born 25 July 1969
It would be a year before Kitty saw her.

1971 Crete, on "our" beach: time with these three grandchildren

1971 With Carole's daughter Dawn, Born 24 November

1972 Lunch at Agios Nikolaos, Crete

1973 Christmas: Kitty, Carole and Nellie

1974 August: Back - Ray, me, Carole, Merv holding Dawn, Jack
Front: Carl, Kitty with Winn, Kathryn

1974 Hallowe'en
Dawn on Annie's lap, me, Kitty, Nellie; Kathryn and Carole front

1974, Christmas morning and presents opened
I'm back left, Jack and Carole in front of me, Ray in the papa-san chair. Winn, Dawn and Kathryn centre. Kitty front, Merv far right.

1975 Kitty with Carole's younger daughter Claire, born 4 June

1975 Cousins: Winn, Dawn holding Claire, Kathryn, Carl

Happy Holidays

1978 Annie's 70th Birthday - Men from left: Fred, Arthur, Tom, Jack
Front: Nellie, Annie, Kitty, Edna, with Mary now playing the fool!

1978 Kitty and Annie at the house, with Arthur and Brenda

HIS DARLING KITTY

1982 Kitty and her boys, Winn and Carl

Early 1980s, Christmas fun
Me, Claire, Carole, Dawn; friends Frankie and Alistair hold Kitty

1986 100th Birthday of Jack's Aunt Liza
Back from left: Brothers Bern, Jack, Bob and his partner Olwyn
Middle: Claire, Liza, Kitty - Front: Dawn

1987 Annie and Kitty in the garden at Beighton

HIS DARLING KITTY

1989 Grandson Winn and his wife Sylvia visit

1991, Kathryn with Luke, born 12 February

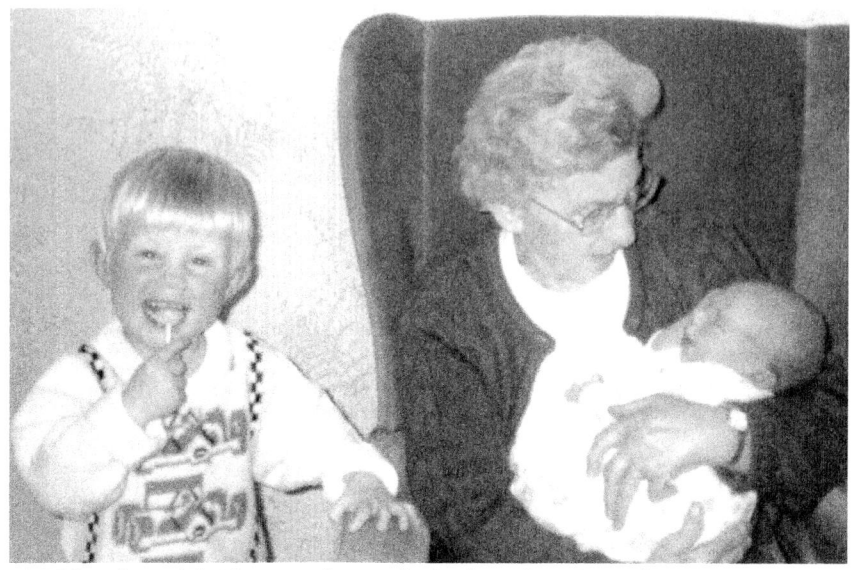

1993 Luke with Kitty and new baby brother Ryan born 2 August

1993 Kitty enjoys herself giving Ryan the giggles

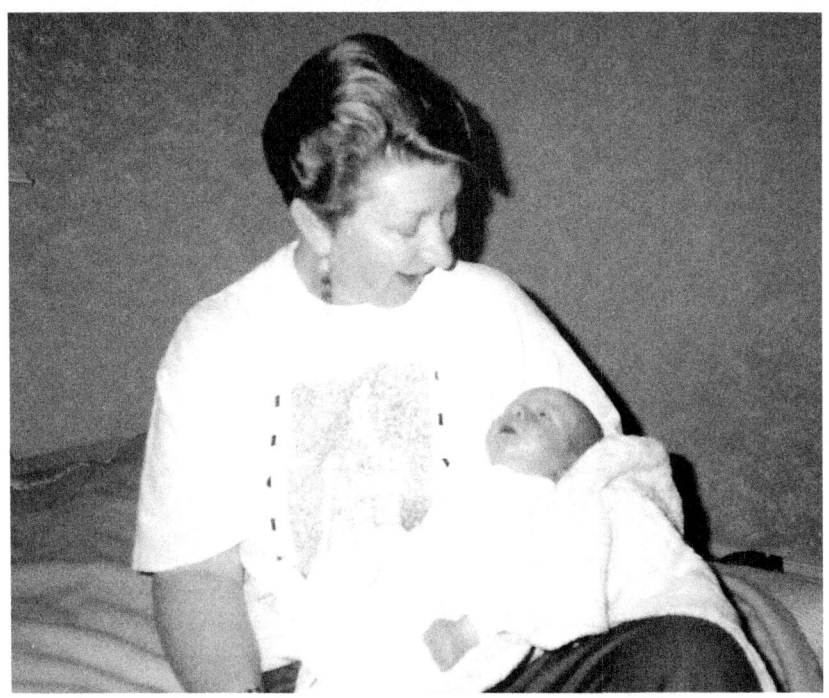

1996 Me with Carl's son Bryce, born 19 May

1996 John's sister Pam and her husband Kevin from Australia over for a visit - and a pub lunch! Jack, Kevin, Pam, Kitty and Carole

1999 August On the beach at Brighton with Carole

Jack makes a good cushion!

HIS DARLING KITTY

2000 Four generations: Kathryn, her daughter Shannon (born 11 June) on Kitty's lap, me

2000, Diamond Wedding: Kitty meets Carl's son Loren, born 1 July
From left: Me, Gwen (Jack's sister-in-law), Jack, Kitty, Carl, Bryce

The Anniversary Couple
Still as much in love as ever

2001 Carl and his two boys

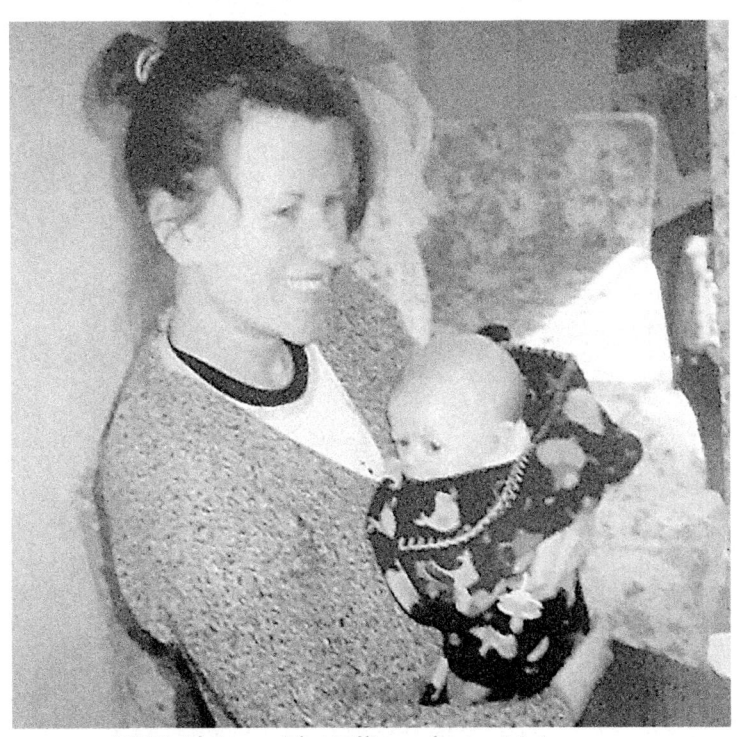

2003 Claire with William, born 11 January

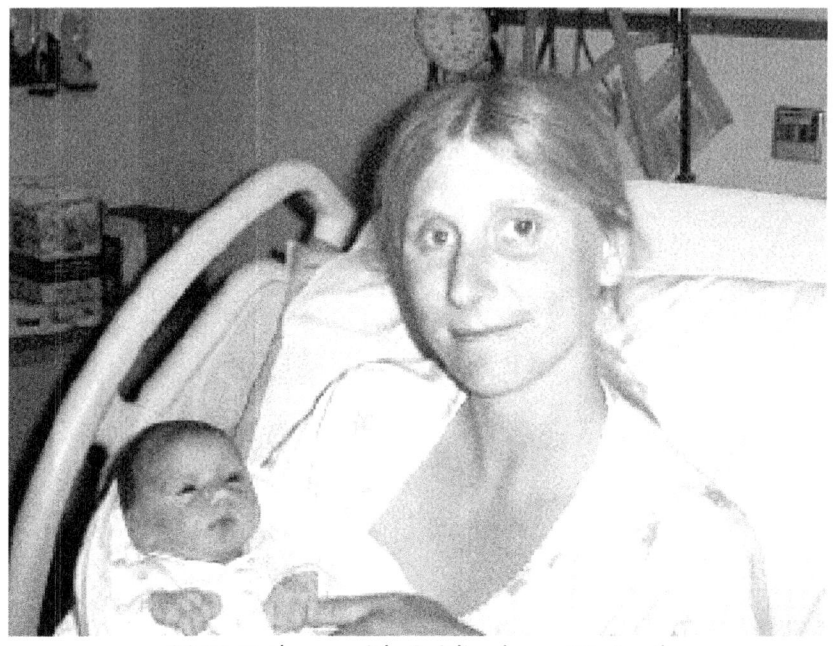

2003 Kathryn with Caitlin, born 23 April

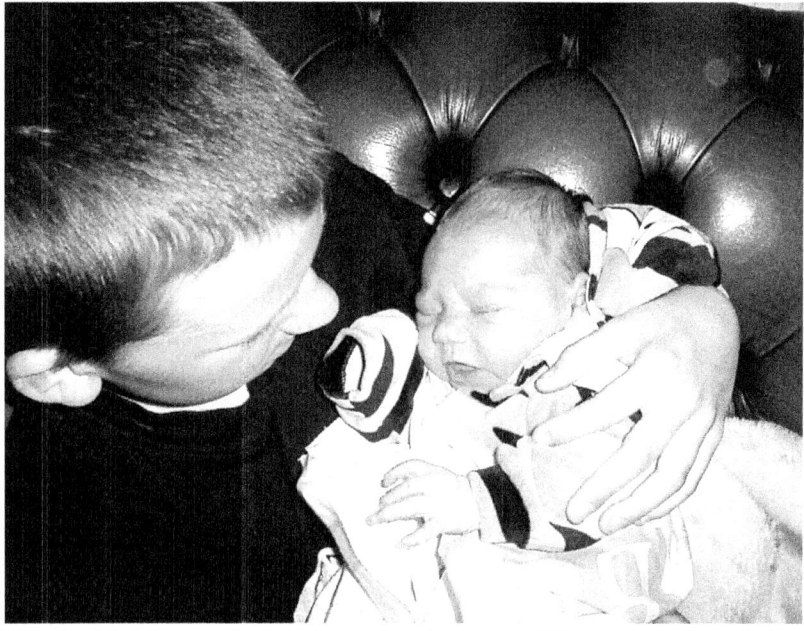

Ryan holds his new baby sister. Look at the difference in hand size!

HIS DARLING KITTY

2004 Dave with Oli, Jack with Toby, Kitty with - Kitty! Dawn

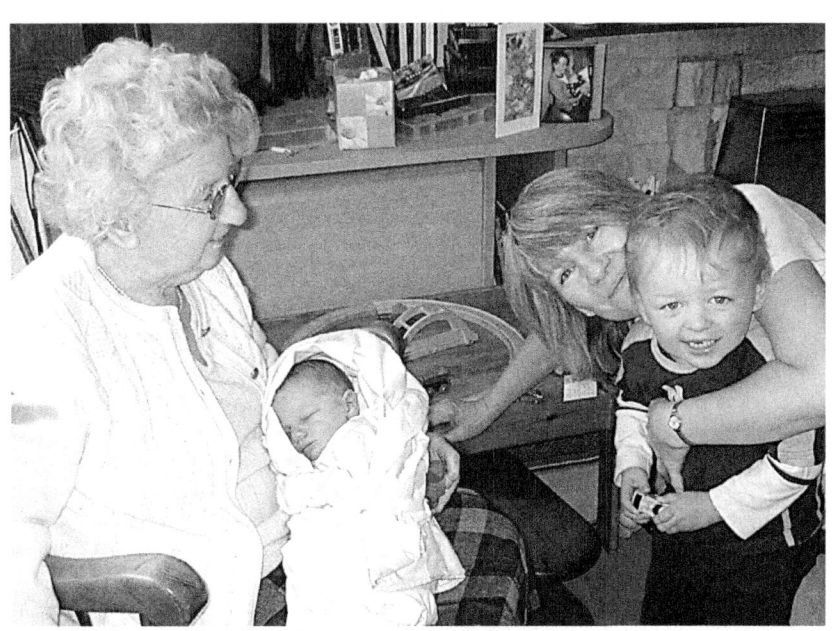

2005 Kitty holds Claire's new baby son Orin, born 11 May, with Carole and William getting into the picture.

2005 Trying on Carole's cycle helmet
"Suits you, modom!"

2005 Family Christmas Lunch: Kitty is interested.
From left opposite: John, Jack, Toby, William, Claire

2006 Bryce and Loren

2006 Ryan, Shannon, Luke, Caitlin

2007 Did I hear, "Say cheese?"

2008 Oli, Kitty, Toby

2008 Orin and William

2008 Kitty loved it when we took Leo down with us.

2008 Another Family Christmas Lunch
Left from front: Young Kitty, Dawn, Oli, full and tired Jack
Right from front: Replete Carole, Kitty, me, John

2009 Winn's visit

2010 Carl's visit, last weekend before the move to Salvete

2010, 3 October moving in

2010 9 October gathered for the Platinum Wedding Anniversary

Kitty and Jack, the anniversary couple

2011 in the lounge at Salvete
Back: Me, Winn. Front: Carole, Jack, Kitty, Dawn

2012 Birthday Visit – Kitty loved balloons as well as flowers

2012 December- the love of Kitty's life has gone but she finds some comfort in family, here with Carl.

At peace: Kitty's ashes lie encased in her beloved bluebell woods

TIME AND PLACE - Also see MAPS

EARLY YEARS
Hackenthorpe and Beighton

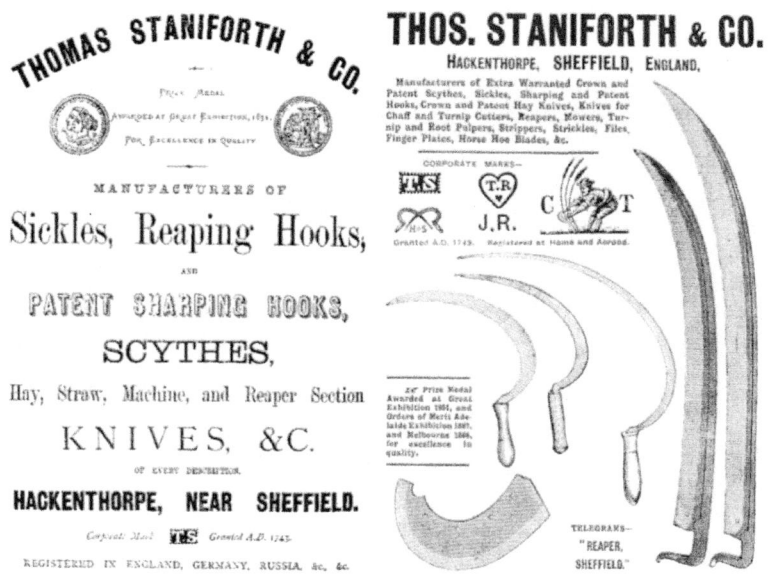

Two old advertisements

Netherthorpe Farm House, all that's left of the farm

Birley Colliery

A Hackenthorpe Terrace Row
Kitty would have been born in a house like these.

Hackenthorpe School, attended by Kitty's 3 eldest siblings

Newspaper of 1921

26 Cairns Road now - no real change, other than windows

Cairns Road, 26 far right.
24, where Mrs Clarke and later Brenda lived, adjoining left
The Avenue opposite, in the foreground, leads to Rosemary Road.

Parade on the High Street 1924
I wonder if Kitty was taken to see it.

Church of St Mary the Virgin (St Mary's), showing some of the graves that so scared Kitty.

School Road, with the school Kitty attended far left
Kitty would have started school in 1925.

The Infant Class in 1925-1926. Which little girl do you think is Kitty? She isn't behind the tear in the photo!

The old Beighton School is now a Nursery School but the buildings are little changed

Butcher's shop on the High Street.
Perhaps this is where Bertha went to buy the pigs' heads.

Bottom end of the High Street, showing Ochre Dike

Looking up the High Street, cinema on the right

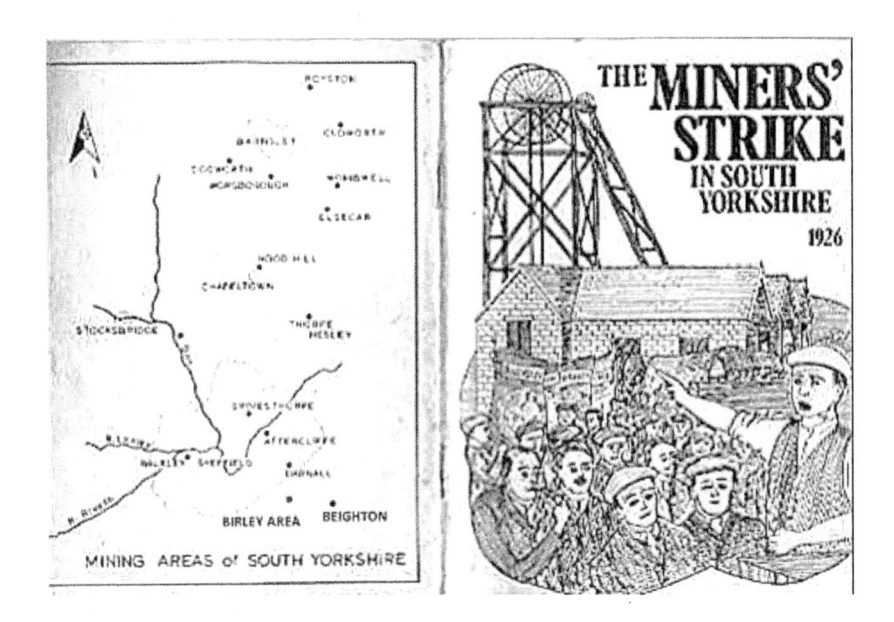

Pamphlet on the Miners' 1926 Strike
All locations approximate

172 Robin Lane now. Number 1 originally, the village expanded beyond it in the post WWII building boom.

It must have been after the miner's strike that the family moved, as Kitty went to school from Cairns Road for at least two years.

Robin Lane looking towards Woodhouse Lane
172 is on the corner of Rosemary Road

Brookhouse Colliery, opened 1929
Sited on the outskirts of Beighton, on the road to Swallownest

The Coke Ovens, fed from Brookhouse Colliery
The gas that was a by-product was used in the manufacture of domestic gas at the nearby gas works.
Each of these would have made a prime target for the Luftwaffe.

Cow Lane, where the bomb fell that blew Edna across the kitchen, as it looks today

LATER YEARS
Bletchley and Fenny Stratford

Looking from Brooklands Road toward Bletchley Road, St Margaret's Church on the left corner. Early 1900s

St Margaret's Church Interior

A steam train passing over the old railway bridge, where the Buckingham Road enters Bletchley.

Bletchley Station 1930s

Station Approach

Station Approach, looking back towards Buckingham Road Bletchley Park is on the right as you look at the picture.

Station Entrance

Bletchley Park Stable Yard Entrance
Kitty may have worked in any of the buildings you see.

The tin shops, on the left just past the railings

One of the well-known little tin shops.

Looking back along Bletchley Road to the station and Buckingham Road beyond.
The tin shops are out of view on the right.

The Park Hotel is the building furthest left. Reg's butcher shop was close by, coming into Bletchley. The new flyover is in the background.

The butcher's shop dressed for Christmas!
I'm afraid I don't know the year. But you wouldn't be allowed to do that nowadays.

Bletchley Road looking into Bletchley from just beyond the tin shops. Entrance to station goods yard near left. Co-op department store is just beyond the two awnings in the distance.

Moving along, WH Smith, bookseller and newsagent, near left: the Co-op still some distance away.

Looking from the Co-op along Bletchley Road
The white building was an extension to the Co-op, added in the 1930s: the original brick building to the right in this picture.

Co-op in the 1950s, rebuilt after a fire. The original building has been replaced and the store extended to its left.

Bletchley Road looking towards Fenny - Cambridge Street near left.

Central Gardens looking towards Bletchley Road entrance Cambridge Street behind the tennis courts on the right

Central Gardens
Western Road is in the background.
Tennis courts are to left

Past the Central Gardens Bletchley Road Entrance
The Studio Cinema is on the left, just beyond the parked truck.

Studio Cinema

Beyond the Studio Cinema

Looking back to the Studio (the large white sided building) on the right, beyond the shops and New Inn pub.

The row of shops included Gilroy's, where Kitty shopped for clothes, a leather goods shop Conway's, and the Castle Wool shop where she purchased her knitting wool.

Fenny Stratford (Fenny) High Street, part of the Watling Street, which became the "Monkey Run" once out of the town.
The Roman Watling Street ran from Shrewsbury to Dover, via London.

The Monkey Run, beyond Fenny station on the left, where you see the signal arm.

Fenny Station
Looking from Fenny towards Bow Brickhill up on the hill
The station entrance is via the ramp on the far right, that leads to the Watling Street by Stag Bridge.

The Ramp

Victoria Road, Fenny
Looking towards St Martin's Church Hall

Aylesbury Street, Fenny

The former Tetley Tea Factory
Corner of Osborne Street and Clifford Avenue

Gas and solid fuel cookers and heaters on display
Gas lighting was still being used in many homes at the time.

Jack's brother Don stands in the doorway.

Stewartby

Stewartby a few years before Kitty moved to the village. Wavell Close is lower right, behind the railway line. The "New Houses" are being built top right.

Later years: school far left on The Crescent, then the 4 detached houses. Kitty and Jack's bungalow faces the green, to the left of the avenue leading to the community hall behind them.

Sports Day - the grandstand backs onto the Club.

1958 Another fancy-dress competition - this time at Stewartby Sports Day. Kitty made Carole the Queen of Heart's costume - and the tarts on display.

Stewartby Co-op on the right, phone box beside it and Club behind.

Front of the Co-op

An old picture of the hall but little has changed.

Hall front today

Above the porch you can clearly see the beehive, symbol of industry.

Steam train approaches Stewartby Halt

View across to Stewartby from Ampthill Park

Front of Stewartby Club

2005, after the 65th Anniversary Party. The Club looks here as it did when built.

Another from 2005

Toby and Oli outside the bungalow. The back kitchen bay window is far left.

The Chequers on the Ampthill Road – a pub now sadly closed

The Pilgrim's Progress, Bedford

The Red Lion, Elstow

The Toby Carvery, Bedford

EXTRAS

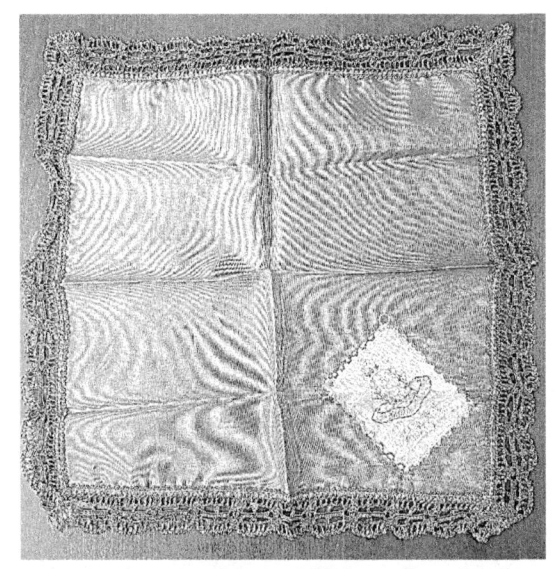

RAMC Sweetheart Silk Handkerchief

Kitty and Jack's Wedding Cake

My Baptism Certificate, kept by Kitty

> Wed
> Nothing happening here yet, when I stepped off the bus at Bedford yesterday Carole was waiting and I said to her "you should be in hospital" her reply "Wish I was." She did look very well so perhaps that is a good sign. I went to Clapham till 8pm, Beryl and Wal popped in to see how things are. They didn't stop long. Carole was pleased to have had your letter she will be writing when baby is born. This seems to be it for now. So Cheerio & Tons of love across to you all. Yours as always Mum & Dad
>
> FOR BIDDY RAY
> X X X X X
> X X X X
> X X X X
> X X X X
> WITH LOVE
>
> FOR OUR KATHRYN
> X X X X X
> X X X X X
> X X X X X
> X X X X X
> X X X X X
> TONS of LOVE FROM Nan.

A letter to me from Kitty, early November 1971

> Coffee Walnut Cake.
>
> Cream 4 oz Marg. and 4 oz sugar. add 2 eggs one at a time. Mix in 1 tablespoon Coffee essence. Fold in 4 ozs self raising flour with 2 ozs chopped Walnuts. Turn into 2 7 ins sandwich tins. Bake in moderate oven 360 F 25 - 30 mins.
>
> Filling
>
> Cream 2 ozs Marg add 4 ozs icing sugar, 1 teaspoon coffee essence, 2 teas milk beat well. Sandwich cake with two thirds of mixture, edge cake top with remainder. Centre icing add 1 teaspoon coffee essence and 2 teasp warm water to 2 ozs icing sugar beat till smooth and glossy pour on cake. decorate with walnuts.

Kitty's hand written recipe for Coffee Walnut Cake, sent to me in a letter. This was a firm favourite with all who tasted it!

Dawn had the workbox table that Jack made Kitty. This is what she found when she looked inside.

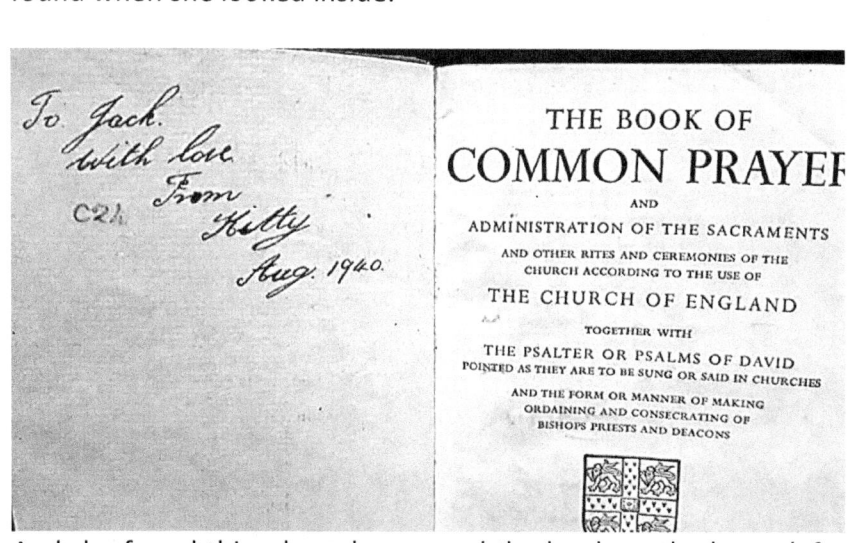

And she found this when she opened the book on the lower left of the previous photograph.

WARTIME
A Small Selection of Government Posters and Images
Kitty would have seen all these and many more.

Propaganda for Commonwealth Forces

Promoting the government's evacuation programme.

Many London mothers must have been tempted to bring their evacuee children back home when the skies were quiet.

There were a number of "Keep Mum" posters, advising against careless talk. Perhaps the most well-known had the slogan, "Be like Dad, keep Mum!"

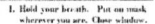

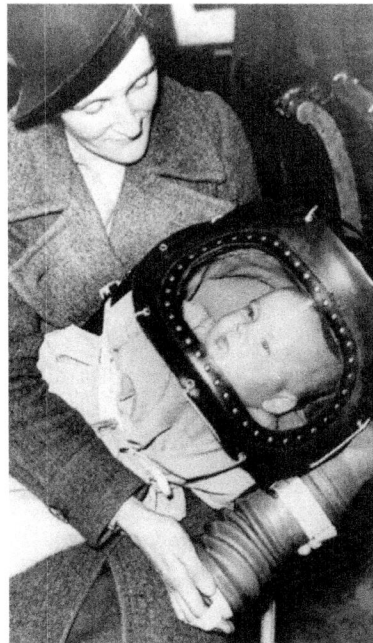

Even babies had gas masks

A 2000-lb. Aerial Bomb uses 600 pounds of scrap metals

A Medium Tank uses 15 tons of scrap metals

A 35,000-ton Battleship uses 20,000 tons of scrap metals

A 3-inch Anti-aircraft Gun uses 3 tons of scrap metals

GET IN THE SCRAP

Everything from saucepans to metal railings was collected for scrap, to be melted down for the war effort.

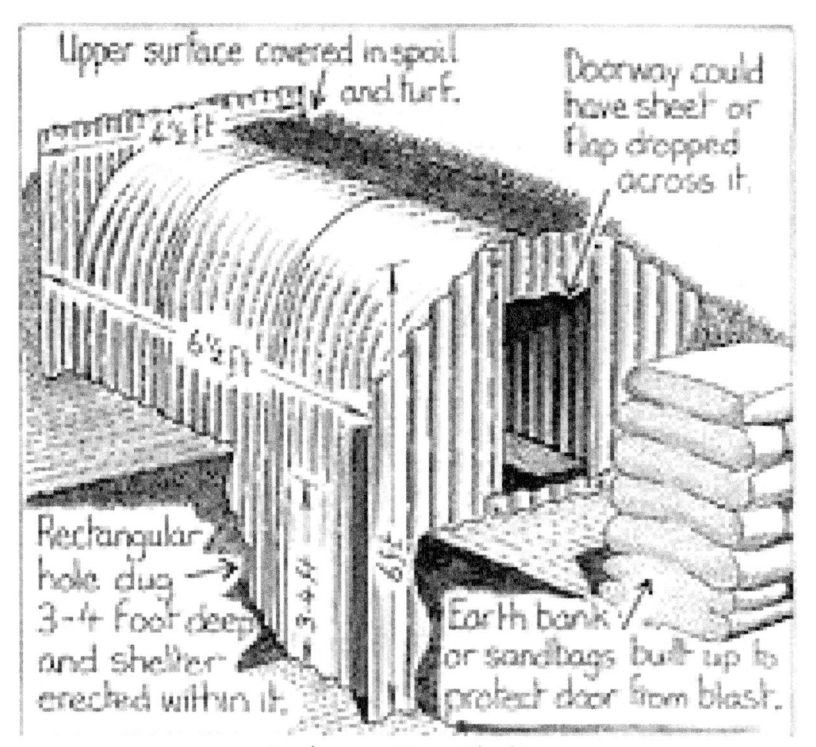

Anderson Type Shelter

Family enters a shelter, carrying gas mask boxes

Advertising the Morison Shelter

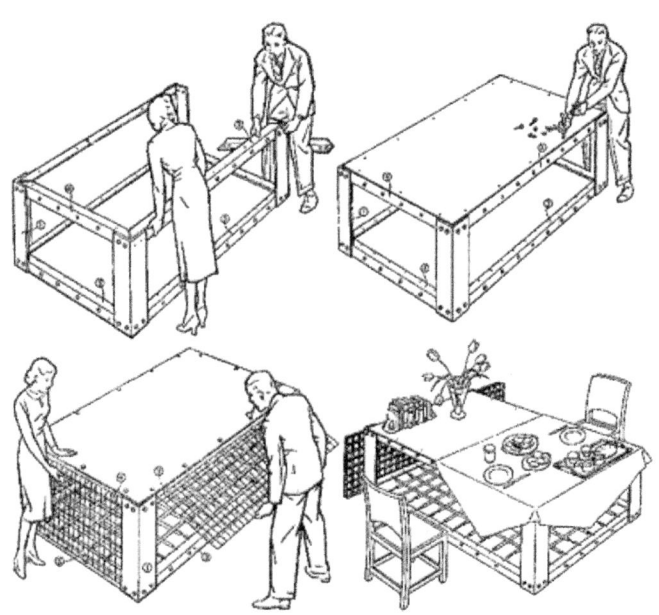

Assembly Instructions

In Use as a Table

Better safe than sorry!

EPILOGUE

Writing this book was both a labour of love and a real struggle. The factual information wasn't so difficult. Trying to capture Kitty herself was altogether another matter. I hope I have managed to give you at least some sense of her essence and character, though my task there remains frustratingly incomplete.

My own story, and that of Jack, are told elsewhere. The books are all available on Amazon.

Autobiographical:

Bucks, Beds and Bricks
In No Particular Order

Biographical:

Jack Blane
His Darling Kitty

Kitty is present in them all, and in my book Variegated Verse. She remains too a very real presence in the hearts of all who loved her.

Both Jack and his darling Kitty, our lovely, loving, mother, grandmother great grandmother and so much more to so many, will always be sorely missed. Yet the ripples of their lives remain, reaching out through the generations.

You will find the family tree on My Heritage in the name Jean Blane. It carries much more information - on both Kitty and Jack's families.

APPENDIX

Early Family	294
Family Trees	
Wallis	298
Packard	300
Family Records	310
Wallis	311
Packard	345
Kitty Blane	359
Maps	368
Home Towns and Villages	
Hackenthorpe	386
Beighton	391
Bletchley	395
Stewartby	401

EARLY FAMILY

We have so far traced the Roper branch of Kitty's maternal family back to 1350, with John Roper and his wife born Margaret Herbenieur. William Eyre, also born 1350, was their son John's father-in-law.

On Kitty's paternal side we can "only" trace the family back as far as 1673 with Anna Hickingbotham, in so far as known birthdates go.

The earliest members of one branch of Kitty's maternal side were to be found in Norfolk and Suffolk. All Kitty's other forebears seem to have been born and lived in an area bordered by Nottingham in the South and Sheffield in the North, including North Derbyshire.

Early generations on both sides had very varied occupations, although many did work in agriculture, and later in the coal mines.

Joseph Jepson born 1785, and his son James, were lead miners. His son Timothy was a blacksmith. Did I say varied occupations? I hadn't even known there were lead mines in Derbyshire until I came across the reference in the 1851 census.

I discovered then that lead had been mined in the area since Roman times and was a valuable commodity. Two centres were Wirksworth and Cromford, both homes to several generations of the family.

Other known occupations range through lace makers and cotton bleachers to a police officer and quarrymen.

I was intrigued that both Henry Packard born 1810, and his son William born 1837, were scythe grinders. In my imagination, scythe grinders were itinerant workers who went from farm to farm to grind the scythes used for harvesting.

Now I have learned that in fact these ancestors would have worked in a mill that manufactured a variety of metal implements. Grinding the metal was the final stage before the fitting of any handle.

That was a grimmer occupation than the one in my imagination. Different stones were used for grinding the different implements. Scythe grinders worked on the largest grinding stones.

In the early 1800's the grinding process changed from using mainly wet stones to dry stones instead. One reason was that the price the men were paid for each piece of grinding work had been cut - and using a dry stone was faster.

Unfortunately, this form of grinding created a lot of dust. The dust was inhaled by the grinders, causing a serious respiratory disease known as Grinders Asthma.

In 1851 (from the census), Henry was living in Beighton but his three youngest children had been born in Hackenthorpe.

Thomas Staniforth & Co was founded by Thomas Staniforth in 1743 with workshops on Main Street, Hackenthorpe. We don't have any direct evidence but this being a sickle, scythe and tool making company, it seems more than reasonable to believe that

Henry worked there.

In the same census we see that his son William (Kitty's grandfather), then aged 14, was also a scythe grinder, presumably working for the same company.

By the time of the 1871 census William was living in Totley and it's uncertain as to where he was then working. However, the most likely place would be the nearby Abbeydale Works.

The earliest Wallis for whom I've found a record but not yet a birth date is George Wallis, who married in 1693. His son George, born 1694, died in 1780.

According to a family tree compiled by Herbert Wallis (1844-1922), a direct descendant, the younger George was in the saddlery business. He was also Churchwarden of St Alkmund's Church, Derby in 1768 and 1769. Many family members were baptised, married and buried at St Alkmund's over the years.

Also on Kitty's paternal side, her great grandfather Thomas Wallis is recorded in the 1851 census as an agricultural labourer. By 1871, he was a cottager. In those day, this was a farm worker who lived in a tied cottage.

The upside of such an arrangement was that the rent was either part of your wages or very cheap. The downside was that if you lost your job, you also lost your home.

Thomas' son Frederick had a varied career. His occupation is listed as Carter in the 1871 census. His wife Sarah had been working as a nurse prior to her marriage, also noted in the 1871 census.

I think that she was most likely a children's nursemaid, since at sixteen years old she was living as a servant with the family for whom she worked.

By the 1881 census, when Frederick and Sarah were visiting the Brownson's, her parents, his occupation is given as police constable. In 1891 and 1901 he was foreman in a colliery.

The 1911 census records him as Farmer at Netherthorpe Farm, Aston cum Aughton. In the same census his fourth child, Kitty's Uncle Frederick, was recorded as Helper on Farm.

Too early for Kitty to remember, Annie had to look after their brother Fred, dragging him off to school with her. In the summer holidays both Annie and Fred went to Netherthorpe Farm, helping with the haymaking. Fred helped with the horses too, which he loved.

By 1921 Kitty's Uncle Frederick was a Carter Contractor, hiring out carts and other vehicles, but appears to have still been living on the farm. His father Frederick had died in 1917.

Kitty's brother Fred would ideally have liked to work on a farm, like his grandfather and uncle. But such jobs became fewer and the family gave up Netherthorpe Farm. Fred ended up, as was the case with so many others, working in a local coal mine.

JEAN FLANNERY
FAMILY TREES

WALLIS

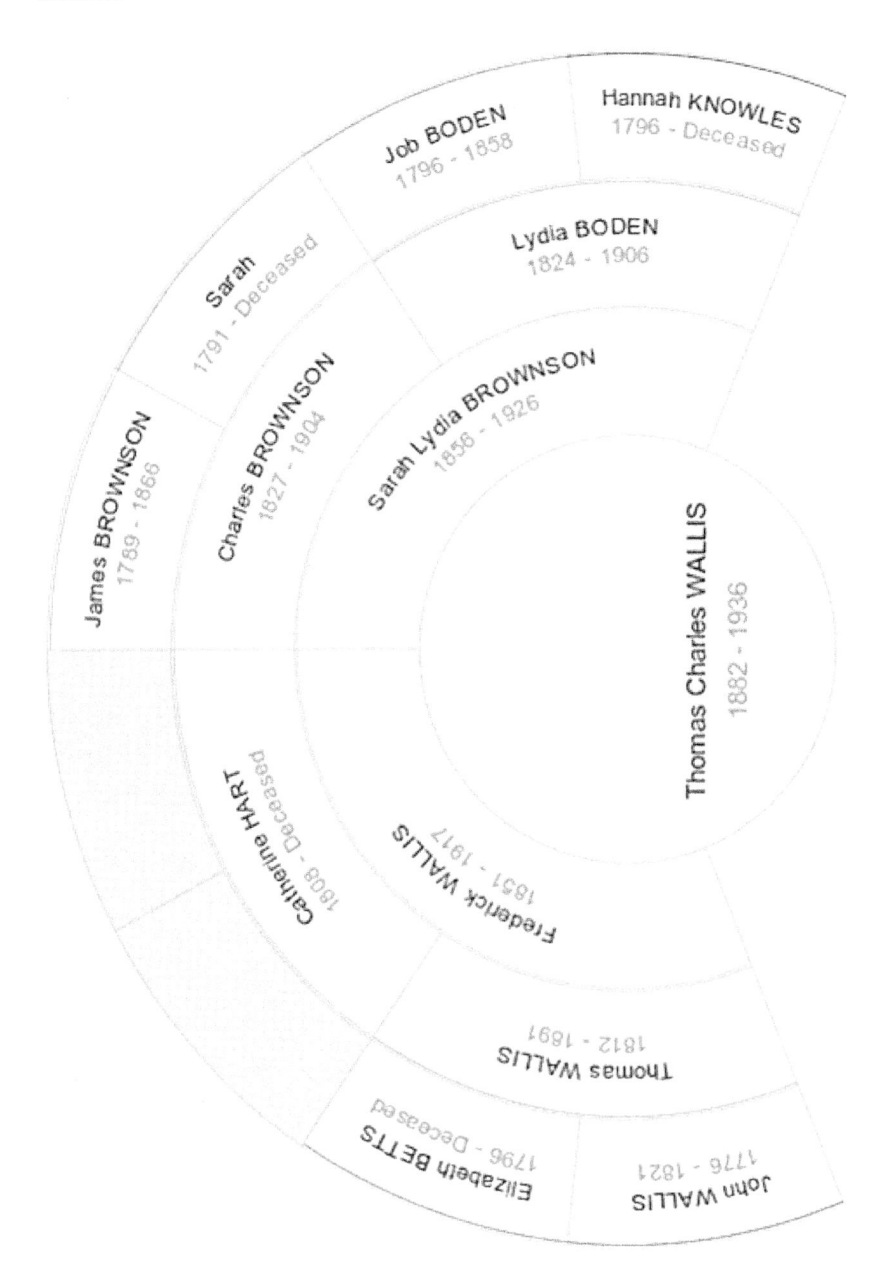

- Thomas Charles WALLIS 1882 - 1936
  - Sarah Lydia BROWNSON 1856 - 1926
    - Charles BROWNSON 1827 - 1904
      - James BROWNSON 1789 - 1866
      - Sarah 1791 - Deceased
    - Lydia BODEN 1824 - 1906
      - Job BODEN 1796 - 1858
      - Hannah KNOWLES 1796 - Deceased
  - Frederick WALLIS 1851 - 1917
    - Thomas WALLIS 1812 - 1891
      - John WALLIS 1776 - 1821
      - Elizabeth BETTS 1796 - Deceased
    - Catherine HART 1808 - Deceased

Fan Chart

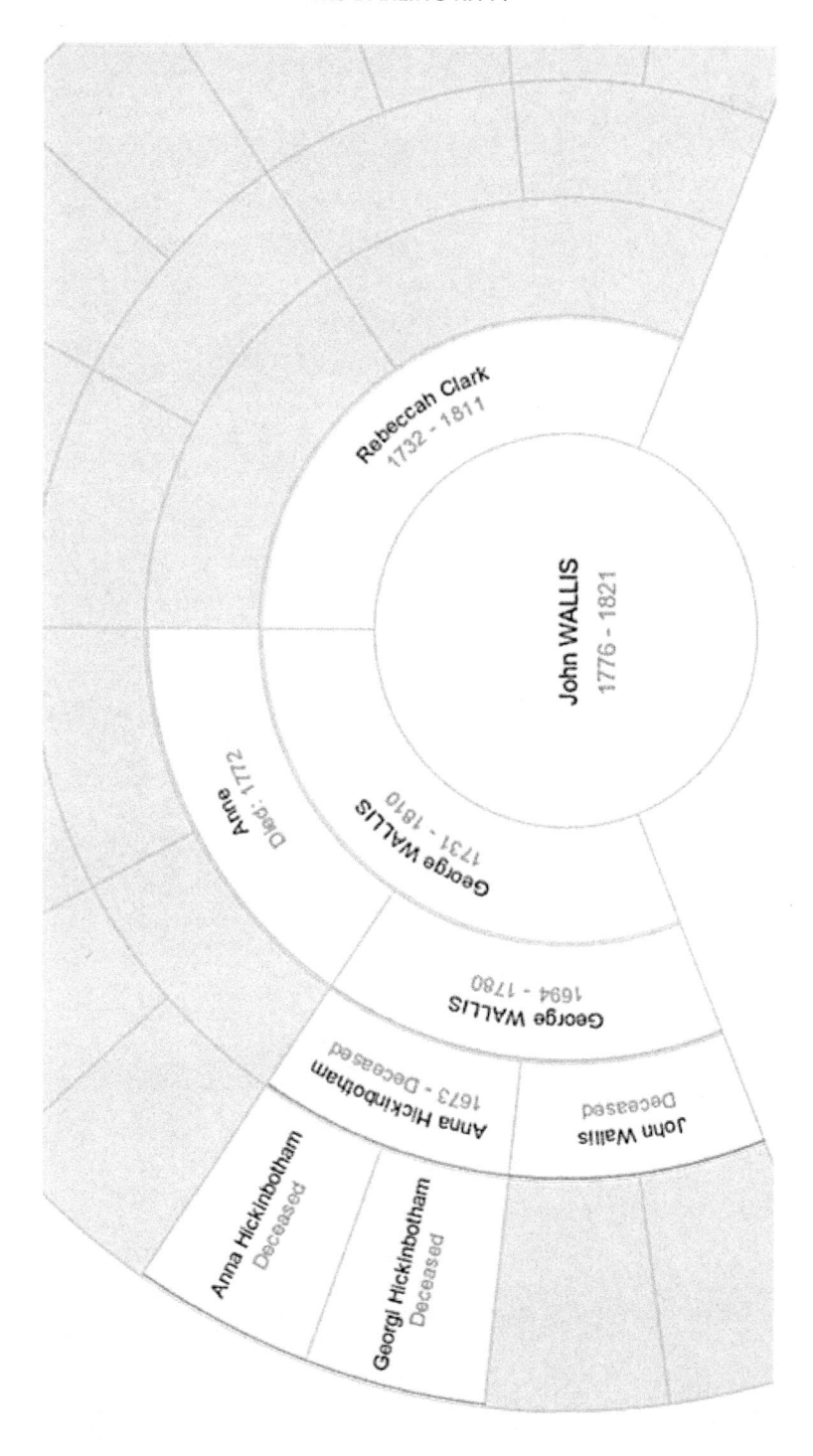

- **John WALLIS** 1776 - 1821
  - Rebeccah Clark 1732 - 1811
  - George WALLIS 1731 - 1810
    - George WALLIS 1694 - 1780
      - John Wallis, Deceased
      - Anna Hickinbotham 1673 - Deceased
        - Anna Hickinbotham, Deceased
        - Georgi Hickinbotham, Deceased
    - Anne, Died: 1772

PACKARD

- Bertha Annie PACKARD 1880 - 1947
  - Elizabeth Ann BIGGIN 1840 - 1905
    - William BIGGIN 1815 - 1847
      - George Biggin 1781 - 1850
      - Mary Ann Biggin 1816 - Deceased
    - Mary Ann JEPSON 1810 - 1852
      - Joseph JEPSON 1785 - Deceased
      - Mary 1781 - Deceased
  - William Henry PACKARD 1837 - 1859
    - Henry PACKARD 1810 - 1863
      - George PACKARD 1761 - 1843
      - Margaret McCLOUD 1761 - 1842

HIS DARLING KITTY

- Elizabeth Smith 1657 - 1728
- Sarah WHITING 1686 - 1758
- Roger Brock 1657 - 1747
- Edward BROCK 1682 - 1758
- Amy BROCK 1727 - Deceased
- George PACKARD 1761 - 1843
- George PACKARD 1733 - Deceased

JEAN FLANNERY

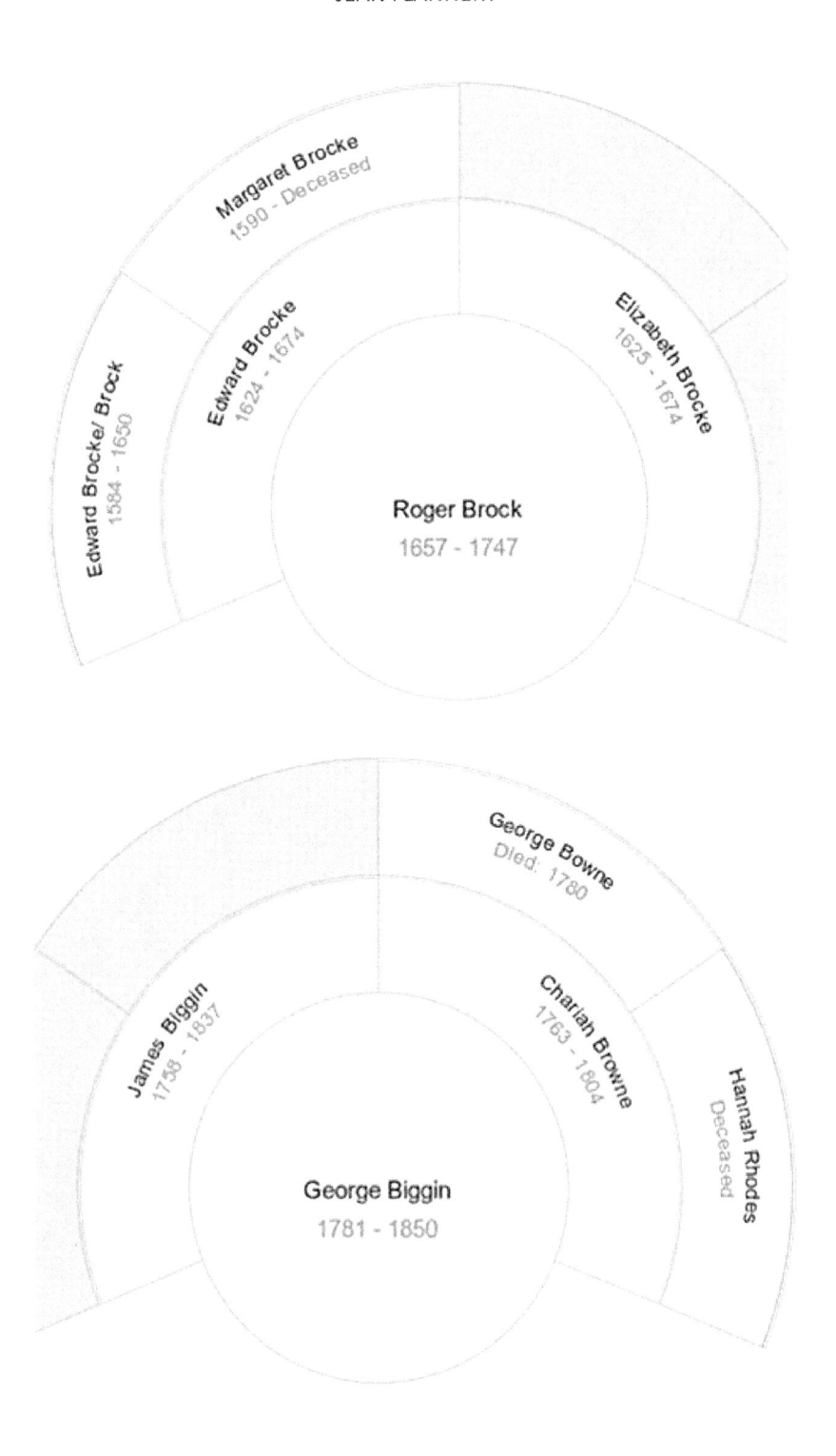

Roger Brock
1657 - 1747

- Edward Brocke 1624 - 1674
  - Edward Brocke/Brock 1584 - 1650
  - Margaret Brocke 1590 - Deceased
- Elizabeth Brocke 1625 - 1674

George Biggin
1781 - 1850

- James Biggin 1758 - 1837
- Charian Browne 1763 - 1804
  - George Bowne Died: 1780
  - Hannah Rhodes Deceased

HIS DARLING KITTY

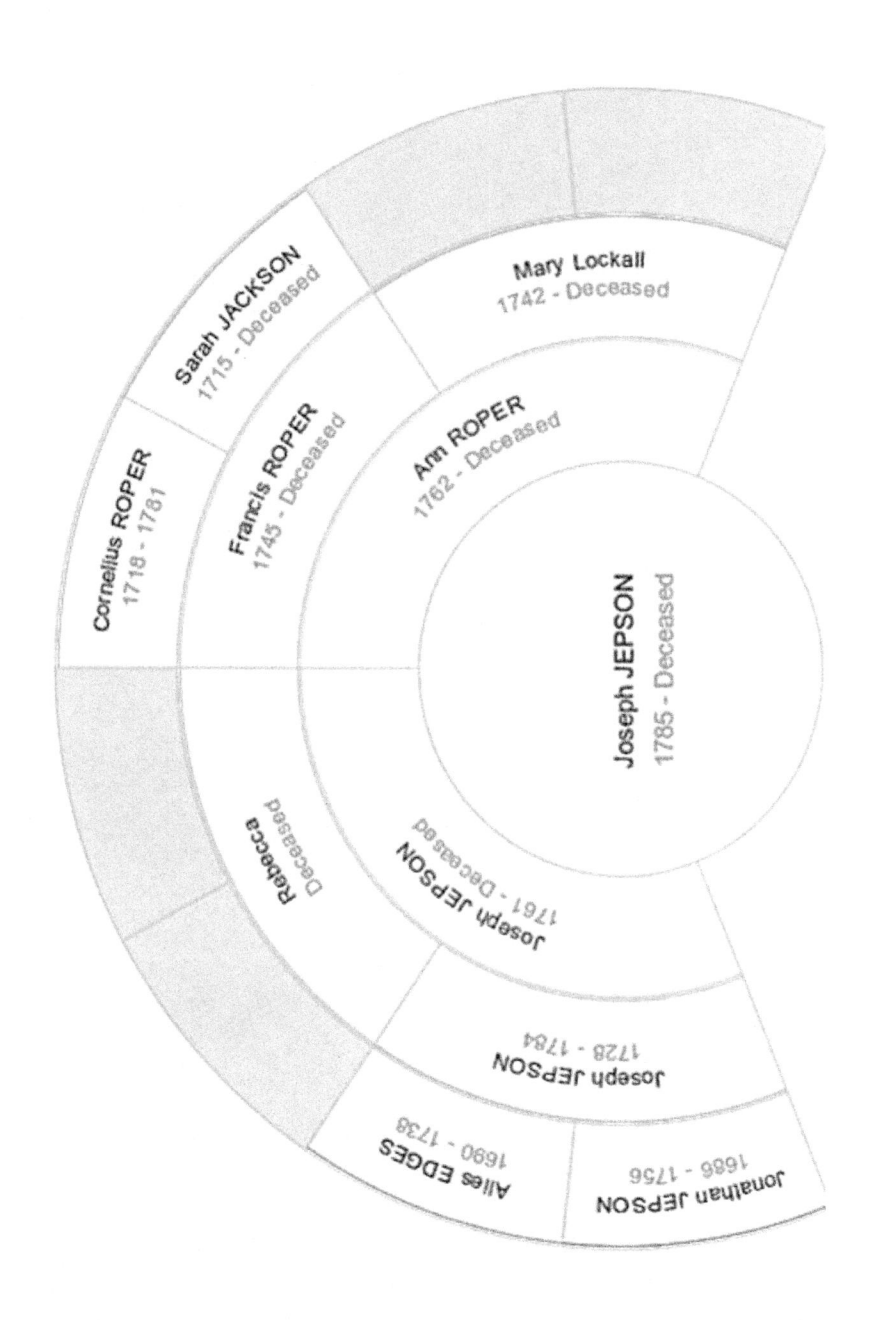

- Joseph JEPSON — 1785 - Deceased
  - Ann ROPER — 1762 - Deceased
    - Francis ROPER — 1745 - Deceased
      - Cornelius ROPER — 1718 - 1781
      - Sarah JACKSON — 1715 - Deceased
    - Mary Lockall — 1742 - Deceased
  - Joseph JEPSON — 1761 - Deceased
    - Joseph JEPSON — 1728 - 1784
      - Jonathan JEPSON — 1686 - 1756
      - Alles EDGES — 1690 - 1738
    - Rebecca — Deceased

JEAN FLANNERY

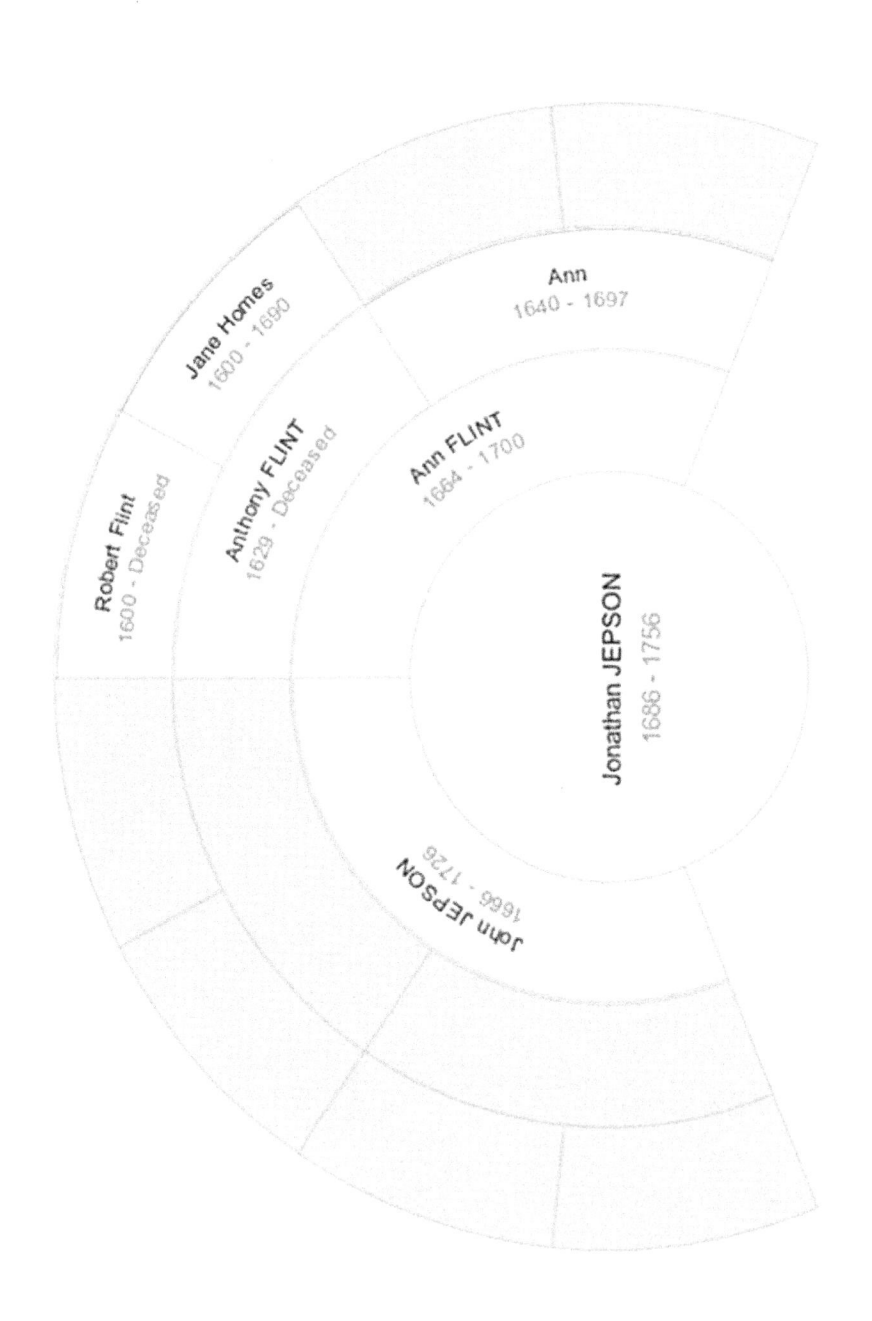

- Jonathan JEPSON 1686 - 1756
  - Ann FLINT 1664 - 1700
    - Anthony FLINT 1629 - Deceased
      - Robert Flint 1600 - Deceased
      - Jane Homes 1600 - 1690
    - Ann 1640 - 1697
  - John JEPSON 1666 - 1726

HIS DARLING KITTY

Cornelius ROPER
1718 - 1781

- Sarah BEARDSLEY
  1683 - 1725
- Cornelius ROPER
  1681 - Deceased
  - Dorothy RIVINGTON
    1640 - 1687
  - Anthony ROPER
    Died: 1692
    - Edward ROPER
      1614 - 1692
    - Ann
      1616 - Deceased

JEAN FLANNERY

Edward ROPER
1614 - 1692

Ann Baston
1595 - 1644

Thomas ROPER
1595 - 1650

Maria Wanndell
1574 - 1651

John Roper
1560 - 1631

Matilda Bouteshall
1528 - 1579

Thomas Roper
1500 - 1579

HIS DARLING KITTY

Thomas Roper
1500 - 1579

Elizabeth Sadler
1470 - Deceased

Henry Roper
1465 - Deceased

Emmotta Gell
1432 - 1480

Hugh Roper
1429 - 1490

Isolda Roper
1410 - 1470

Richard Furneux
1400 - 1470

JEAN FLANNERY

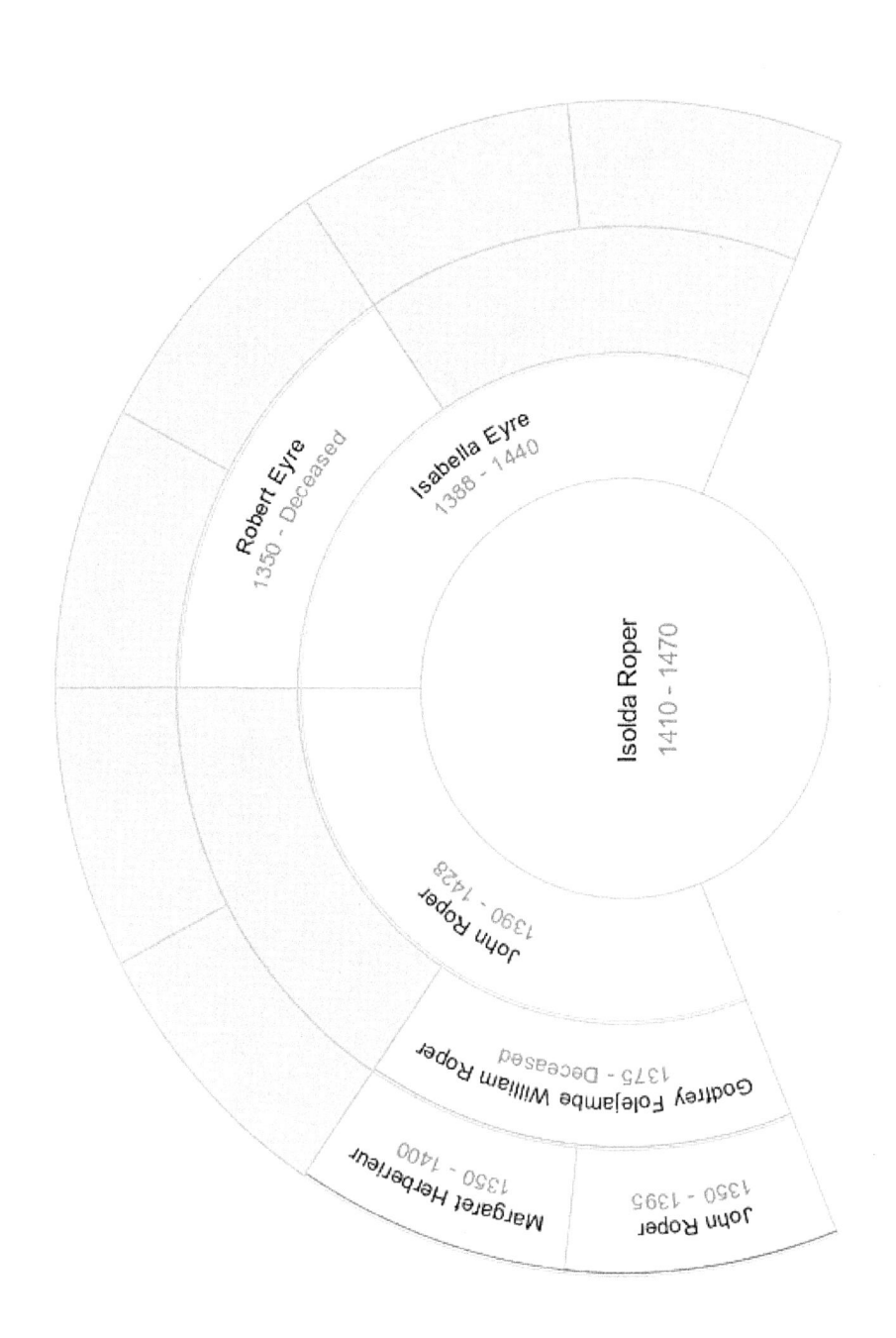

- Isolda Roper 1410 - 1470
  - Isabella Eyre 1388 - 1440
    - Robert Eyre 1350 - Deceased
  - John Roper 1390 - 1428
    - Godfrey Foljambe William Roper 1375 - Deceased
      - John Roper 1350 - 1395
      - Margaret Herberteur 1350 - 1400

Richard Furneux
Deceased

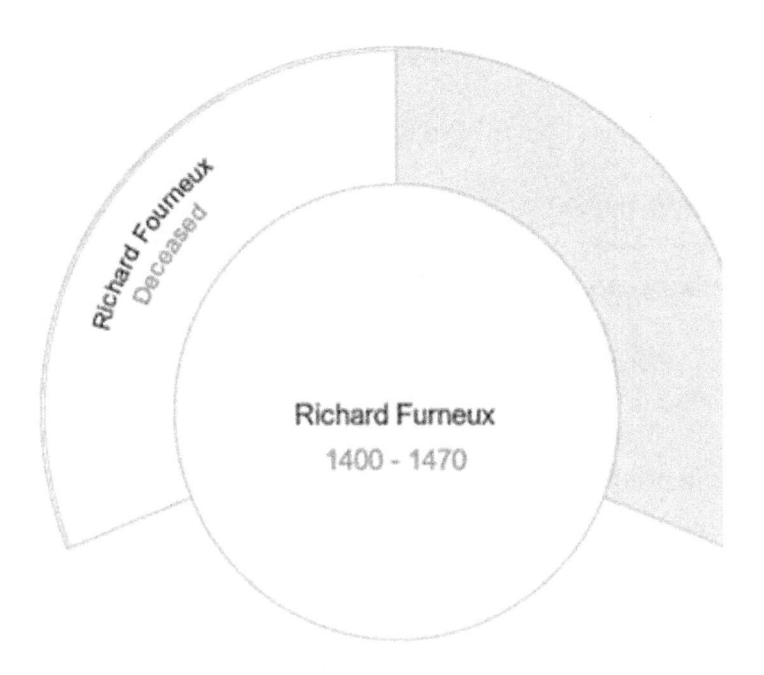

Richard Furneux
1400 - 1470

I have included this last small branch of the tree, with Isolda Roper's father-in-law, as it does complete the family lines. That is to say, it completes them to date. But since I have been adding finds almost to the present day, there is no telling who else might show up.

RECORDS

All transcripts are from official records, though the family records are far too numerous to include more than a sample here.

This is the earliest record I've found of Netherthorpe Farm.

Included in the Dissolution of the Monasteries, the priory was gifted by Henry VIII in 1538 to Frances Talbot, 5th Earl of Shrewsbury - born in Sheffield. Did he gift the farm lease to Joan?

Although the priory itself was located near Worksop, Nottinghamshire, it owned extensive lands estimated at 2,330 acres and was located less than 10 miles from Netherthorpe. In 1291 the priory received a temporality from Sheffield Rectory of £10, equivalent in 2021 to over £12,000 (Bank of England).

```
Quitclaim by Joan Cutloffe of Tuxforthe, Henry Matley of
the same, scholar, her natural...
```

Reference:	C 146/7537
Description:	Quitclaim by Joan Cutloffe of Tuxforthe, Henry Matley of the same, scholar, her natural son, and others, to Sir Nicholas Styrley of Styrley, knight, of their interest in the lease of a farm called 'Netherthorpe' formerly of the dissolved priory of Worsope. 3 . Henry [VIII]. English.
Note:	Seal
Date:	[c 1539]
Held by:	The National Archives, Kew
Legal status:	Public Record(s)
Closure status:	Open Document, Open Description

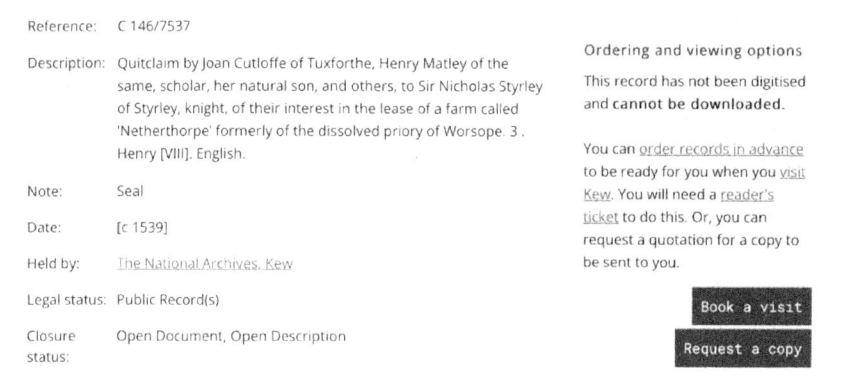

Ordering and viewing options

This record has not been digitised and cannot be downloaded.

You can order records in advance to be ready for you when you visit Kew. You will need a reader's ticket to do this. Or, you can request a quotation for a copy to be sent to you.

Book a visit

Request a copy

Transcript from British History Online:

(Filed in) Yorkshire [West Riding]

Quitclaim by Joan Cutloffe of Tuxforthe, Henry Matley of the same, scholar, her natural son, and others, to Sir Nicholas Styrley of Styrley, knight, of their interest in the lease of a farm called 'Netherthorpe' formerly of the dissolved priory of Worsope 3. Henry [VIII]. English. Seal

WALLIS

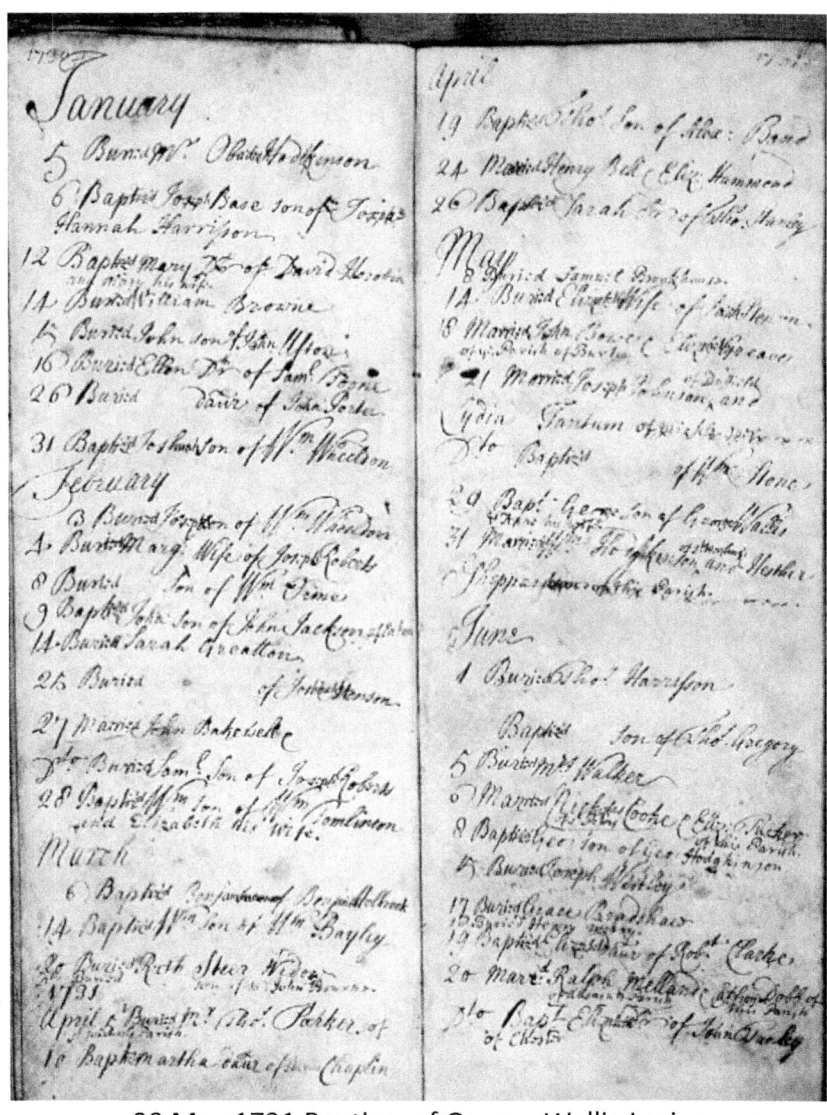

29 May 1731 Baptism of George Wallis Junior
St Alkmund, Derby Parish Register

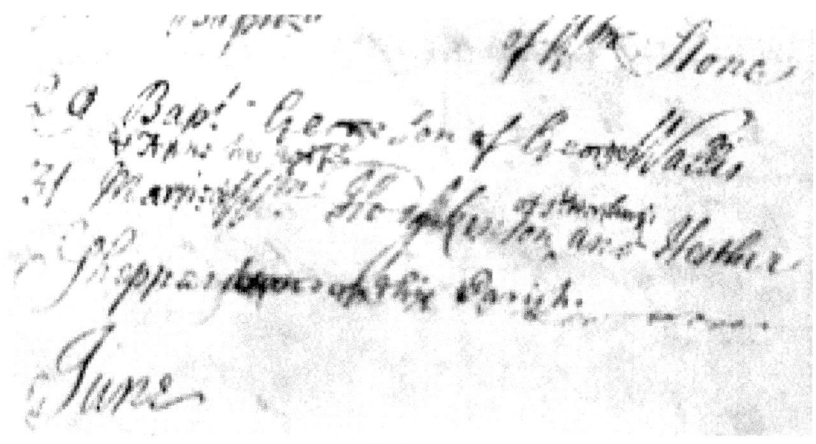

Entry

Name	**George Wallis**
Sex	**Male**
Christening Date	**29 May 1731**
Christening Place	**Derby, Derbyshire, England, United Kingdom**
Christening Place (Original)	**Derby, St.Alkmund, Derby, England**
Father's Name	**George Wallis**
Father's Sex	**Male**
Mother's Name	**Anne**
Mother's Sex	**Female**

George Wallis's Parents and Siblings   OPEN

George Wallis	Father	M
Anne	Mother	F

29 May 1731 Baptism Transcript
George Wallis

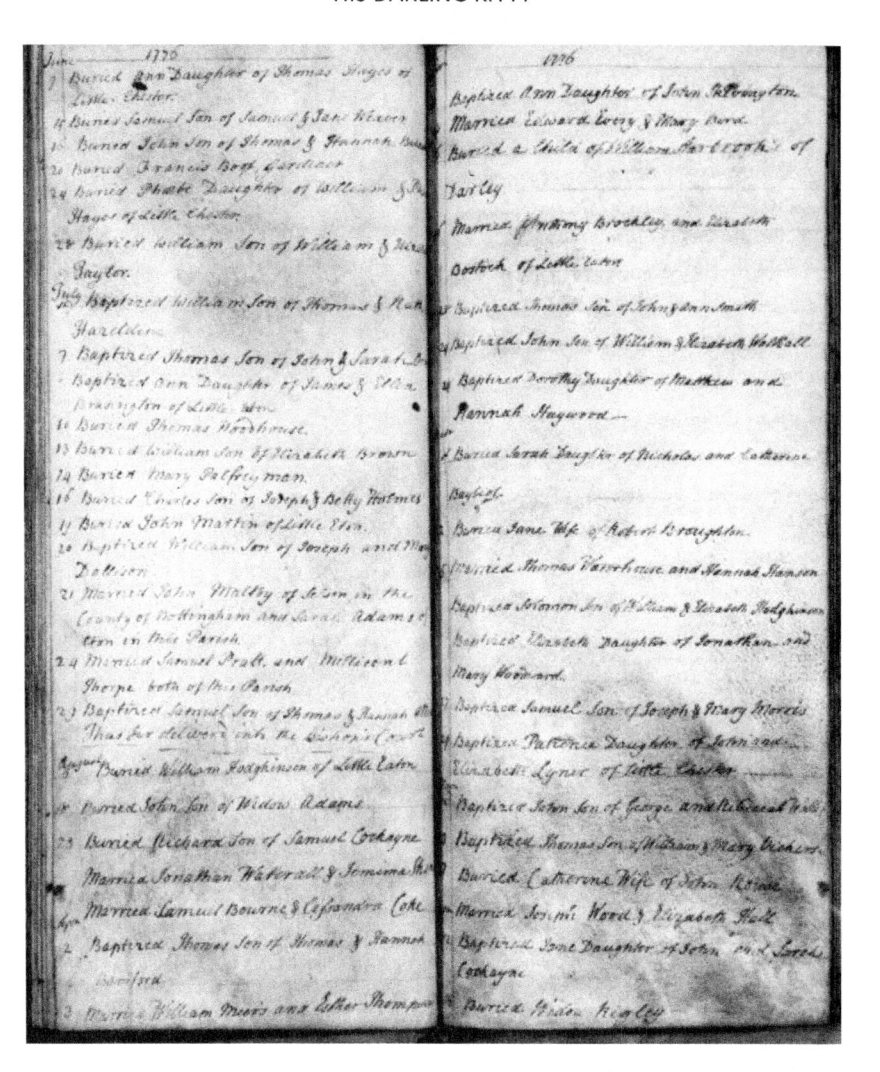

3 November 1776 Baptism of John Wallis
St Alkmund Parish Register

John Wallis
England Births and Christenings, 1538-1975

Name:	John Wallis
Sex:	Male
Christening Date:	3 Nov 1776
Christening Place:	Derby, Derbyshire, England, United Kingdom
Christening Place (Original):	Derby, St.Alkmund, Derby, England
Father's Name:	George Wallis
Father's Sex:	Male
Mother's Name:	Rebeccah
Mother's Sex:	Female

John Wallis, Baptism Transcript

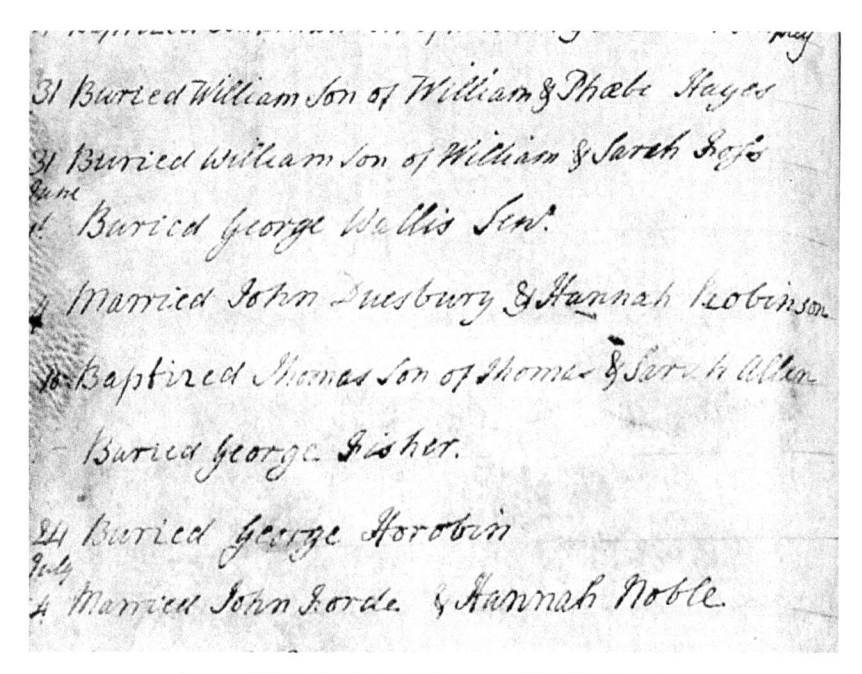

June 1780 Burial of George Wallis Senior
St Alkmund Parish Register

HIS DARLING KITTY

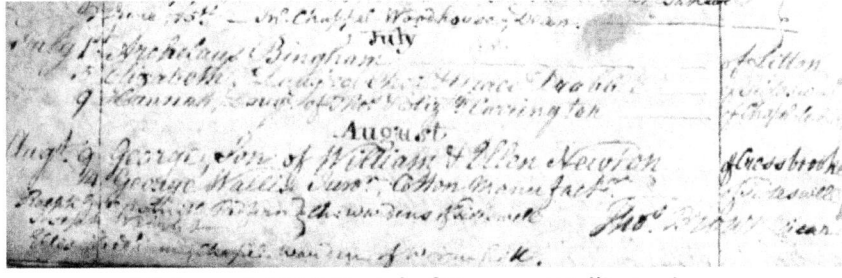

14 August 1810 Burial of George Wallis Junior
St John the Baptist Tideswell, Church Register

George Wallis
England, Derbyshire, Church of England Parish Registers, 1537-1918

Event Type:	Burial
Name:	George Wallis • Edit
Death or Burial Date:	14 Aug 1810 • Edit
Death or Burial Place:	Tideswell, Derbyshire, England, United Kingdom

Burial Transcript

25 December 1822 Marriage of Job Biden and Hannah Knowles
Matlock Parish Register

Name: **Job Boden**

Sex: **Male**

Marriage Date: **25 Dec 1822**

Marriage Place: **Matlock, Matlock, Derbyshire, England**

Spouse's Name: **Hannah Knowles**

Spouse's Sex: **Female**

Job Boden and Hannah Knowles, Marriage Transcript

Name: **Lydia Boden**

Sex: **Female**

Christening Date: **14 Mar 1824**

Christening Place: **Matlock, Derbyshire, England, United Kingdom**

Christening Place (Original): **Matlock, Derby, England**

Birth Date: **18 Feb 1824**

Father's Name: **Job Boden**

Father's Sex: **Male**

Mother's Name: **Hannah**

Mother's Sex: **Female**

14 March 1824 Lydia Boden Birth, Matlock

Charles Brownson
England Births and Christenings, 1538-1975

Name:	Charles Brownson
Sex:	Male
Christening Date:	3 Aug 1828
Christening Place:	Cromford, Derbyshire, England, United Kingdom
Christening Place (Original):	Saint Mary, Cromford, Derby, England
Father's Name:	James Brownson
Father's Sex:	Male
Mother's Name:	Sarah
Mother's Sex:	Female

3 August 1828, Charles Brownson Christening
St Mary's Church, Cromford

1841 Census Joseph Jepson
Wife Mary; sons James, Timothy and William

Name	**James Brownson**
Sex	**Male**
Age	**50**
Event Date	**1841**
Event Place	**Wirksworth, Derbyshire, England, United Kingdom**
Event Place (Original)	**Wirksworth, Derbyshire, England**
Registration District	**Bakewell**
Birth Year (Estimated)	**1787-1791**
Birthplace	**Derbyshire**
Event Type	**Census**
Page Number	**6**
Piece/Folio	**198/6**
Registration Number	**HO107**

Other People on This Record   OPEN ALL

Charles Brownson	M	12	Derbyshire	˅
Abele Brownson	M	10	Derbyshire	˅
George Brownson	M	8	Derbyshire	˅
Sarah Brownson	F	50	Derbyshire	˅
Marey Brownson	F	15	Derbyshire	˅
Emilia Brownson	F	14	Derbyshire	˅

1841 Census James Brownson

Strangely, his wife Sarah's name is listed below those of 3 of his children.

26 December 1848
Marriage of Charles Brownson and Lydia Boden

Matlock Parish Register

Charles Brownson
England, Derbyshire, Church of England Parish Registers, 1537-1918

Name:	Charles Brownson • Edit
Sex:	Male
Marital Status:	Single
Father's Name:	James Brownson • Edit
Marriage Date:	25 Dec 1848 • Edit
Marriage Place:	Matlock, Matlock, Derbyshire, England • Edit
Spouse's Name:	Lydia Boden
Spouse's Sex:	Female
Spouse's Marital Status:	Single
Spouse's Father's Name:	Job Boden

Marriage Transcript

Name	Charles Bronson
Sex	Male
Age	23
Event Date	1851
Event Place	Matlock, Derbyshire, England
Registration District	Bakewell
Birth Year (Estimated)	1828
Birthplace	Cromford, Derbyshire
Marital Status	Married
Occupation	Baker
Relationship to Head of Household	Head
Event Type	Census
Page Number	14
Piece/Folio	2150 / 188
Registration Number	HO107

Charles Bronson's Spouses and Children   OPEN ALL

Lydia Bronson	Wife	F	24	Matlock, Derbyshire	∨
James Bronson	Son	M	2	Matlock, Derbyshire	∨
Anna Bronson	Daughter	F	1	Matlock, Derbyshire	∨

1851 Census Charles Brownson

Note the incorrect spelling of the surname on the transcript, such errors not unusual in the early censuses. But errors occur even in transcripts of the 1921 census records, recently released.

Event Type	**Census**
Name	**John Wallis**
Sex	**Male**
Age	**75**
Event Date	**1851**
Event Place	**Wilford, Nottinghamshire, England**
Registration District	**Basford**
Birth Year (Estimated)	**1776**
Birthplace	**Long Eaton, Derbyshire**
Marital Status	**Married**
Occupation	**Agl Labourer**
Relationship to Head of Household	**Head**
Page Number	**16**
Piece/Folio	**2128 / 576**
Registration Number	**HO107**

John Wallis's Spouses and Children   OPEN ALL

Elizabeth Wallis	Wife	F	77	East Leak, Nottinghamshire	⌄
Thomas Wallis	Son	M	39	Wilford, Nottinghamshire	⌄
John Wallis	Son	M	10	Wilford, Nottinghamshire	⌄
Phoebe Wallis	Daughter	F	8	Wilford, Nottinghamshire	⌄
Edward Wallis	Son	M	6	Wilford, Nottinghamshire	⌄
Henry Wallis	Son	M	3	Wilford, Nottinghamshire	⌄

1851 Census John Wallis

The young children are those of his son Thomas.
You will note that at 77 years old, John is still working as an agricultural labourer - no old age pension in those days.

Thomas Wallis
England and Wales Census, 1851

Name:	Thomas Wallis
Sex:	Male
Age:	39
Event Date:	1851
Event Place:	Wilford, Nottinghamshire, England
Registration District:	Basford
Birth Year (Estimated):	1812
Birthplace:	Wilford, Nottinghamshire
Marital Status:	Married
Occupation:	Agl Labourer
Relationship to Head of Household:	Son
Page Number:	16
Piece/Folio:	2128 / 576
Registration Number:	HO107

Household	Role	Sex	Age	Birthplace
John Wallis	Head	Male	75	Long Eaton, Derbyshire
Elizabeth Wallis	Wife	Female	77	East Leak, Nottinghamshire
Thomas Wallis	Son	Male	39	Wilford, Nottinghamshire
Catherine Wallis		Female	43	Clifton, Nottinghamshire
John Wallis	Son	Male	10	Wilford, Nottinghamshire
Phoebe Wallis	Daughter	Female	8	Wilford, Nottinghamshire
Edward Wallis	Son	Male	6	Wilford, Nottinghamshire
Henry Wallis	Son	Male	3	Wilford, Nottinghamshire
Fredric Wallis	Son	Male	0	Wilford, Nottinghamshire

1851 Census Thomas Wallis
This gives a fuller picture of the household.

Sarah Lydia Brownson
England and Wales Birth Registration Index, 1837-2008

Name:	Sarah Lydia Brownson
Event Date:	1856
Event Place:	Bakewell, Derbyshire, England
Registration District:	Bakewell
Volume:	7B
Affiliate Line Number:	40
Registration Quarter:	Apr-May-Jun
Registration Year:	1856

1856 Sarah Lydia Brownson Birth

Sarah Lydia Brownson
England Births and Christenings, 1538-1975

Name:	Sarah Lydia Brownson
Sex:	Female
Christening Date:	6 Jul 1856
Christening Place:	Matlock, Derbyshire, England, United Kingdom
Christening Place (Original):	Matlock, Derby, England
Father's Name:	Charles Brownson
Father's Sex:	Male
Mother's Name:	Lydia
Mother's Sex:	Female

6 July 1856 Sarah Lydia Brownson Christening

Charles Brownson
England and Wales Census, 1861

Name:	Charles Brownson
Sex:	Male
Age:	34
Event Date:	1861
Event Place:	Matlock, Derbyshire, England, United Kingdom
Event Place (Original):	Matlock, Derbyshire, England
Registration District:	Bakewell
Birth Year (Estimated):	1827
Birthplace:	Cromford, Derbyshire
Marital Status:	Married
Occupation:	Labourer
Relationship to Head of Household:	Head
Page Number:	8
Piece/Folio:	2542 / 41
Registration Number:	RG09

Household	Role	Sex	Age	Birthplace
Charles Brownson	Head	Male	34	Cromford, Derbyshire
Lydia Brownson	Wife	Female	34	Matlock, Derbyshire
James Brownson	Son	Male	12	Matlock, Derbyshire
Charles Brownson	Son	Male	9	Matlock, Derbyshire
Sarah Brownson	Daughter	Female	4	Matlock, Derbyshire
Elizabeth Brownson	Daughter	Female	3	Matlock, Derbyshire

1861 Census, Charles Brownson
Sarah Lydia's middle name omitted

Thomas Wallis
England and Wales Census, 1861

Name:	Thomas Wallis
Sex:	Male
Age:	49
Event Date:	1861
Event Place:	Wilford, Nottinghamshire, England, United Kingdom
Event Place (Original):	Wilford, Nottinghamshire, England
Registration District:	Basford
Birth Year (Estimated):	1812
Birthplace:	Wilford, Nottinghamshire
Marital Status:	Married
Occupation:	Agricultural Labourer
Relationship to Head of Household:	Head
Page Number:	2
Piece/Folio:	2446 / 130
Registration Number:	RG09

Household	Role	Sex	Age	Birthplace
Thomas Wallis	Head	Male	49	Wilford, Nottinghamshire
Cath Wallis	Wife	Female	52	Ryall, Nottinghamshire
Charles Wallis	Son	Male	23	Wilford, Nottinghamshire
John Wallis	Son	Male	20	Wilford, Nottinghamshire
Phebe Wallis	Daughter	Female	18	Wilford, Nottinghamshire
Henry Wallis	Son	Male	13	Wilford, Nottinghamshire
Frederic Wallis	Son	Male	10	Wilford, Nottinghamshire

1861 Census, Thomas Wallis

Name	James Brownson
Age	77
Death Date	1866
Death Place	Bakewell, Derbyshire, England
Event Type	Death
Registration District	Bakewell
Page	451
Volume	7B
Affiliate Line Number	354
Registration Quarter	Jan-Feb-Mar
Registration Year	1866
Birth Year (Estimated)	1789

1866 James Brownson Death

Name	James Brownson
Age	77
Death or Burial Date	7 Feb 1866
Death or Burial Place	St Giles, Matlock, Derbyshire, England
Event Type	Burial
Birth Year (Estimated)	1789

7 February 1866 James Brownson Burial
St Giles Church, Matlock

Name	James Brownson
Probate Date	9 Mar 1866
Probate Place	Derbyshire, England, United Kingdom
Probate Place (Original)	Derby
Death Date	4 Feb 1866
Beneficiary's Name	Sarah Brownson

9 March 1866 James Brownson Probate

Name	Sarah L Brownson
Sex	Female
Age	16
Event Date	1871
Event Place	Withington, Lancashire, England, United Kingdom
Event Place (Original)	Withington, Lancashire, England
Sub-District	Didsbury
Enumeration District	7
Birth Year (Estimated)	1855
Birthplace	Matlock, Derbyshire
Marital Status	Unknown
Occupation	Nurse
Relationship to Head of Household	Servant
Entry Number	9

Other People on This Record

Name	Sex	Age	Place
Henrietta M Provis	F	11	Manchester, Lancashire
Helen Ada Provis	F	8	Manchester, Lancashire
Frederick B Provis	M	6	Manchester, Lancashire
Chas Wm Provis	M	3	Manchester, Lancashire
Robert S Provis	M	2	Withington, Lancashire
Frank M Provis	M	1	Withington, Lancashire
Eden Ogg	F	49	Manchester, Lancashire
Annie Louisa Leigh	F	20	Winsford, Cheshire

1871 Census, Sarah Lydia Brownson
Living with and working for the Provis family, in Lancashire

HIS DARLING KITTY

Thomas Wallis
England and Wales Census, 1871

Name:	Thomas Wallis
Sex:	Male
Age:	59
Event Date:	1871
Event Place:	Wilford, Nottinghamshire, England, United Kingdom
Event Place (Original):	Wilford, Nottinghamshire, England
Sub-District:	Wilford
Enumeration District:	10
Birth Year (Estimated):	1812
Birthplace:	Wilford, Nottinghamshire
Marital Status:	Married
Occupation:	Cottager
Relationship to Head of Household:	Head

Household	Role	Sex	Age	Birthplace
Thomas Wallis	Head	Male	59	Wilford, Nottinghamshire
Catherine Wallis	Wife	Female	63	Wilford, Nottinghamshire
Phabe Wallis	Daughter	Female	28	Wilford, Nottinghamshire
Frederick Wallis	Son	Male	20	Wilford, Nottinghamshire
Mary C Wallis	Granddaughter	Female	3	Nottingham, Nottinghamshire

1871 Census Thomas Wallis, now a Cottager

Frederick Wallis
England and Wales Census, 1871

Name:	Frederick Wallis
Sex:	Male
Age:	20
Event Date:	1871
Event Place:	Wilford, Nottinghamshire, England, United Kingdom
Event Place (Original):	Wilford, Nottinghamshire, England
Sub-District:	Wilford
Enumeration District:	10
Birth Year (Estimated):	1851
Birthplace:	Wilford, Nottinghamshire
Marital Status:	Unknown
Occupation:	Carter
Relationship to Head of Household:	Son

1871 Census Frederick Wallis, working as a Carter

Frederick Wallis
England and Wales Census, 1881

Name:	Frederick Wallis
Sex:	Male
Age:	28
Event Date:	1881
Event Place:	Matlock, Derbyshire, England
Registration District:	Bakewell
Birth Year (Estimated):	1853
Birthplace:	Wilford, Nottinghamshire, England
Marital Status:	Married
Occupation:	Police Constable
Relationship to Head of Household:	Son In Law
Page Number:	11
Piece/Folio:	3450/58
Registration Number:	RG11

Household	Role	Sex	Age	Birthplace
Charles Brownson	Head	Male	56	Cromford, Derbyshire, England
Lydia Brownson	Wife	Female	56	Matlock, Derbyshire, England
Abel Brownson	Son	Male	14	Matlock, Derbyshire, England
Frederick Wallis	Son In Law	Male	28	Wilford, Nottinghamshire, England
Sarah L Wallis	Daughter	Female	24	Matlock, Derbyshire, England

1881 Census, Frederick Wallis at his in-laws' home
Occupation has changed from Carter to Police Constable

Thos Wallis
England and Wales Census, 1881

Name:	Thos Wallis
Sex:	Male
Age:	69
Event Date:	1881
Event Place:	Wilford, Nottinghamshire, England
Registration District:	Basford
Birth Year (Estimated):	1812
Birthplace:	Wilford, Nottinghamshire, England
Marital Status:	Married
Occupation:	Labourer
Relationship to Head of Household:	Head
Page Number:	4
Piece/Folio:	3339/144
Registration Number:	RG11

Household	Role	Sex	Age	Birthplace
Thos Wallis	Head	Male	69	Wilford, Nottinghamshire, England
Catherine Wallis	Wife	Female	73	Whysell, Leicestershire, England

1881 Census, Thomas Wallis
Still working as a labourer at 69 years old

Thomas Charles Wallis
England Births and Christenings, 1538-1975

Name:	Thomas Charles Wallis
Sex:	Male
Christening Date:	28 Nov 1883
Christening Place:	Derbyshire, England, United Kingdom
Christening Place (Original):	Derbyshire, England
Father's Name:	Frederick Wallis
Father's Sex:	Male
Mother's Name:	Sarah Lydia Wallis
Mother's Sex:	Female

28 November 1883 Christening of Thomas Charles Wallis
Kitty's Father

Name	Frederick Wallace
Sex	Male
Age	40
Event Date	1891
Event Place	Eckington, Derbyshire, England, United Kingdom
Event Place (Original)	Eckington, Derbyshire, England
Enumeration District	21
Registration District	Chesterfield
Birth Year (Estimated)	1851
Birthplace	Nottinghamshire, England
Marital Status	Married
Occupation	Colliery Foreman
Relationship to Head of Household	Head
Event Type	Census
Event Place Note	Gleadless Road
Page Number	9
Piece/Folio	2771/ 67
Registration Number	RG12

Frederick Wallace's Spouses and Children OPEN ALL

Sarah L Wallace	Wife	F	34	Derbyshire, England	∨
Thomas C Wallace	Son	M	9	Derbyshire, England	∨
Harry Wallace	Son	M	4	Derbyshire, England	∨
Fred Wallace	Son	M	3	Derbyshire, England	∨
Frank Wallace	Son	M	0	Derbyshire, England	∨

1891 Census Frederick Wallis

Note another incorrect spelling of a surname. This is obviously Kitty's grandfather Frederick, now a Colliery Foreman.

Frederick Wallis
England and Wales Census, 1901

Event Place Note:	Birdfield
Name:	Frederick Wallis
Sex:	Male
Age:	48
Event Date:	31 Mar 1901
Event Place:	Eckington, Derbyshire, England, United Kingdom
Event Place (Original):	Eckington, Derbyshire, England
Sub-District:	Eckington
Registration District:	Chesterfield
Birth Year (Estimated):	1853
Birthplace:	Wilford, Nottinghamshire
Marital Status:	Married
Occupation:	COAL SCREEN FOREMAN
Relationship to Head of Household:	Head
Page Number:	9
Piece/Folio:	29
Schedule Type:	65

Household	Role	Sex	Age	Birthplace
Frederick Wallis	Head	Male	48	Wilford, Nottinghamshire
Sarah Lydia Wallis	Wife	Female	44	Matlock, Derbyshire
Thomas Charles Wallis	Son	Male	19	Matlock, Derbyshire
Harry Wallis	Son	Male	14	Cutthorpe, Derbyshire

1901 Census Frederick Wallis
Still working at the colliery

JEAN FLANNERY

Fred Wallis
England and Wales Census, 1911

Tools

Name:	Fred Wallis
Sex:	Male
Age:	23
Event Date:	1911
Event Place:	Aston cum Aughton, Yorkshire, England, United Kingdom
Event Place (Original):	Aston Cum Aughton, , Yorkshire (West Riding), England
Sub-District:	Aston
Sub-District Number:	1
Enumeration District:	1
Registration District:	Rotherham
District Number:	511
Birth Year (Estimated):	1888
Birthplace:	Cuthorpe, Derbyshire
Marital Status:	Single
Occupation:	HELPER ON FARM
Number in Family:	8
Relationship to Head of Household:	Son
Document Type:	3
Page Number:	1
Source Page Type:	6
Piece/Folio:	57
Registration Number:	RG14
Schedule Type:	28
House Name:	NETHERTHORPE FARM

Household	Role	Sex	Age	Birthplace
Frederick Wallis	Head	Male	58	Wilford, Nottinghamshire
Sarah Lydia Wallis	Wife	Female	54	Matlock, Derbyshire
Fred Wallis	Son	Male	23	Cuthorpe, Derbyshire
Frank Wallis	Son	Male	20	Ridgeway, Derbyshire
Albina Bensford Wallis	Granddaughter	Female	2	Swallownest, Yorkshire
Reuben Rippery	Boarder	Male	37	Ridgeway, Yorkshire
John Edward Greaves		Male	27	Laughton In Le Morthen, Yorkshire
Ida Brightmore	Visitor	Female	14	Hollinsend, Yorkshire

1901 Census Kitty's Uncle Fred

334

Charles Brownson
England and Wales Death Registration Index 1837-2007

Event Type:	Death
Registration District:	Bakewell
Name:	Charles Brownson
Age:	80
Death Date:	1904
Death Place:	Bakewell, Derbyshire, England
Volume:	7B
Affiliate Line Number:	95
Registration Quarter:	Jul-Aug-Sep
Registration Year:	1904
Birth Year (Estimated):	1824

1904 Charles Brownson Death

Charles Brownson
England, Derbyshire, Church of England Parish Registers, 1537-1918

Event Type:	Burial
Name:	Charles Brownson
Age:	80
Death or Burial Date:	27 Aug 1904
Death or Burial Place:	St Giles, Matlock, Derbyshire, England
Birth Year (Estimated):	1824

27 August 1904 Charles Brownson Burial

31 March 1902 Thomas Charles Wallis and Bertha Annie Packard Marriage Certificate

Bertha Annie Packard
mentioned in the record of Thomas Charles Wallis

Name:	Bertha Annie Packard
Age:	21
Sex:	Female
Father:	William Packard
Husband:	Thomas Charles Wallis

Other information in the record of Thomas Charles Wallis
from England Marriages, 1538-1973

Name:	Thomas Charles Wallis
Sex:	Male
Age:	20
Birth Year (Estimated):	1882
Marital Status:	Single
Father's Name:	Frederick Wallis
Father's Sex:	Male
Spouse's Name:	Bertha Annie Packard
Spouse's Sex:	Female
Spouse's Age:	21
Spouse's Birth Year (Estimated):	1881
Spouse's Marital Status:	Single
Spouse's Father's Name:	William Packard
Spouse's Father's Sex:	Male
Marriage Date:	31 Mar 1902
Marriage Place:	Ridgeway, Derbyshire, England, United Kingdom

Marriage Transcript

Thomas Charles Wallis
England and Wales Census, 1911

Name:	Thomas Charles Wallis
Sex:	Male
Age:	29
Event Date:	1911
Event Place:	Beighton, Derbyshire, England, United Kingdom
Event Place (Original):	Beighton, Bank View Hackenthorpe Near Sheffield, Derbyshire, England
Sub-District:	Eckington
Sub-District Number:	4
Enumeration District:	4
Registration District:	Chesterfield
District Number:	438
Birth Year (Estimated):	1882
Birthplace:	Matlock, Derbyshire
Marital Status:	Married
Occupation:	COAL MINE WEIGHMAN ABOVE GROUND
Number in Family:	6
Relationship to Head of Household:	Head
Document Type:	3
Page Number:	1
Source Page Type:	6
Piece/Folio:	19
Registration Number:	RG14
Schedule Type:	10

Household	Role	Sex	Age	Birthplace
Thomas Charles Wallis	Head	Male	29	Matlock, Derbyshire
Bertha Annie Wallis	Wife	Female	29	Eckington, Derbyshire
Florence Ellen Wallis	Daughter	Female	7	Ridgeway, Derbyshire
Annie Edith Wallis	Daughter	Female	2	Hackenthorpe, Derbyshire
Charles Hammond Moorhouse	Visitor	Male	40	Rotherham, Yorkshire
Clara Moorhouse	Visitor	Female	42	Aston, Yorkshire

1911 Census Thomas Charles Wallis

Name	Frederick Wallis
Sex	Male
Age	58
Event Date	1911
Event Place	Aston cum Aughton, Yorkshire, England, United Kingdom
Event Place (Original)	Aston Cum Aughton, , Yorkshire (West Riding), England
Sub-District	Aston
Sub-District Number	1
Enumeration District	1
Registration District	Rotherham
District Number	511
Birth Year (Estimated)	1853
Birthplace	Wilford, Nottinghamshire
Marital Status	Married
Occupation	FARMER
Number in Family	8
Relationship to Head of Household	Head
Event Type	Census
Document Type	3
Page Number	1
Source Page Type	6
Piece/Folio	57
Registration Number	RG14
Schedule Type	28
House Name	NETHERTHORPE FARM

1911 Census Frederick Wallis, now a Farmer

Fred Wallis
England and Wales Census, 1911

Name:	Fred Wallis
Sex:	Male
Age:	23
Event Date:	1911
Event Place:	Aston cum Aughton, Yorkshire, England, United Kingdom
Event Place (Original):	Aston Cum Aughton, , Yorkshire (West Riding), England
Sub-District:	Aston
Sub-District Number:	1
Enumeration District:	1
Registration District:	Rotherham
District Number:	511
Birth Year (Estimated):	1888
Birthplace:	Cuthorpe, Derbyshire
Marital Status:	Single
Occupation:	HELPER ON FARM
Number in Family:	8
Relationship to Head of Household:	Son
Document Type:	3
Page Number:	1
Source Page Type:	6
Piece/Folio:	57
Registration Number:	RG14
Schedule Type:	28
House Name:	NETHERTHORPE FARM

Household	Role	Sex	Age	Birthplace
Frederick Wallis	Head	Male	58	Wilford, Nottinghamshire
Sarah Lydia Wallis	Wife	Female	54	Matlock, Derbyshire
Fred Wallis	Son	Male	23	Cuthorpe, Derbyshire
Frank Wallis	Son	Male	20	Ridgeway, Derbyshire
Albina Berisford Wallis	Granddaughter	Female	2	Swallownest, Yorkshire
Reuben Rippery	Boarder	Male	37	Ridgeway, Yorkshire
John Edward Greaves		Male	27	Laughton In Le Morthen, Yorkshire
Ida Brightmore	Visitor	Female	14	Hollinsend, Yorkshire

1911 Census Kitty's Uncle Fred, more complete record

In Loving Memory

A sudden change, I in a moment fell,
I had not time to bid my friends farewell
Think this not strange, death happens unto all,
This day was mine, to-morrow you may fall.

NETHERTHORPE FARM,
ASTON.

IN LOVING MEMORY OF

Frederick Wallis,

The beloved Husband of Sarah Lydia Wallis,

Who departed this life October 11th, 1917,

Aged 64 Years,

And was interred at Aston Cemetery, October 15th. 1917.

1917 In Memoriam card: Frederick Wallis Senior
Card front, left and right interior

Name	**Frederick Wallis**
Age	**64**
Death Date	**1917**
Death Place	**Rotherham, Yorkshire, England**
Event Type	**Death**
Registration District	**Rotherham**
Page	**699**
Volume	**9C**
Affiliate Line Number	**71**
Registration Quarter	**Oct-Nov-Dec**
Registration Year	**1917**
Birth Year (Estimated)	**1853**

1917 Frederick Wallis Senior Death Transcript

19 February 1920 Kitty's Birth Certificate

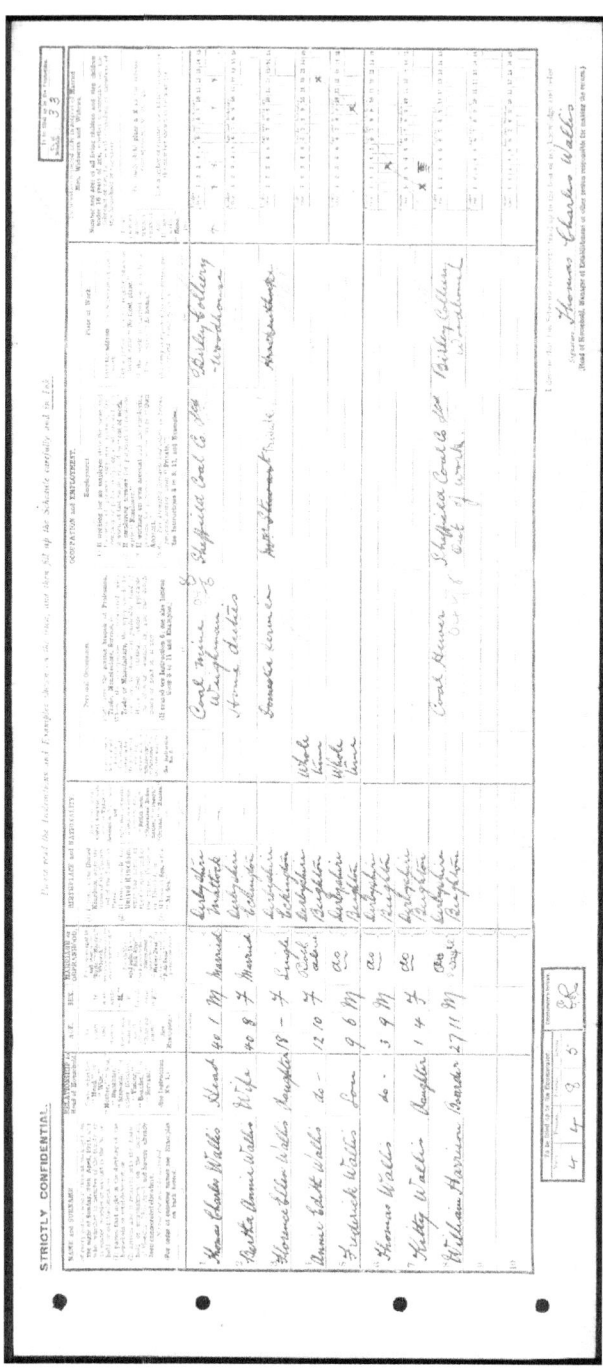

1921 Census Thomas Charles Wallis
In his own handwriting, all we have of Kitty's father himself.

HIS DARLING KITTY

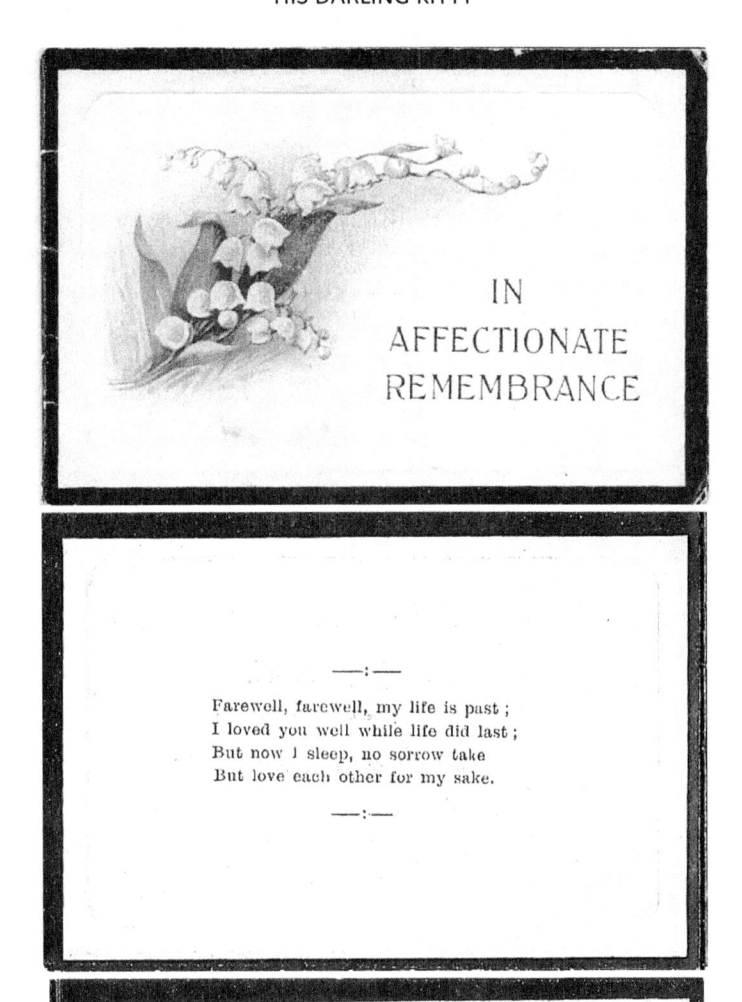

IN AFFECTIONATE REMEMBRANCE

Farewell, farewell, my life is past ;
I loved you well while life did last ;
But now I sleep, no sorrow take
But love each other for my sake.

IN LOVING MEMORY OF

Sarah Lydia Wallis

The beloved wife of the late Frederick Wallis,

Who departed this life December 6th, 1926,

Aged 70 years and 6 Months,

And was interred at Aston Cemetery,
December 11th, 1926.

1926 In Memoriam card Sarah Lydia Wallis

Thomas C Wallis
England and Wales Death Registration Index 1837-2007

Tools

Event Type:	Death
Registration District:	Chesterfield
Name:	Thomas C Wallis
Age:	55
Death Date:	1936
Death Place:	Chesterfield, Derbyshire, England
Volume:	7B
Affiliate Line Number:	117
Registration Quarter:	Oct-Nov-Dec
Registration Year:	1936
Birth Year (Estimated):	1881

1936 Thomas Charles Wallis Death

Name	**Frederick Wallis**
Death Date	**1940**
Death Place	**Nottinghamshire, England, United Kingdom**
Death Place (Original)	**Nottinghamshire**
Page	**884**
Volume	**7B**
Affiliate Line Number	**92**

1940 Frederick Wallis Junior, Kitty's Uncle, Death

PACKARD

Name	Edward Brock
Sex	Male
Spouse's Name	Sarah Whiting
Spouse's Sex	Female
Marriage Date	3 Oct 1717
Marriage Place	South Elmham All Saints and St Nicholas, Suffolk, England
Marriage Place (Original)	South Elmham-St. Nicholas, Suffolk, England
Source Details	item 23
Reference	Items 23-25

3 October 1717 Edward Brock Marriage

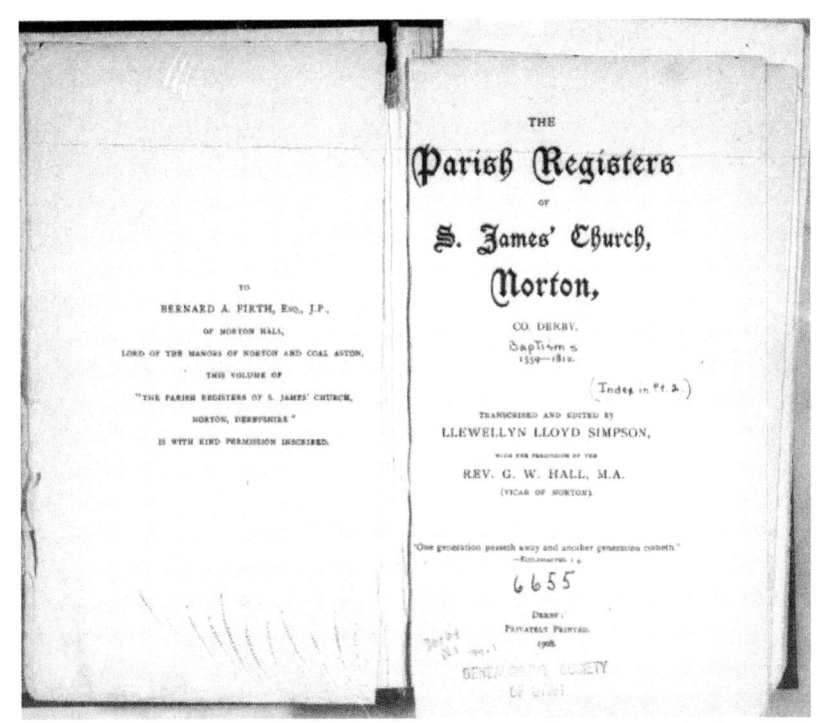

St James' Church Norton, Yorkshire: Parish Register including 1810

312 Norton Parish Registers	[1810]	Baptisms.		313
Mary Ann, d. Willm. and Elizabeth Armsby, Margathway		...fred, s. Joshua and Mary Hewitt, Bradway	17 Feb.	1811
Mary Ann, d. Edward and Elizabeth Butler, Jordanthorpe	21 June	...hn, s. William and Elizabeth Booker, Greenhill	17 Feb.	,,
Elizabeth, d. Thomas and Katurah Cavile, Bolehill	22 June	...orge, s. George and Elizabeth Richardson, Hill-top	3 Mar.	,,
Mary, d. Thomas and Elizabeth Ashton, Hemsworth	25 June	...irza, d. Jonathan and Melicent Barstow, Crabtree-bank	22 Mar.	,,
Hester, d. Jonathan and Ann Greaves, Four lane Ends	6 Aug	...ester, d. Thomas and Elizabeth Garfitt, Snowhill	22 Mar.	,,
Thomas, s. John and Millicent Wolstenholme, Hempard-lane	6 Aug	...annah, d. Joseph and Sarah Wainright, Greenhill	21 Ap	
Wm. John, s. John and Nanny Ramey, Hemsworth	6 Aug	...enry, s. George and Sarah Siddall, L. N.	16 June	
Hierom Valentine, s. Hierom and Ann Rodger, Hemsworth	15 Aug	...orge, s. John and Elizabeth Rose, Backmoor	30 June	
Lydia, d. John and Elizabeth Richardson, L. N.	10 Aug	...n, d. Edward and Elizabeth Butler, Jordanthorpe	10 July	
William, s. John and Elizabeth Linley, Hemsworth	30 Aug	...illiam, s. John and Rebecca Fox, Hemsworth	12 July	
Elizabeth, d. William and Elizabeth Swift, Woodseats	3 Sep.	...seph, s. James and Sarah Gill, Wetlands	25 July	
Sidney, s. George and Sarah Rhoades, Newfield-green	7 Sep.	...hn, s. William and Mary Yeardley, Ecclesfield	4 Aug.	
John, s. Jonathan and Ann Booth, Woodseats	14 Sep.	...hn, s. Johnson and Ann Vicars, Herdings	4 Aug.	,,
James, s. Joshua and Hester Jarvis, Hazlehurst	28 Oct.	...ry Ann, d. John and Mary Bargbe, Lightwood	5 Aug.	,,
Joseph, s. Luke and Dorothy Duckworth, Backmoor	31 Oct.	...omas, s. William and Mary Bingham, Backmoor	5 Aug	
Henry, s. George and Margaret Packard, Sicke	7 Nov	...illiam, s. George and Mary Redfearn, Greenhill	23 Aug	
Ann, d. Peter and Sarah Linley, Bolehill	2 Dec	...lliam, s. John and Elizabeth Gillatt, Margathway	9 Sep.	
Elizabeth, d. John and Catharine Parkes, Greenhill	9 Dec	...n, d. Joseph and Hannah Parks, Greenhill	15 Sep.	
Robert, s. Joseph and Sarah Sykes, Greenhill	11 Dec	...n, d. William and Mary Frith, Backmoor	15 Sep.	
Thomas, s. Thomas and Ann Lee, Margathway	25 Dec	...hn, s. James and Rebecca Reaney, Greenhill	22 Sep.	
P. Robinson, Vic. R. Robinson, Cu.	29 Dec	...omas, s. Joseph and Hannah Hallam, Hemsworth	26 Sep.	
Mark, s. Isaac and Hannah Biggin, Greenhill	13 Jan	...es, s. Anthony and Frances Wolstenholme, Greenhill	24 Nov.	
James, s. John and Elizabeth Reaney, Derbyshire-lane	20 Jan	...nces, d. Peter and Sarah Linley, Bolehill	1 Dec.	
John, s. Samuel and Elizabeth Wolstenholme, Hempard-lane	23 Jan	...n, d. John and Elizabeth Wilkinson, Woodseats	3 Dec.	,,
James, s. James and Ann Kilner, Snow-hill	1 Feb	...n, d. Thomas and Elizabeth Biggin, Greenhill	8 Dec.	,,

Joseph, s. Luke and Dorothy Duckworth, Backmoor .. .. 7 Nov
Henry, s. George and Margaret Packard, Sicke 2 Dec
Ann, d. Peter and Sarah Linley, Bolehill .. 9 Dec
Elizabeth, d. John and Catharine Parkes,

2 December 1810 Baptism of Henry Packard
St James' Church Norton

25 October 1840 Baptism of Ann Biggin
Parents William and Mary Ann
Christ Church, Dore Derbyshire

Wm Biggin
England and Wales Census, 1841

Name:	Wm Biggin
Sex:	Male
Age:	25
Event Date:	1841
Event Place:	Sheffield, Yorkshire, England, United Kingdom
Event Place (Original):	Sheffield, Yorkshire, Yorkshire West Riding, England
Registration District:	Ecclesall Bierlow
Birth Year (Estimated):	1812-1816
Birthplace:	Yorkshire
Page Number:	22
Piece/Folio:	1334/48
Registration Number:	HO107

Household	Role	Sex	Age	Birthplace
Wm Biggin		Male	25	Yorkshire
Mary Biggin		Female	25	Yorkshire
Ann Biggin		Female	0	Yorkshire

1841 Census William Biggin

Name	**William Biggin**
Sex	**Male**
Death or Burial Date	**27 Apr 1847**
Death or Burial Place	**Dore, Derbyshire, England, United Kingdom**
Death or Burial Place (Original)	**Dore, Derbyshire, England**

27 April 1847 William Biggin Burial

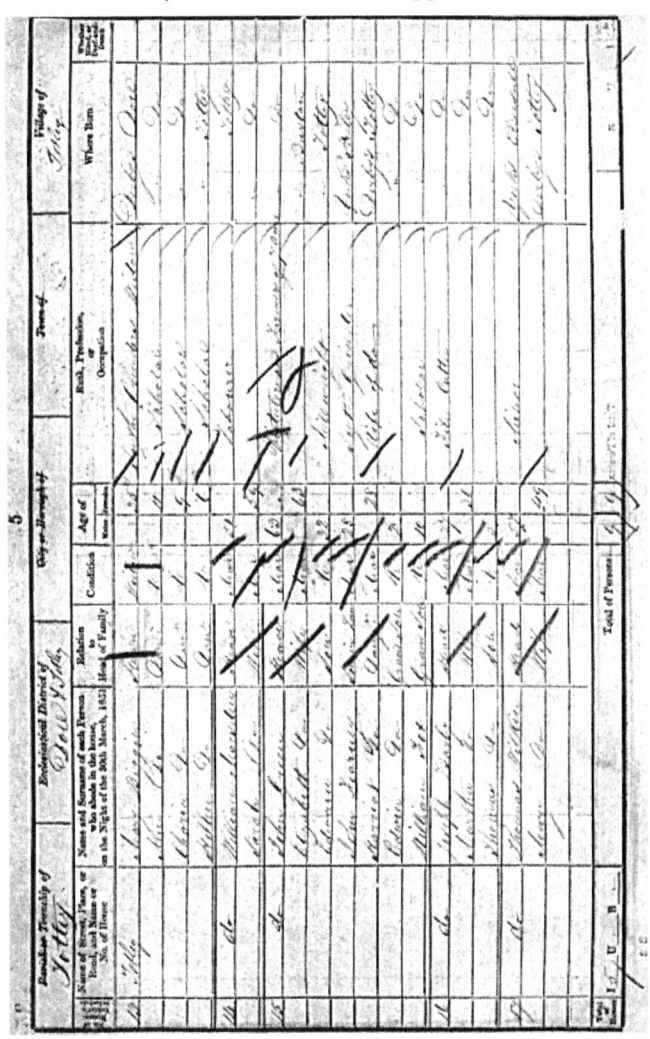

1851 Census Mary (Ann) Biggin, Scythe Grinder's Widow

Name	**Mary Biggin**
Sex	**Female**
Age	**35**
Event Date	**1851**
Event Place	**, Yorkshire,Yorkshire (West Riding), England**
Registration District	**Ecclesall Bierlow**
Birth Year (Estimated)	**1816**
Birthplace	**Dore, Derbyshire**
Marital Status	**Widow**
Occupation	**Scythe Grinders Widow**
Relationship to Head of Household	**Head**
Event Type	**Census**
Page Number	**5**
Piece/Folio	**2336 / 354**
Registration Number	**HO107**

Mary Biggin's Spouses and Children   OPEN ALL

Ann Pinder	Daughter	F	11	Dore, Derbyshire
Charia Pinder	Daughter	F	9	Dore, Derbyshire
Helen Pinder	Daughter	F	6	Totley, Derbyshire

Transcript

What is very odd about this transcript, even more so than many others, is the surname given to the daughters. It is quite clearly the right family.

Henry Packard
England and Wales Census, 1851

Name:	Henry Packard
Sex:	Male
Age:	41
Event Date:	1851
Event Place:	Beighton, Yorkshire, Yorkshire (West Riding), England
Registration District:	Rotherham
Birth Year (Estimated):	1810
Birthplace:	Hansworth, Derbyshire
Marital Status:	Married
Occupation:	Scythe Grinder
Relationship to Head of Household:	Head
Page Number:	7
Piece/Folio:	2343 / 24
Registration Number:	HO107

Household	Role	Sex	Age	Birthplace
Henry Packard	Head	Male	41	Hansworth, Derbyshire
Mary A Packard	Wife	Female	42	Gleadless, Yorkshire
William Packard	Son	Male	14	Conisbro, Yorkshire
Ann Packard	Daughter	Female	12	Notting Mill Dore, Derbyshire
Henry Packard	Son	Male	10	Little Cornn Ecclesall, Derbyshire
Maria Packard	Daughter	Female	9	Woodhouse, Yorkshire
Eliza Packard	Daughter	Female	7	Hackenthorpe, Derbyshire
Peter Packard	Son	Male	5	Hackenthorpe, Derbyshire
Jane Packard	Daughter	Female	3	Hackenthorpe, Derbyshire

1851 Census Henry Packard
Eldest son is William Henry

Name	Henry Packard
Gender	Male
Birth	Circa 1811
	📍 Hamsworth, Derbyshire
Residence	1861
	📍 Totley Moor, Fotley, Yorkshire, England
Age	50
Marital status	Married
Occupation	Scythe Grinder and Gun Maker
Inhabited	1
Wife	Mary Packard
Children	Mary Jane Packard
	Joe Packard
	Thomas Packard
	Fredrick Packard
	Adelia Packard
	Ellinor Packard

1861 Census Henry Packard

Just for interest, I discovered that after Mary Ann died in 1852 Henry married Mary Bradbury, 17 years his junior, that same year.

5th April 1871 baptism of Thomas and Walter Packard, Kitty's uncles. Dore, Derbyshire

William Packard
England and Wales Census, 1871

Event Type:	Census
Name:	William Packard
Sex:	Male
Age:	34
Event Date:	1871
Event Place:	Yorkshire West Riding, England, United Kingdom
Event Place (Original):	Totley, Totley, Yorkshire (West Riding), England
Sub-District:	Hallam, Upper
Enumeration District:	5
Birth Year (Estimated):	1837
Birthplace:	Cunsbro, Yorkshire
Marital Status:	Married
Occupation:	Scythe Grinder
Relationship to Head of Household:	Head

Household	Role	Sex	Age	Birthplace
William Packard	Head	Male	34	Cunsbro, Yorkshire
Ann Packard	Wife	Female	30	Owrleton, Yorkshire
Samuel Packard	Son	Male	9	Totley, Derbyshire
William Packard	Son	Male	6	Totley, Derbyshire
Thomas Packard	Son	Male	2	Totley, Derbyshire
Walter Packard	Son	Male	0	Totley, Derbyshire
Mary Biggin	Mother-in-law	Female	55	Dove, Derbyshire
Thomas Packard	Apprentice	Male	16	Dove, Derbyshire

1871 Census William Packard

Perhaps Mary was now living with his family.
Also note that he has an apprentice numbered in the household.

11 April 1873 Baptism of Walter and Mary Edith Packard, Kitty's Aunt and Uncle. Dore, Derbyshire

It is the earliest definite indication so far of fraternal twins in the family. So this "inheritance" of ours comes from the Biggin line.

Annie Packard
England and Wales Birth Registration Index, 1837-2008

Name:	Annie Packard
Event Date:	1880
Event Place:	Chesterfield, Derbyshire, England
Registration District:	Chesterfield
Volume:	7B
Affiliate Line Number:	159
Registration Quarter:	Oct-Nov-Dec
Registration Year:	1880

1880 Bertha Annie: birth registered simply as Annie

Name	William Packard
Gender	Male
Birth	Circa 1837 Conisboro, Yorkshire
Residence	1881 Ford Lane, Ford Lane, Derbyshire, England
Age	44
Marital status	Married
Occupation	Scythe Grinder
Inhabited	1
Wife	Elizabeth A Packard
Children	Samuel Packard William Packard Thomas Packard Walter Packard Elizabeth A Packard Frank Packard Herbert Packard Bertha A Packard

1881 Census William Packard

William Packard
England and Wales Census, 1891

Event Place Note:	Ford Lane
Name:	William Packard
Sex:	Male
Age:	53
Event Date:	1891
Event Place:	Eckington, Derbyshire, England, United Kingdom
Event Place (Original):	Eckington, Derbyshire, England
Enumeration District:	23
Registration District:	Chesterfield
Birth Year (Estimated):	1838
Birthplace:	Yorkshire, England
Marital Status:	Married
Occupation:	Scythe Grinder
Relationship to Head of Household:	Head
Page Number:	24
Piece/Folio:	2771/ 100
Registration Number:	RG12

Household	Role	Sex	Age	Birthplace
William Packard	Head	Male	53	Yorkshire, England
Ann Packard	Wife	Female	51	Derbyshire, England
Walter Packard	Son	Male	19	Derbyshire, England
Elizabeth Packard	Daughter	Female	16	Derbyshire, England
Frank Packard	Son	Male	14	Derbyshire, England
Herbert Packard	Son	Male	12	Derbyshire, England

1891 Census William Packard
Note that Elizabeth Ann's first name has been omitted.

Bertha Annie Packard
England and Wales Census, 1901

Event Place Note:	Highlane
Name:	Bertha Annie Packard
Sex:	Female
Age:	20
Event Date:	31 Mar 1901
Event Place:	Eckington, Derbyshire, England, United Kingdom
Event Place (Original):	Eckington, Derbyshire, England
Sub-District:	Eckington
Registration District:	Chesterfield
Birth Year (Estimated):	1881
Birthplace:	Totley, Derbyshire
Marital Status:	Single
Occupation:	SERVANT DOMESTIC
Relationship to Head of Household:	Servant
Page Number:	6
Piece/Folio:	27
Schedule Type:	38

Household	Role	Sex	Age	Birthplace
William Allison	Head	Male	44	Olleston, Nottinghamshire
Harriet Allison	Wife	Female	42	Ridgeway, Derbyshire
Frank Allison	Son	Male	21	Ridgeway, Derbyshire
Willie Allison	Son	Male	18	Ridgeway, Derbyshire
Henry Osborne Allison	Son	Male	8	Ridgeway, Derbyshire
Oliver Allison	Son	Male	0	Ridgeway, Derbyshire
Bertha Annie Packard	Servant	Female	20	Totley, Derbyshire

1901 Census Bertha Packard

KITTY BLANE

29 September 1939 National ID Register
Kitty was staying with her mother in Beighton

9 October 1940 Kitty and Jack's Marriage Certificate

MARRIAGE OF MR. JACK BLANE

The wedding took place at St. Martin's Church, Bletchley, on Wednesday, of Mr. Jack Blane, sixth son of Mr. and Mrs. C. Blane, of 14, Brooklands Rd., Bletchley, and Miss Kitty Wallis, youngest daughter of the late Mr. Wallis and Mrs. T. C. Wallis, of Sheffield. The Rev. C. A. Wheeler (Vicar) conducted the ceremony.

The bride, who was given away by her brother-in-law, Mr. R. Cutts, wore white broche taffeta over net, a head-dress and coronet of lilies, and silver shoes. Her bouquet consisted of red roses. The bride was attended by two maids-of-honour, Mrs. T. and Mrs. F. Wallis, a small bridesmaid, Miss Brenda Gee (niece of bride), and a page, Master Charles Wallis (bride's nephew). The maids of honour were attired in pale pink net and organdie over taffeta, shoulder length veils, with coronets of pink leaves and roses, and silver shoes. Their bouquets were of deep pink carnations. The small bridesmaid was dressed in pale blue net and organdie over taffeta, with Victorian bonnet in pink and blue taffeta. She carried a posy of Michaelmas daisies. Master Charles Wallis wore pale blue satin and white shoes. The bridegroom gave gold horseshoe brooches to the maids of honour, a gold bangle to the bridesmaid and a regimental tiepin to the page. The bride's gift to the bridegroom was a leather wallet and the groom's gift to the bride, a string of pearls.

Mr. Martin Blane (bridegroom's brother) was best man, and Mr. Bernard Blane was groomsman.

A reception held at St. Martin's Hall was attended by 30 guests.

Several cheques were among the 35 presents Mr. and Mrs. Blane received. The gifts also included a cut-glass salad bowl and cake knife from Premier Press Employees where the bride is employed, and a £3 cheque from London Brick Co. employees, where the bridegroom was employed before joining H.M. Forces. The bridegroom is on seven days' leave.

Local Newspaper Report

JEAN FLANNERY

CERTIFIED COPY of an ENTRY OF BIRTH
Pursuant to the Births and Deaths Registration Acts, 1836 to 1929.

Registration District **NORTH BUCKS**

Birth in the Sub-District of **BLETCHLEY** in the **COUNTY OF BUCKINGHAM**

1944.

No.	When and Where Born	Name, if any	Sex	Name and Surname of Father	Name and Maiden Surname of Mother	Rank or Profession of Father	Signature, Description and Residence of Informant	When Registered	Signature of Registrar	Baptismal Name, if added after Registration of Birth
487	Tenth October 1944. 12, Cambridge Street, Bletchley. U.D.	Jean	Girl	Jack Blane	Kitty Blane formerly Wallis	L/Corporal No. 7266456 R.A.M.C. (Clerk)	K. Blane Mother 12, Cambridge Street, Bletchley.	Twenty fifth October 1944.	E. V. Truckfield Registrar	

I, ERNEST VICTOR TRUCKFIELD, Registrar of Births and Deaths for the Sub-District of BLETCHLEY in the COUNTY OF BUCKINGHAM do hereby certify that this is a true copy of the Entry No. 487 in the Register Book of Births for the said Sub-District, and that such Register Book is now legally in my custody.

WITNESS MY HAND the 25th day of October 19 44

E. V. Truckfield
Registrar of Births and Deaths.

CAUTION.—Any person who (1) falsifies any of the particulars on this Certificate, or (2) uses it as true, knowing it to be falsified, is liable to Prosecution.

1944 October Jean Birth Certificate

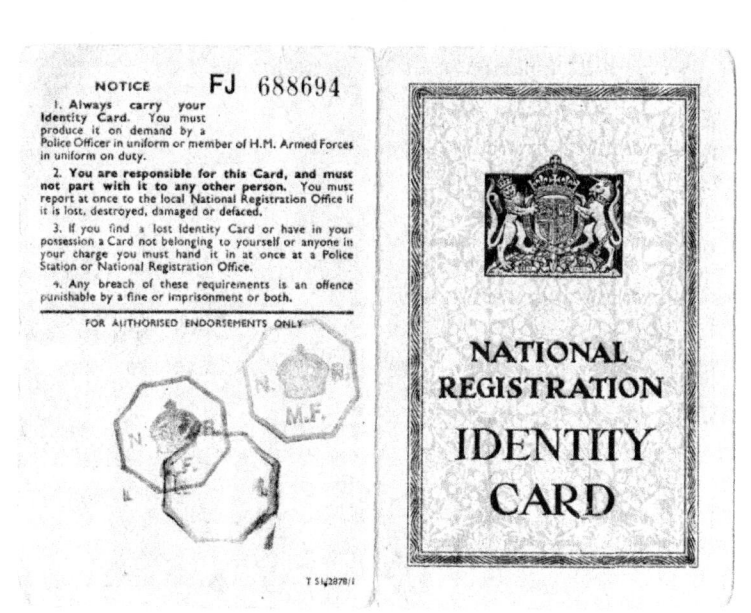

Kitty's National Identity Card Cover

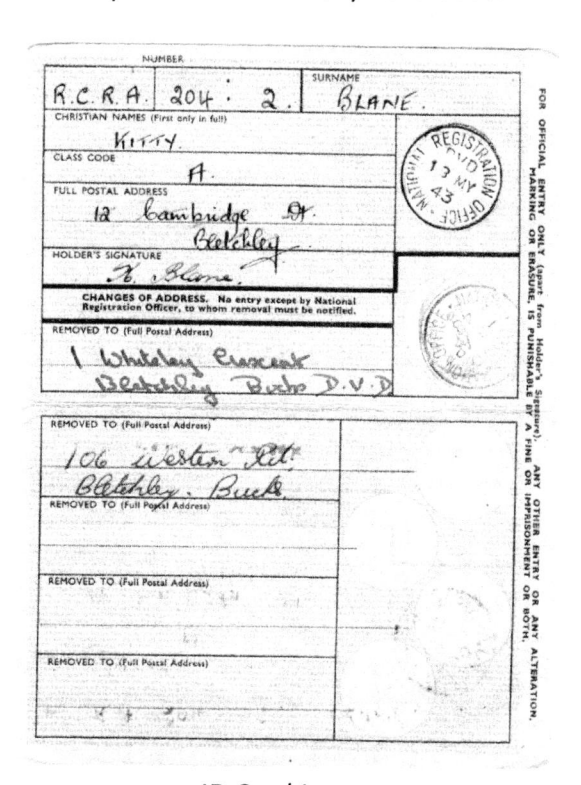

ID Card Inner

1954 Kitty's NHS Card

1973 Kitty's Smallpox Vaccination Record

Flight Certificate

This is to Certify that

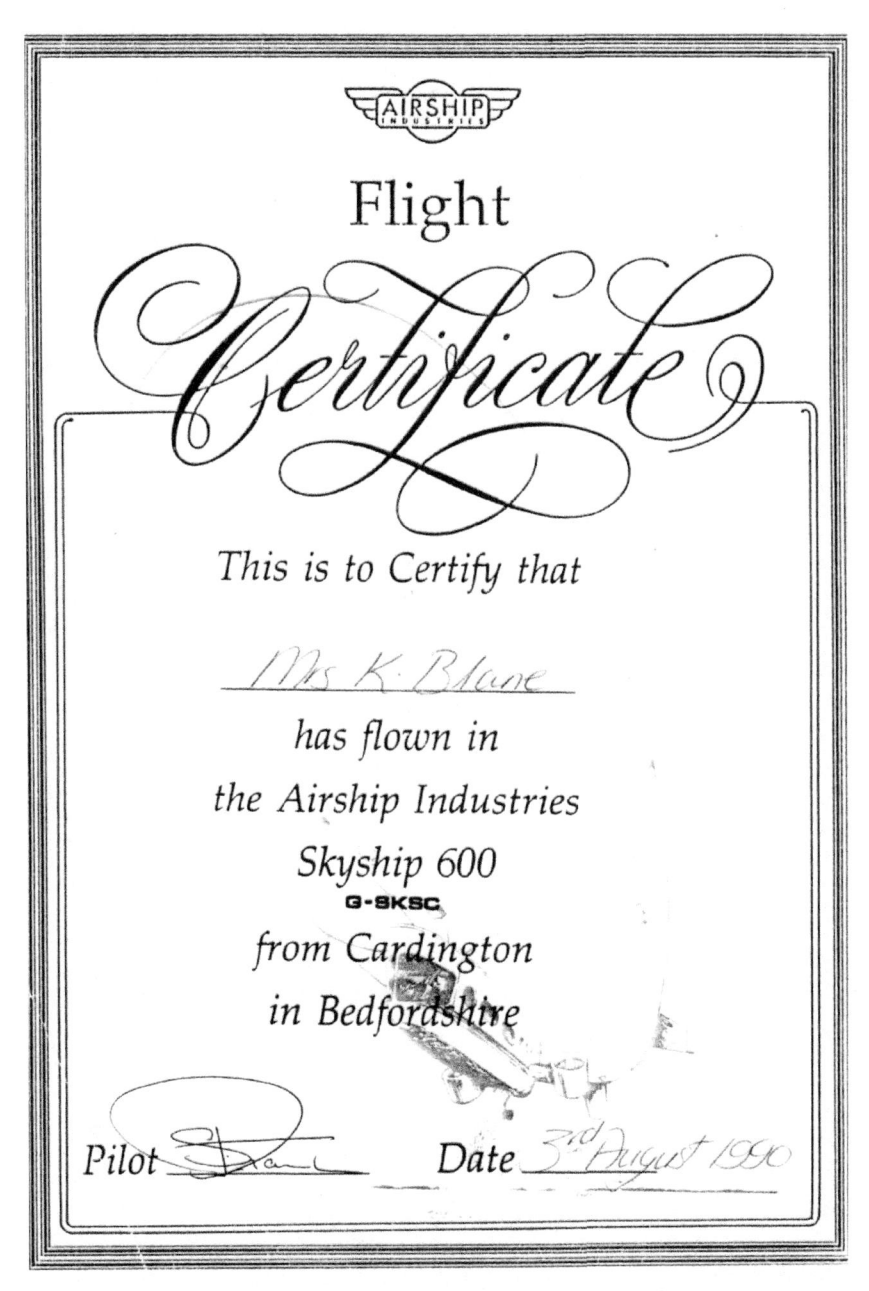

Mrs K. Blane

has flown in

the Airship Industries

Skyship 600

G-SKSC

from Cardington

in Bedfordshire

Pilot _____   Date 3rd August 1990

3 August 1990 Kitty's Airship Flight Certificate

BAV 787544

CERTIFIED COPY OF AN ENTRY
Pursuant to the Births and Deaths Registration Act 1953

DEATH

Entry No. 229

Registration district: Bedford
Administrative area: The Borough of Bedford
Sub-district: Bedford

1. **Date and place of death**
   Eighth December 2012
   Salvete 15 Rothsay Place Bedford

2. **Name and surname**
   Jack BLANE

3. **Sex:** Male

4. **Maiden surname of woman who has married:** —

5. **Date and place of birth**
   Fourteenth August 1918
   Bletchley Buckinghamshire

6. **Occupation and usual address**
   Club Secretary-Sport and Social (retired)
   Husband of Kitty BLANE Housewife (retired)
   Salvete 15 Rothsay Place Bedford

7. (a) **Name and surname of informant**
   Carole HULATT
   (b) **Qualification**
   Daughter
   Present at the death
   (c) **Usual address**
   Flat 14 Russell Court Bushmead Avenue Bedford Bedfordshire

8. I certify that the particulars given by me above are true to the best of my knowledge and belief
   Signature of informant: C Hulatt

9. **Cause of death**
   I (a) Metastatic Prostate Cancer
   II Frailty
   Certified by D C Fenske MBBS

10. **Date of registration**
    Thirteenth December 2012

11. **Signature of registrar**
    S E Chandler
    Deputy Registrar

Certified to be a true copy of an entry in a register in my custody.

Signed: SE Chandler { Deputy Registrar

Date 13.12.2012

System No. 507748204 CAUTION: THERE ARE OFFENCES RELATING TO FALSIFYING OR ALTERING A CERTIFICATE AND USING OR POSSESSING A FALSE CERTIFICATE. ©CROWN COPYRIGHT

WARNING: A CERTIFICATE IS NOT EVIDENCE OF IDENTITY.

8 December 2012 Jack Death Certificate

HIS DARLING KITTY

BBC 919640

CERTIFIED COPY OF AN ENTRY
Pursuant to the Births and Deaths Registration Act 1953

DEATH

Entry No. 99

Registration district	Bedford
Sub-district	Bedford
Administrative area	The Borough of Bedford

1. **Date and place of death**
   Sixth September 2014
   Salvete 15 Rothsay Place Bedford

2. **Name and surname**
   Kitty BLANE

3. **Sex**
   Female

4. **Maiden surname of woman who has married**
   WALLIS

5. **Date and place of birth**
   Nineteenth February 1920
   Chesterfield Derbyshire

6. **Occupation and usual address**
   Housewife
   Widow of Jack BLANE Secretary - Sports And Social Club (retired)
   Salvete 15 Rothsay Place Bedford

7. (a) **Name and surname of informant**
   Carole HULATT

   (b) **Qualification**
   Daughter

   (c) **Usual address**
   14 Russell Court Bushmead Avenue Bedford Bedfordshire

8. I certify that the particulars given by me above are true to the best of my knowledge and belief
   C Hulatt
   Signature of informant

9. **Cause of death**
   I (a) Vascular Dementia

   Certified by John Murphy MBBCh

10. **Date of registration**
    Ninth September 2014

11. **Signature of registrar**
    Y Prudham
    Registrar

Certified to be a true copy of an entry in a register in my custody.

*Superintendent Registrar
*Registrar
*Strike out whichever does not apply

Date 9.9.2014

CAUTION: THERE ARE OFFENCES RELATING TO FALSIFYING OR ALTERING A CERTIFICATE AND USING OR POSSESSING A FALSE CERTIFICATE. ©CROWN COPYRIGHT

System No. 510807196

WARNING: A CERTIFICATE IS NOT EVIDENCE OF IDENTITY.

6 September 2014 Kitty Death Certificate

MAPS

Link to Old Maps Website	369
Approximate Locations of Family Homes	370
Beighton Area	372
Beighton	374
Hackenthorpe	376
Bletchley Park	377
Bletchley/Bedford Area	378
Bletchley and Fenny Stratford	380
Far Bletchley	382
Stewartby	384

Link to Old Maps

Copying and pasting the link below will take you to the National Library of Scotland collection of old maps. There you can find originals of area and town maps from the era.

Browse at your leisure!

https://maps.nls.uk/os/6inch-england-and-wales/?fbclid=IwAR1rfQpPBpjZpqNccDHR2pxCM05nYz7QCzAKqUwg6ELfzZnVKCsLOiNJf1E

Ordnance Survey Maps - Six-inch England and Wales, 1842-1952

The most comprehensive, topographic mapping covering all of England and Wales from the 1840s to the 1950s. Two editions for all areas, and then regular updates in the 20th century for urban or rapidly changing areas.

Browse the maps:

- As individual sheets using a zoomable map of England and Wales
- As a seamless zoomable overlay layer (1888-1913) on modern satellite imagery and OS maps
- As a seamless zoomable layer (1888-1913) side-by-side with modern satellite imagery and OS maps ← **Click here**
- By map sheet number (eg. Oxfordshire IX.NW) – county text lists

See also:

Approximate Locations of Family Homes

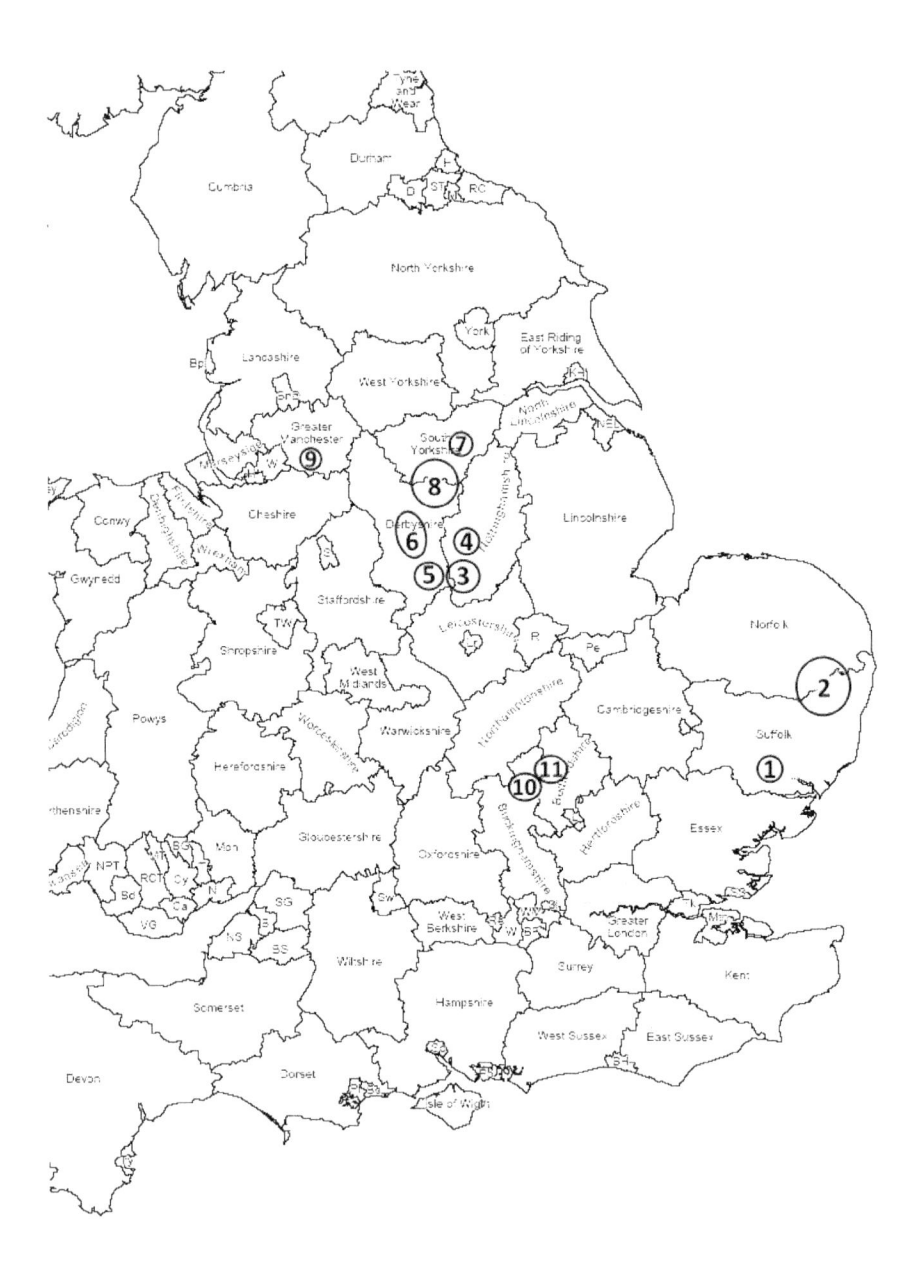

Key

1   Sudbury, Suffolk

2   Suffolk/Norfolk

3   Nottinghamshire/Derbyshire

4   Basford, Nottinghamshire

5   Derby

6   Going north, all in Derbyshire:
     Wirksworth
     Matlock
     Bakewell

7   Conisborough

8   Area around the Yorkshire/Derbyshire border where the other family locations are placed.

9   Withington, Lancashire

10   Bletchley, Buckinghamshire

11   Stewartby, Bedfordshire

Beighton Area Family Locations

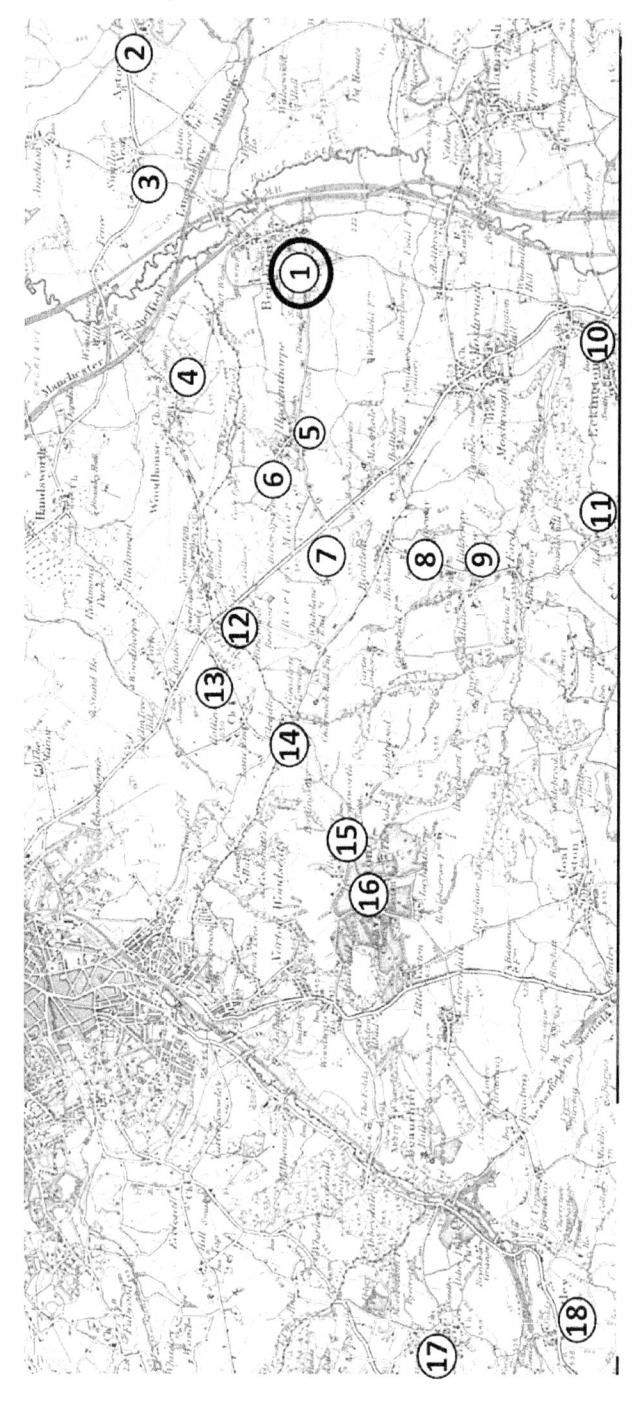

It is less than 4 miles (about 6 km) from Beighton to Eckington as the crow flies.

Key

1	Beighton
2	Netherthorpe
3	Swallownest
4	Woodhouse
5	Hackenthorpe
6	Owlthorpe
7	Birley
8	Ridgeway
9	Ridgeway Moor
10	Eckington
11	Marshlane
12	Birley Vale Colliery
13	Hollins End
14	Gleadless
15	Hemsworth
16	Norton
17	Dore
18	Totley

Beighton

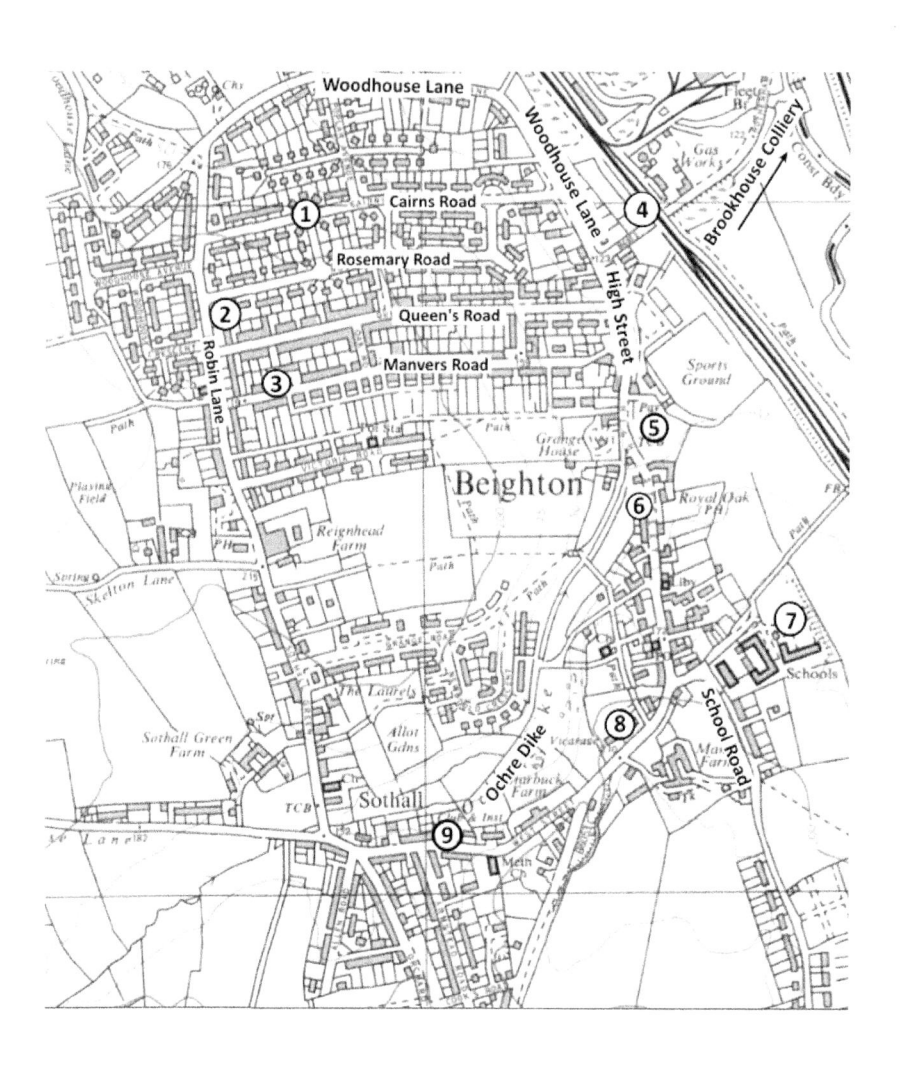

Key

1	26 Cairns Road
2	172 Robin Lane
3	164 Manvers Road
4	Railway Station
5	Miners' Welfare Club
6	Cinema
7	School
8	St Mary the Virgin Church
9	Sothall Club

Hackenthorpe

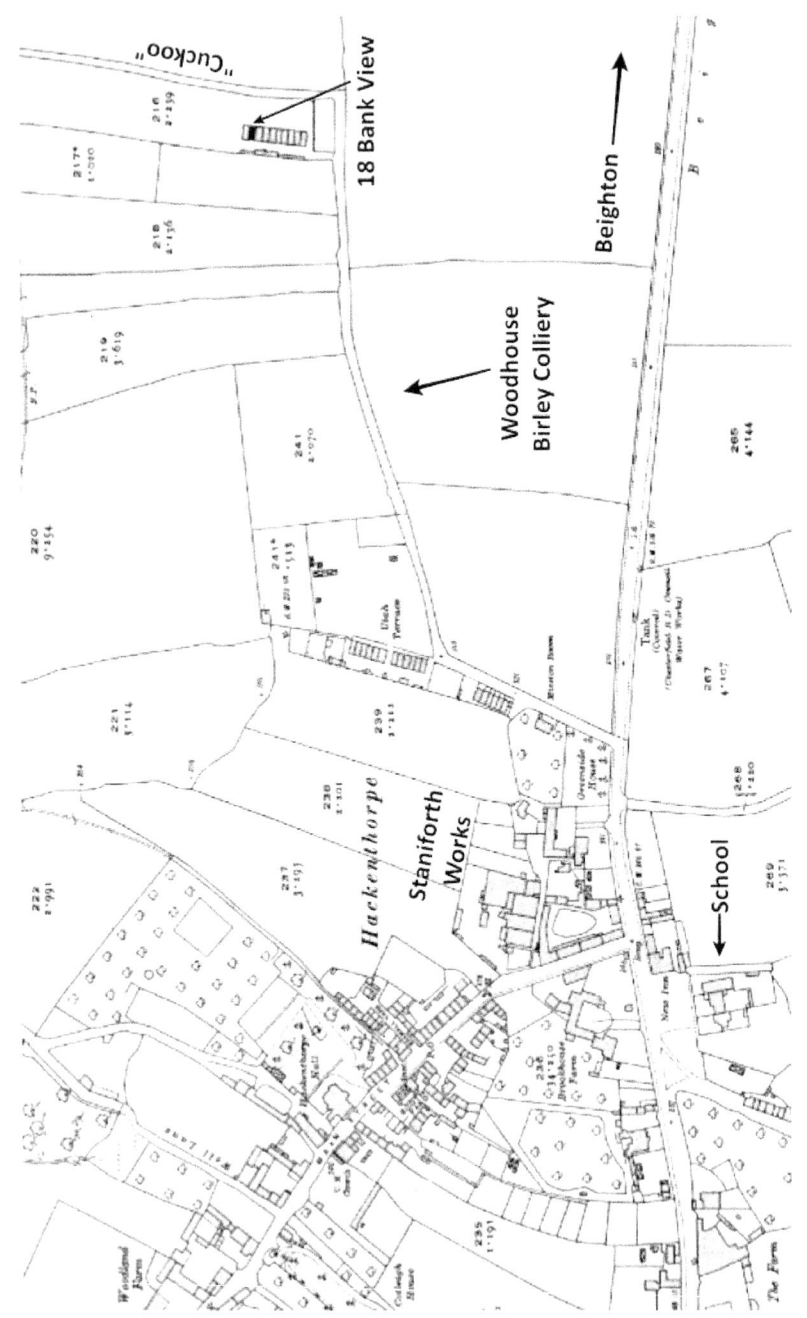

Places of interest are marked, directions marked.

Bletchley Park

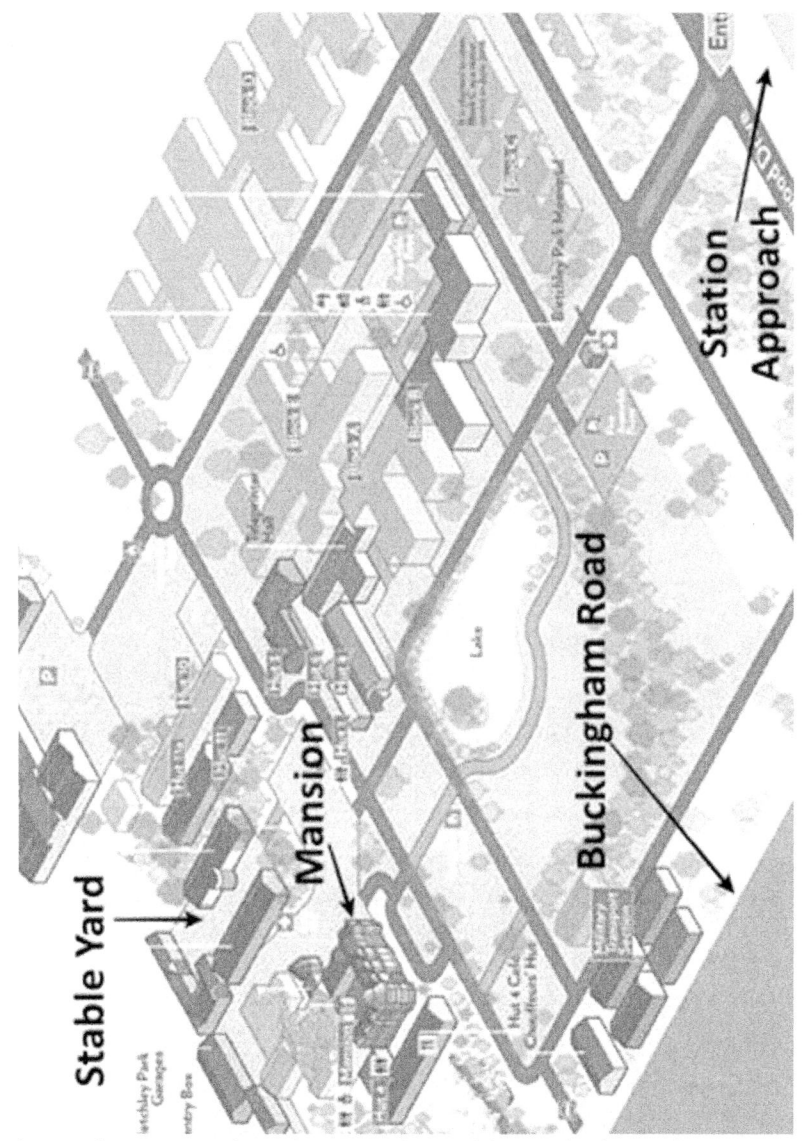

The park as it is today, showing the stable yard where the Premier Press was housed.

Bletchley/Bedford Area

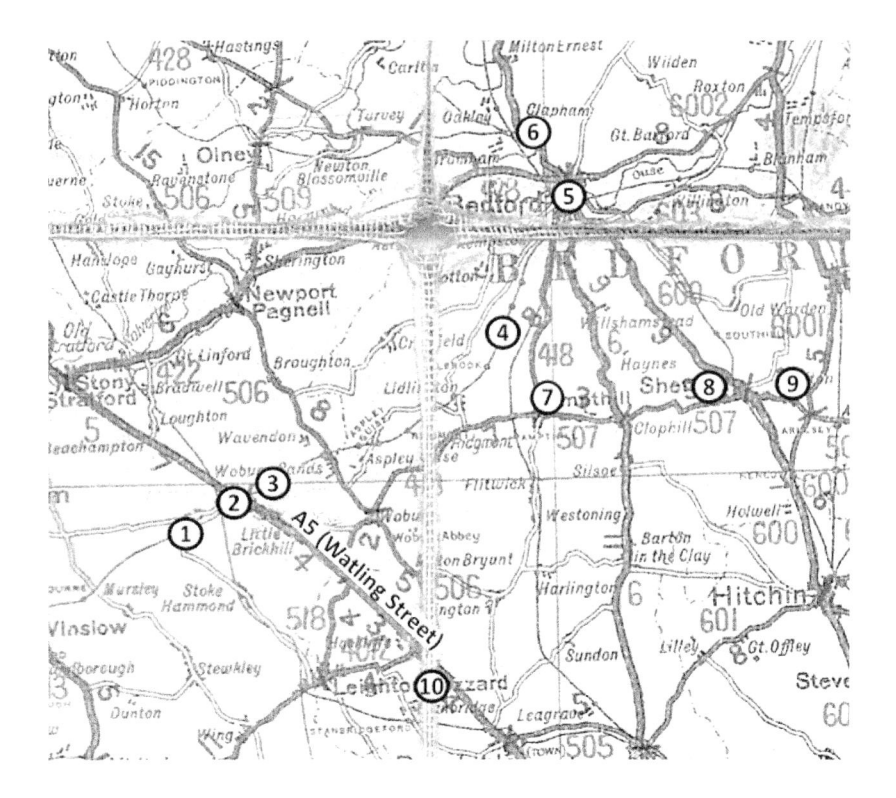

This was taken from an old map, which is unfortunately undated. It shows both roads and railway lines.

The railway line on which places are marked was known until the mid-1960s as the Oxbridge Line, running from Oxford in the west to Cambridge in the east. After Beeching took his axe to the railway system (you can look it up!), all that remained was the stretch of line between Bletchley and Bedford. The distance by rail from one to other is about 15 miles (just over 24 km).

I don't know what route Kitty took to Leighton Buzzard on her bike but suspect it was via back roads not marked on this map.

Key

1	Far Bletchley

2	Bletchley and Fenny Stratford

3	Bow Brickhill

4	Stewartby

5	Bedford

6	Clapham

7	Ampthill

8	Chicksands

9	Clifton

10	Leighton Buzzard

JEAN FLANNERY

Bletchley and Fenny Stratford, Main Area in Kitty's Day

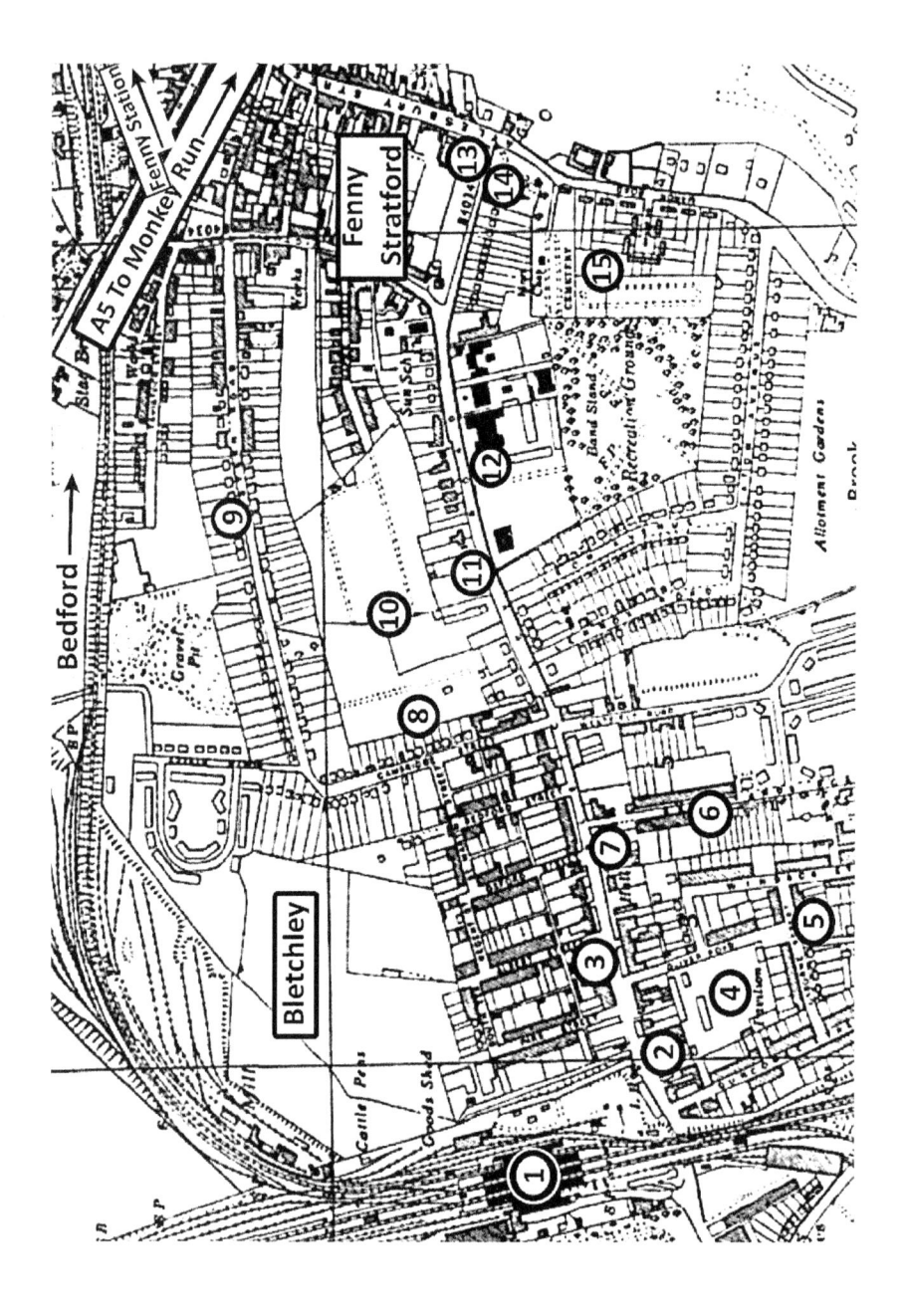

Key

1   Bletchley Railway Station

2   Reg's Butcher Shop

3   Co-op

4   Cattle and General Market

5   Tetley Tea Factory

6   14 Brooklands Road, Jack's Parents

7   St Margaret's Church

8   12 Cambridge Street

9   106 Western Road

10   Central Gardens

11   Studio Cinema

12   School

13   St Martin's Church

14   St Martin's Church Hall

15   Cemetery

Far Bletchley

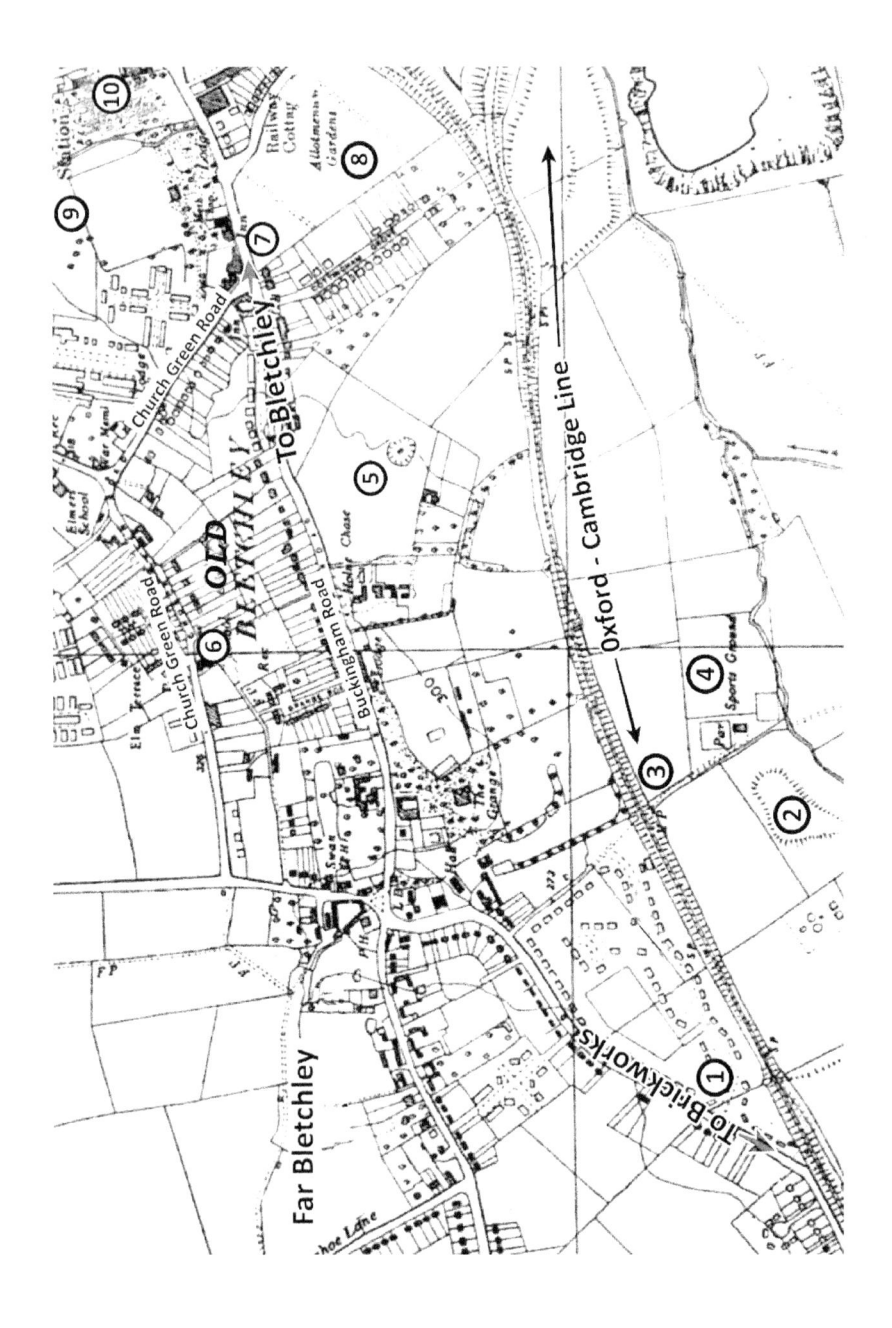

Key

1   1 Whiteley Crescent

2   Brickworks knothole

3   Path to LBC Sports Field

4   Sports Field

5   Pond in Holne Chase Spinney

6   Church Green Road C of E Primary School

7   Bus stop at bottom of Church Green Road

8   Jack's allotment

9   Bletchley Park

10 Bletchley Station Approach

Stewartby

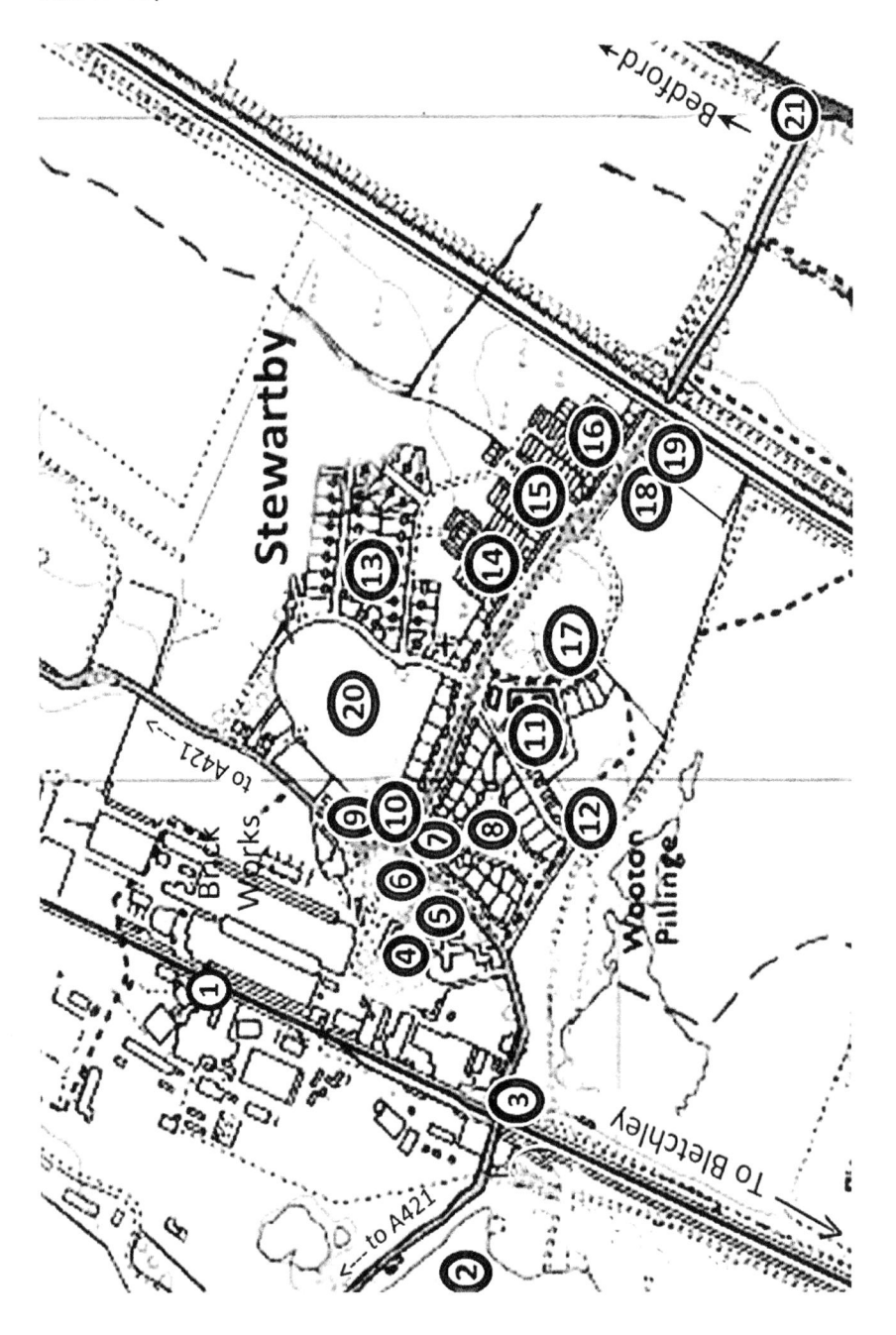

Key

1 Brickworks
2 Knothole
3 Stewartby Halt
4 Swimming Pool
5 Laboratory
6 Bus Stop
7 Village Hall
8 Churchill Close
9 Stewartby Club
10 Co-op/Post Office
11 Schools
12 Old School Sports Field
13 "New Houses"
14 Alexander Close
15 Montgomery Close
16 Wavell Close, home from 1954-1998
17 Sir Malcolm Stewart Homes, The Crescent Home from 1998-2010
18 Carter's Farm, later site of more bungalows
19 Allotments, also later site of more bungalows
20 Sports Field
21 Bus Stop at Stewartby Turn, Ampthill Road

HOME TOWNS AND VILLAGES

HACKENTHORPE

The first mention of the name appears to be in Anglo-Saxon records. A village by the name of Eckingthorp, the name itself of Anglo-Saxon origin, is mentioned in the Derbyshire land owners lists of the 9th century. However, the area was settled by the Vikings much earlier.

Eckingthorp bears a resemblance to the modern names of Hackenthorpe and Eckington, translating to "The hamlet of Eck's people." Hackenthorpe's name though is far more likely to have originated from the Old Norse for "Hachen's outlying farmstead."

A hamlet at the time, it stood on the edges of the "Great Forest," which extended over a vast area of land. Today the only remnant of the Great Forest is Sherwood Forest, most known for the legend of Robin Hood.

Following the invasion of England by the Angles and Saxons in the 5th and 6th centuries, the settlements were on the Mercia side of the border between the kingdoms of Mercia and Northumbria.

Both were prone to invasion by Northumbria, being so close to the border. The border itself was the nearby Shire Brook, which continued to act as a border between Derbyshire and Yorkshire.

Hackenthorpe and Beighton were both on the Derbyshire side and Hackenthorpe, having no Anglican church of its own, came to be included in the parish of Beighton.

Shire Brook today

The modern name of Hackenthorpe came into use during the 14th century, at a time when local dialects began to shape the names of villages and hamlets.

In its early years the hamlet was surrounded by farmland and forest. Serfs worked for their local lord of the manor, who owned the land on which they lived. They were also given the right to farm strips of land for their own subsistence and had the protection of the lord.

Work for the lord would include more than farming. The local forest was a source of charcoal, used to fuel furnaces for smelting the iron that was mined in shallow pits.

Hackenthorpe Hall is one of the oldest buildings still standing in the village. It was built in 1653 by John and Alice Newbould.

By then, coal was also mined in shallow pits and used to heat the homes of the wealthier residents of the hamlet.

Hackenthorpe Hall

During the 18th century the area began to see more industrial development. Coal mining, milling and brick kilns were found in what had now grown to a village as well as in the area to the north, known as Birley.

In 1743 the Staniforth Works was opened on Main Street. It was a workshop used for the smithing of farm tools such as scythes and sickles. The Staniforth family already owned multiple sickle grinding wheels along the Shire Brook. The works building still stands, with the old smithy pond behind it.

in 1877 the Birley East Pit was opened and began producing up to 500 tons of coal daily. Local employment now began to shift from sickle smithing and farming to coal mining.

Birley Colliery

The 1894 Local Government Act introduced District and Parish councils. Hackenthorpe was now a parish in its own right. But it didn't have its own Anglican Church, Christ Church, until 1899. Even that was initially a Chapel of Ease, as St Margaret's in Bletchley, but this for Beighton's Church of St Mary the Virgin.

Christ Church today

With the population of the village growing steadily thanks to the coal mines, the colliery owners began buying land and building terraced housing for the workers. Many of these terraces, including those on Bank View where Kitty was born, have since been demolished.

In 1921 the population of the Chesterfield registration district, which included Hackenthorpe, was just under 165,000 in 35,350 homes. I have been unable to find the number living in the village itself.

Its incorporation into the city of Sheffield brings Hackenthorpe's history into the modern era. Although many of the residents protested this move, it was made official 1 April 1967.

After so many centuries Hackenthorpe, though remaining a parish, was no longer a separate village and no longer in Derbyshire but in Yorkshire. It is now classified as a historic township of Sheffield. Despite this, it retains a sense of identity.

BEIGHTON

The first mention of Beighton also comes from 9th century Anglo-Saxon records of Derbyshire land owners. The village was then known as Bectune, meaning "The farm by the brook."

In the Domesday Book of 1086, the hamlet was noted as having just 15 households, the land being owned by Roger the Poitevin (Roger de Poitou), an Anglo-Norman aristocrat.

A moated castle was said to exist in the village, according to a reference from the 13th century describing how "the tower of the former castle" was to be seen in a field named Castle Mead. The Enclosure Plan for the village and a plan made in 1792 indicate a site by the river Rother that may have formed a moat. However, no evidence remains and nothing more is known.

The parish church of St. Mary the Virgin dates back to c1150. The first documented mention of the church is in an undated deed written during the reign of Edward I (1272–1307).

Prior to the 20th century, farming and smithing were the primary forms of employment. The Ochre Dyke stream was used to power grinding and water wheels during this time period.

Employment here too shifted towards mining during the latter part of the 19th century, with numerous mines being opened in the area - most notably Brookhouse Colliery and Birley Collieries.

The small Birley Vale colliery was working by 1856, but it wasn't until the Birley East pit opened that really significant amounts of coal were being mined. The early days saw some terrible accidents, due to dreadful working conditions. These were in part what led to the 1926 miners' strike.

The shaft for Brookhouse was sunk late for the area, in 1930.

In 1958 there had been an accident at Brookhouse Colliery that became known as the "Overwind" incident. It happened when a new electrical winding system on the miners' shaft cage broke, causing it to fall to the bottom of the shaft.

Miner William Wild recalls the event: "It was sheer hell down there. The cage was a mass of bodies thrown against each other and the pit bottom was full of moans and groans."

There were thankfully no fatalities, in part due to colleagues who carried the injured a mile to safety.

Brookhouse Colliery ceased production in 1985.

Beighton had its own railway station and many residents travelled to and from Sheffield and beyond by train. The station sadly closed in 1954.

Beighton Station

The Station Master in peaked cap stands on the platform, his staff around him.

Due to the village's close proximity to the river Rother, a good number of major flooding events have occurred over the years.

I think the Railway Inn has suffered here.

Beighton too became incorporated into Sheffield city in 1967. It is officially recognised as an electoral ward that includes Hackenthorpe and other local villages similarly now historic townships of Sheffield. However, Beighton too still retains a sense of identity.

Beighton also retains three working men's clubs: Beighton Top Club, the Miners Welfare Club and Sothall Club.

The Miners Welfare Club

Perhaps the last time Kitty was in the Miner's Welfare Club was for her nephew Brian's wedding reception. Brenda's reception had also been held here, following the service in St Mary's church.

The Crystal Peaks shopping centre on the outskirts of Beighton was opened in 1988. Now local people, including those in the surrounding "villages," no longer have to go further afield to do their shopping.

BLETCHLEY

Ken Barrow took this view, looking east towards Bletchley Road, from the railway bridge. The London Brick Company's AEC Mercury, passing the Park Hotel, dates the photograph to around 1958. The row of tin shops visible just past the railings on the left were very popular and included Mr Hurst's bicycle shop, Elizabeth's hat shop and the finest fish and chip shop in town.

Jack would recognise this view from his younger days, the buildings unchanged for decades. The Co-op butcher's shop, managed by Reg, stood on the "apron" just beyond the Park Hotel. The Co-op department store is the white building rear left.

The original Bletchley was the area that became known as Old Bletchley and Far Bletchley. It was a satellite of Fenny Stratford.

The town's name, meaning Blæcca's clearing, is Anglo-Saxon. It was first recorded in the 12th century as Bicchelai, then in the 13th Century as Blechelegh, and from the 14th to the 16th century as Blecheley. The area that we know simply as Bletchley was first known as Central Bletchley, to distinguish it from the older town area.

Just to the south of Fenny Stratford was the Romano-British town, Magiovinium, lying on both sides of the Roman road, the Watling Street (see Monkey Run!)

The town had developed with the coming of the railway. Bletchley became an important junction on the London Euston line. The Grand Union Canal, running close to the Watling Street, was no longer a main artery for traffic after the coming of the railways. Fenny Stratford lessened in importance as Bletchley grew.

Bletchley Station, another view

Tin Shops, another view

Quite soon after passing these, on this side of the road and further down the other, the pavement widened to become very spacious.

The largest shop in Bletchley, a little further along into the town and still on the left, was the Co-op department store. There were a great many small, independent shops in both Bletchley and Fenny Stratford but very few that were part of a chain. And there was certainly only the one real department store.

In 1911 Bletchley became the name of the Urban District that included Fenny Stratford. The population of the combined parishes was 5,166 in that year, as they began to merge.

By 1921 the combined population was still only around 5,500. In 1951, following the end of WWII, its population had grown to 10,919.

Throughout the time Kitty lived there, Bletchley remained a very pleasant, small market town.

The cattle market site held animal sales on one day a week and a general market on another. Each summer a funfair also set up on the market site.

Cattle market - sheep sales today!

Industry included brick making, and the railway was a major employer in the town. In Fenny Stratford, Akroyd Stuart manufactured one of the first heavy oil engines.

Brush manufacturing began in the late 19th century and continued for over 60 years. Fenny Stratford's other industries included a timber yard and saw mill, a printing works, tea packing factory, and an iron foundry. Fenny Stratford also contained one of Britain's first telephone repeater stations. The station was powered by a locally produced Akroyd Stuart engine. Repeater stations were necessary, as early long-distance telephone circuits had to be amplified around every 50 miles.

During World War II, as everyone now knows, Bletchley Park was the centre of secret decoding operations. At the time, all that local residents there not employed there knew, was that it was a top-secret establishment. That much was obvious. It also brought a temporary influx of residents into the area until after the war.

Bletchley Park Manor House

Operating "Colossus"

Bletchley Park housed the Post Office Management School after WWII and is now home to the National Museum of Computing.

By mid-1952 the Council had agreed terms with five London Boroughs to accept people and businesses from bombed-out sites in London. This trend, known as the London Overspill, continued through the 1950s and 1960s, both the permanent population and the economy correspondingly growing.

Bletchley continued to expand and its economy prosper until the early 1970s. In 1971 the combined population of Bletchley and Fenny Stratford was 30, 642. But in the late 1960s it had become a suburb of the new city of Milton Keynes.

Parts of the town were cut off from one another by new road building. Cambridge Street and Western Road were one continuous thoroughfare until a dual carriageway was built that sliced them in two.

There was also no longer a direct access to Buckingham Road through the town. These are among the reasons why neither Jack nor Kitty had any desire to visit Bletchley in later life.

With the opening of Central:MK, Milton Keynes' shopping mall, Bletchley went into a commercial decline. But there are plans for revival, with a large sports and event stadium there already.

STEWARTBY

The Stewart family had been directors of the London Brick Company from 1900. They were instrumental in developing the brickworks at Stewartby, which had grown into the largest in the world by the time we were there.

There were more than thirty brick kiln chimneys when we moved to Stewartby. They made a real landmark, especially as four of the central chimneys had, respectively: L, B, C (for London Brick Company) and STEWARTBY written on them, picked out in white bricks.

Even though the chimneys were so tall, when there was no wind and atmospheric conditions were right the smoke sank to the ground, shrouding the bottom of the village. It didn't affect us so badly where we lived but even so the smell of sulphur could be awful at times.

The brick company owned a lot of land around the area. It meant that when one knothole (clay pit) was exhausted they could start digging out another. The laboratory in Stewartby tested the quality of everything, from the clay right through to the finished article; bricks, roofing tiles, hollow blocks and field drainpipes.

Exterior facing bricks, unlike plain interior ones, were made in different colours and textures. Very hard "Rustic" bricks, a pleasant red in colour and rough textured, were used to build all the village houses.

The Stewarts built a so-called model village on the site of the tiny hamlet of Wootton Pillinge, to provide homes for the brickyard workers. The first phase of 210 houses, started in 1926, was completed by the beginning of WWII. It was excellent company housing for workers in those days.

The construction was of high quality, of course using the brickworks' own products. Mains water and electricity were brought into the village, although not gas. Every house had an indoor toilet and bathroom (by no means universal at the time) and a garden.

The village footpaths were made from pieces of broken clay tile, in various shades of mellow deep red, set in cement. The look was unusual and pleasing to the eye. When simply walking you hardly noticed the slight unevenness of the surface, although it was different when pushing a pram - or riding a bike or roller skates.

Stewartby initially comprised one long street running up the village, deviating at intervals to wind around in four "Closes." In these closes the houses were arranged around the road, which bordered a central grassy area. There was no other road exit from them, except for Montgomery Close. From the back of that you could take a road left down to the "New Houses," a small estate built behind the main road some years later.

The largest house in the village, where the works manager lived, was near the club. This was quite separate from the other village houses. The brickworks, club, village hall and Co-op shop (incorporating the post office) were all at the bottom end of the village. Then houses ran along both sides of Stewartby Way, on the flat ground from the brickworks end, as far as a lane just before the school. After that the road started to run uphill.

From this point the ordinary houses were only built on the left side of the road, opposite the school, up to the main London - Bedford railway line. This was known to us all as the Bedpan Line because from Bedford it ran into St Pancras station in London.

Running uphill from the school opposite these houses, in the curve of The Crescent, was a big grassy area. When I was a child only four large houses stood on The Crescent, two detached and two semi-detached, just beyond the school.

Their residents have included at various times the LBC's Chief Chemist, Chief Engineer, Head Planner, the Stewartby Secondary School Head Teacher, and the Scottish Free Church minister.

The ground levelled out again at the roundabout by the top end of The Crescent. There was a wide grassy area between the footpath and main road through the village, on both sides at the bottom end.

Here some large old trees grew, together with younger lime trees planted by the company. Then on the left, where the footpath and grassy area continued, just a row of lime trees marched all the way up the village.

It was after World War II that the main road through the village was named Stewartby Way, the closes called Churchill, Alexander, Montgomery and Wavell, as tributes to those wartime leaders.

The senior school became what was known as a Secondary Modern School. Its entrance was on The Crescent, whereas the building housing the infant and junior schools, although next to it, was actually set back just behind a small grassed area facing Stewartby Way.

The building of the first of the Sir Malcolm Stewart Homes, in one of which my parents later lived, was completed in 1956.

Our house was on the corner of Wavell Close and Stewartby Way.

Wavell Close from Stewartby Way
199 is out of view, right front.

Across Stewartby Way was Carter's Farm.

The roundabout in 1959, Carter's Farm behind it on the right. Beyond are the allotments, a footpath along which blackberry brambles and dog roses grew, and the railway embankment.

Looking down the village from the roundabout in the same year.

All the roundabout planting was done by the groundsmen for as long as the London Brick Company owned the village.

The houses on the corners of Alexander and Wavell Close were next largest in size to those on The Crescent and were semi-detached, whereas most in the village were terraced.

We lived in one of these corner houses on Wavell Close. One on Alexander Close was the village police house. Stewartby had its own village constable (bobby). What was our brick shed, opposite the back door, was his office.

Across a side road from the sports ground was Stewartby United Church. One of the doctors from the GP practice in nearby Kempston came to hold a surgery in a hut next to the church twice a week. There was also a regular mother and baby clinic held there.

The other small estate of houses, the so-called "New Houses," had been built behind here in the early 1950s, running up the hill as far as Montgomery Close.

Groundsmen mowed the grass, planted out the roundabout and took care of the rose beds in the village.

They also cut the thick mass of privet bush outside our house and the other corner houses on Wavell and Alexander Closes, as well as pruning trees and doing any other necessary gardening work.

The whole village looked really lovely. All the houses were kept in excellent condition too, with any problems taken care of by maintenance men employed by the brick company. It certainly was in many ways a truly "model" village.

Stewartby was served by two bus routes, one at each end of the village, and by the Bletchley to Bedford rail service.

Stewartby Halt with its crossing keeper's hut, bank of manual signal levers and the low platform. The crossing keeper's house is just behind the hut.

In the days of steam engines, steps were let down, with a great hiss of steam, from the guard's van for the passengers. Any items such as prams and bicycles were lifted manually onto the train. This arrangement continued until the coming of diesel engines to the line, when the platforms were raised.

The village was virtually self-contained. There was the Co-op grocery shop come post office. The company owned and heavily subsidised a workingmen's club, sports ground with bowling green and other games facilities, the village hall, church, swimming pool, and the infant, junior and senior schools.

The London Brick Company, although it was a limited (public) company, was basically run by the Stewart family who owned a controlling interest.

The Stewart family was very paternalistic, the Stewarts genuinely concerned for the wellbeing of their employees and families. They even considered the schooling needs of the children in surrounding villages. And Sir Malcolm Stewart set up a trust fund in his will to provide free sheltered housing for company pensioners and widows.

That is not to say that the founding director, Sir Halley Stewart, was not controlling. For example, being very Calvinistic, he ruled that no washing could be hung outside on a Sunday. To break this rule meant eviction! But overall, employees and their families did well from the company. And the strict rules died with Sir Halley.

When Hanson took over the London Brick Company in 1984, rent for my parents had gone up to just £9 per week, still subsidised. But the days of subsidised rent then became a thing of the past as the houses were sold off, with first refusal going to existing tenants.

Sadly, in February 2008 brickmaking at Stewartby came to an end. Hanson closed the brickworks. The chimneys did not meet UK sulphur emission regulations.

The brickworks chimneys have now all been demolished and the works site lies derelict. But the village itself has expanded and remains a thriving community of old timers and new comers alike.

There are plans too for yet more houses to be built on the old brickworks site.

Printed in Great Britain
by Amazon